Routledge Revivals

Sensation and Perception

First published in 1961, *Sensation and Perception* aims to cast light upon the nature of perception itself. This, the author believes, can be achieved only through an understanding of the concepts of sensation and perception. A survey of the principal attempts to arrive at such an understanding brings out the fact that perception has most often been assimilated to sensation or judgment. The author believes that both of these views are wrong but that an attention to the history of thought can provide an explanation of the temptation to accept them. A final chapter gives the author's own views on the nature of sensation and perception. As such it would be of interest both to philosophers and to those psychologists who are concerned with the nature of perception.

Sensation and Perception
A History of the Philosophy of Perception

D. W. Hamlyn

First published in 1961
by Routledge & Kegan Paul Ltd.

This edition first published in 2022 by Routledge
4 Park Square, Milton Park, Abingdon, Oxon, OX14 4RN
and by Routledge
605 Third Avenue, New York, NY 10017

Routledge is an imprint of the Taylor & Francis Group, an informa business

© D. W. Hamlyn 1961

All rights reserved. No part of this book may be reprinted or reproduced or utilised in any form or by any electronic, mechanical, or other means, now known or hereafter invented, including photocopying and recording, or in any information storage or retrieval system, without permission in writing from the publishers.

Publisher's Note
The publisher has gone to great lengths to ensure the quality of this reprint but points out that some imperfections in the original copies may be apparent.

Disclaimer
The publisher has made every effort to trace copyright holders and welcomes correspondence from those they have been unable to contact.

A Library of Congress record exists under LCCN: 62001011

ISBN: 978-1-032-32719-8 (hbk)
ISBN: 978-1-003-31645-9 (ebk)
ISBN: 978-1-032-32732-7 (pbk)

Book DOI 10.4324/9781003316459

SENSATION AND PERCEPTION

A History of the Philosophy of Perception

by

D. W. Hamlyn

LONDON
ROUTLEDGE & KEGAN PAUL
NEW YORK: THE HUMANITIES PRESS

First published 1961
by Routledge & Kegan Paul Ltd.
Broadway House, 68–74 Carter Lane
London, E.C.4

Printed in Great Britain
by Richard Clay and Co., Ltd.
Bungay, Suffolk

© *D. W. Hamlyn* 1961

No part of this book may be reproduced
in any form without permission from
the publisher, except for the quotation
of brief passages in criticism

To
Eileen, Nicholas and Catherine

CONTENTS

	PREFACE	*page* ix
1	THE CLASSICAL GREEK PHILOSOPHERS	1
	(i) Introduction	1
	(ii) The Presocratics	5
	(iii) Plato	10
	(iv) Aristotle	17
2	HELLENISTIC PHILOSOPHY	31
	(i) Introduction	31
	(ii) Epicurus	32
	(iii) The Stoa	35
	(iv) Plotinus and Neo-Platonism	39
3	MEDIAEVAL THOUGHT	43
	(i) Introduction	43
	(ii) Augustine	43
	(iii) Aquinas	46
	(iv) Bonaventure	51
	(v) William of Ockham	52
4	THE 17TH CENTURY—AN INTRODUCTION	55
5	THE RATIONALISTS	62
	(i) Descartes	62
	(ii) Malebranche	75
	(iii) Spinoza	82
	(iv) Leibniz	85
6	THE EMPIRICISTS	93
	(i) Introduction	93
	(ii) Locke	94
	(iii) Berkeley	104
	(iv) Hume	116
	(v) Appendix—Reid	124

CONTENTS

7 KANT, HEGEL AND IDEALISM   *page* 131
    (i) Kant   131
    (ii) Hegel and Idealism   140

8 NINETEENTH-CENTURY SENSATIONALISM   147

9 THE REACTION   158

10 THE 20TH CENTURY—SENSE-DATA AND PHENOMENOLOGY   172
    (i) Introduction   172
    (ii) Sense-data   174
    (iii) Phenomenology   181
    (iv) Appendix—20th-century Neurology   184

11 CONCLUSION—SENSATION AND PERCEPTION   186

    BIBLIOGRAPHY   198

    INDEX   205

PREFACE

IN general histories of philosophy trends or tendencies in the treatment of specific problems are liable to be obscured by the necessity of taking a broad view of the field. There may, therefore, be some merit in a history of treatments of a particular philosophical problem or group of problems. In some cases, of course, it is impossible to divorce a philosopher's thought on one subject from his general approach to philosophy. It is not therefore suggested that the treatments of a subject like perception can stand alone; and in some cases a more detailed attention to the background of thought is required than in others. But a history of the main attempts to deal with a single group of problems may have decided philosophical advantages which outweigh the historical disadvantages which accrue from a somewhat artificial restriction of the field. It may be possible as a result to see more clearly the main approaches to the problems and the types of solution suggested, together with the reasons for their adoption. This too may bring with it a clearer insight both into the nature of the problems and into the way to their proper solution.

It is in this spirit that the present work attempts to deal with the concepts of sensation and perception. What perception is and how it is related to its conditions have been problems to philosophers from the beginnings of philosophical inquiry. There have been natural tendencies to assimilate it on the one hand to sensation, to the having of experiences in the most elementary sense, and on the other hand to judgment, to an activity of the mind. The first line of treatment provides an easy way of dealing with the problem of the connection between perception and the physiology of the sense-organs; for if perception is a passive affair, it could well be merely the effect of a stimulation of our sense-organs. But in that case how are we to account for the evident fact that perception in some sense brings knowledge and beliefs about the world? The second line of treatment provides a possible answer to this last problem but further difficulties in respect of the former. The main aim of the present work is, therefore, to chart the most important attempts to deal with these difficulties, and in a final chapter to cut the Gordian knot and try to offer some solution.

But the history of thought is never so tidy as one would wish. Philosophical thought, even in relation to a restricted field, tends to be drawn into side issues and to adopt lines of development for extraneous reasons. In the long run it is perhaps well that it should do so. As a result, histories of philosophy are apt to follow one of three main lines if they are to be more than mere histories of ideas. The first approach, which might be called the 'pure scholarship approach', devotes itself to setting down everything that philosophers have said on a particular subject. The result, only too often, is an inability to see the wood for the trees. At the other extreme is the Hegelian approach, in which the historical facts are made to fit a theory of history and its development. In this the theory often has to ignore the facts. In between there is what is perhaps the method of Aristotle—a survey of the field which is itself interpreted and categorized in contemporary philosophical terms. The scholar may question this, levelling accusations of anachronism, but by this method philosophical issues are less liable to be lost sight of than by an over-strict attention to the niceties of historical fact. The present work probably falls somewhere between the first type of approach and the Aristotelian, but its aim is the same as that of Aristotle's surveys of previous philosophical thought—to cast light upon certain philosophical problems by a history of their treatment.

It is for this reason that no attempt has been made to be absolutely comprehensive. The work is a history of the *main* types of treatment of the problems of perception. While it is inevitably concerned with epistemological issues, many of these issues arise within the philosophy of perception only as a result of a certain conception of perception. The problem of knowledge is a general problem about the possibility of knowledge. Perception raises special problems here only if it be supposed that there is of necessity a gap between our perpetual experiences and the objective world around us which we claim to know. If perception is an entirely subjective matter, then there seems greater reason for scepticism concerning our claims to know the so-called external world. But is perception like this? The conceptual problem—the

PREFACE

problem of the nature of our concept of perception—is thus in a sense prior to the epistemological problem. For this reason, the present work is chiefly concerned with this issue—what perception is. The main lines of treatment are here the most relevant.

I should like to express my debt to my colleagues Dr. R. L. Saw, Dr. R. S. Peters and Mr. A. P. Griffiths, who have between them read the greater part of the manuscript and have made valuable comments and criticisms.

I
THE CLASSICAL GREEK PHILOSOPHERS

(i) INTRODUCTION

INQUIRY into the beginnings of a tradition of philosophical thought inevitably brings with it the realization that certain concepts which are now more or less familiar to us were once not understood at all. The surprise that this realization may bring will perhaps be lessened when it is recognized that the concepts in question are *philosophical* concepts. They are concepts used not in thinking about matters of everyday life, but in thinking about the ways in which we deal with everyday life. Since the concepts which we employ in our thought are reflected in the words which we use, those words may provide a key to the problem whether or not a concept exists at any given time. The works of Homer, for example, the earliest works in Greek Literature, abound in words which were of use in talking about seeing and hearing things. But, as Bruno Snell has pointed out,[1] each word used had a quite distinct function, and there was no one word, for example, summing up the central features of vision. Still less was there a word, like 'perception', which could be of use *in reflecting upon* the processes of seeing and hearing things. Hence there are grounds for the conclusion that Homer had no concept of perception. He was not in the position to think about perception in itself at all.

The word *aesthesis* (αἴσθησις), which is used prolifically in Plato and Aristotle to mean 'sensation' or 'perception', is a word which originated in the 5th century B.C. The verb from which it

[1] Bruno Snell, *The Discovery of the Mind*, ch. 1.

derived (αἰσθάνομαι) can be encountered, as might be expected, a little earlier (in Herodotus, for example), and this verb is itself probably derived from another word with much the same meaning which *is* found in Homer. Plato and Aristotle, therefore, had a word which was of use in reflecting about sense-perception, while Homer did not. It might be objected that they were philosophers by intention, while he was not, and that this explains the difference. This, however, is not sufficient, since, as far as can be seen, the earliest philosophers also lacked a word for perception. The development of philosophical thought goes hand in hand with the development of a suitable language.

Granted that Plato and Aristotle had a word at their disposal for perception, it does not necessarily follow that they possessed the concept of perception, i.e. that they were able to think about perception in a coherent manner. The link between concepts and words is complex. Indeed, philosophers have sometimes possessed certain concepts before having the actual words to go with them. It is possible to have a certain concept and yet show that one has it only by the use of periphrasis. On the other hand, the use of a single word or phrase is not a *proof* of the possession of the concept corresponding to it, since the existence of the word may be accidental only. It is, nevertheless, a straw in the wind.

An example of the difficulties is provided by the evolution of the concept of a quality in Greek thought. It is clear from their writings that the Presocratic philosophers did not have this concept. That is to say, they did not think in terms of qualities at all. They certainly had no single *word* for quality, but their general discussion shows that they did not possess the concept either. Where *we* should talk of qualities they tended to talk of things. The traditional opposites, for example—qualities like heat and cold— were always thought of as things. In the development of Plato's philosophy some sensitivity to the necessity of distinguishing between qualities and things begins to emerge. In the earlier formulations of the Theory of Forms, the Forms correspond to qualities and yet are thought of as, in some sense, things. In the *Theaetetus*,[1] however, Socrates is made to introduce, with apologies, the *word* for quality (ποιότης)—a word literally meaning 'what-sort-of-ness', which was constructed out of the word meaning 'what sort

[1] *Theaetetus*, 182a.

of' (ποῖος) which was already in use. Nevertheless, Plato's problems over qualities were not at an end. The dialogues show that he never thoroughly acclimatized himself to the necessity of making a rigorous distinction in his thought between things and qualities. He could not fully appreciate what it was to think of something as a quality, as distinct from a thing. Aristotle, who, in his doctrine of categories, laid the philosophical foundations of the distinction, sometimes shows by his philosophical discussion that he was not fully at home.

The question whether a philosopher possesses a given concept is a difficult one, and while the use of the corresponding word is an indication in that direction, it is not a *sure* indication. In the field of sense-perception, the situation is more complicated still. Even when the Greek philosophers came to use the word *aesthesis* they tended to use it in a variety of different ways. We find the word used to speak of the senses, the faculty of sense-perception, sensations and the sense-organs, even when there are other words for the purpose. The continued use of the one general word *aesthesis* where there *are* other words might be put down to looseness of expression; but this answer cannot be given in all cases. One important fact stands out—that except by periphrasis the classical Greek philosophers had no way of distinguishing between sensation and perception. Moreover, the failure in the majority of cases to make the distinction even by periphrasis is an indication that they had in general no idea of the necessity of distinguishing the two concepts. Aristotle, perhaps, is on the threshold of making some such distinction, but he does not succeed fully in doing so.

It is possible to distinguish different stages in the evolution of a philosophical concept.

> (1) The stage at which a philosopher possesses neither the concept nor the corresponding word.
> (2) The stage at which a philosopher possesses the concept, at any rate in part (as is revealed by his periphrases or his general discussion of the subject), but at which he does not have at his disposal the corresponding word.
> (3) The stage at which a philosopher possesses both the concept and the word, but at which he is not fully alive to all the implications of the concept, i.e. he has the ability to talk or

think about the subject in a certain way, but he has not fully
reflected upon the implications of his thought.
(4) The stage at which a philosopher has both the concept
and the word, and at which he is also aware of the implications of these.

These stages are not necessarily clear cut, nor is the order necessarily as set out. But it is the most natural and typical order. Moreover, it brings out the complexities of the relation between thought and the use of language. Many modern philosophers have insisted that the use of words is at least a clue to the nature of our concepts. But it is no more than a clue, and the question whether a particular philosopher fully appreciates a certain concept or a certain way of thought is often a very difficult one to answer. On the other hand, it is very difficult to have any appreciation of a concept until one has the corresponding word. The lack of sufficient words in Greek to make a clear distinction between sensation and perception was perpetuated through Latin translations, and the philosophers of the 17th century and afterwards were presented with unnecessary problems by the inheritance of a ready-made philosophical terminology.

These are, of course, not the only sources of philosophical misunderstandings in this sphere. There is also the perennial influence upon philosophical inquiries of physiological speculations and discoveries. That influence has been especially strong at certain periods, e.g. the Presocratic era, the 17th century and today, and it has not always been salutary. A stress upon the physiological conditions of perception tends to foster the belief that our perception of things must necessarily be caused by those things. This results, in turn, in an assimilation of the concepts of sensation and perception. Philosophical insight, therefore, sometimes has to come *in spite of* the influences of physiology and not because of it.

There is another source of misunderstanding which is, so to speak, domestic. Philosophers tend to be hampered, not only by the lack of a sufficiently detailed terminology, but also by the retention of an over-rigorous or too limited scheme of categories. It is a natural tendency for a philosopher to work with a scheme of categories, into which, as he supposes, everything must be fitted. It may happen that recalcitrant candidates are, in consequence, fitted to procrustean beds. A description of a concept and of the implications of its use may sometimes be more illuminating than any number of attempts to fit it into some scheme of classification.

(ii) THE PRESOCRATICS

In Presocratic thought it is possible to trace a development through the first two stages of the evolution of the concepts of sensation and perception, and a partial move into the third stage. It is possible also to see the results of the influence exerted by physiological speculation and discoveries.

To judge from what we know of their writings, the earliest Presocratics showed little interest in sense-perception. Theophrastus, to whose work, the *De Sensu* (a chapter from his history of previous philosophical thought), we owe most of our knowledge of Presocratic writings on perception, mentions nobody before Alcmaeon or Parmenides.[1] Heraclitus makes certain remarks about the reliability of the senses as ways of finding out what he takes to be the truth about the world. Fragment 55,[2] for example, says that he prefers the things of which there is seeing, hearing and learning, but fragment 107 adds that the eyes and ears are bad witnesses for men when their souls do not understand their language. Heraclitus is therefore willing to distinguish between what the senses 'tell us' and the interpretation that is to be put upon this. But these sayings are meant to be understood in the context of Heraclitus's metaphysical theory about the world. This theory, he thinks, men can verify by the use of their senses. The sayings, therefore, have no more general implications.

It is not surprising to find that the earliest theorist about sense-perception was a man who was interested in physiology—Alcmaeon of Croton. Theophrastus (*De Sensu*, 25 ff.) says that he viewed perception as the effect of unlike upon unlike, and that he distinguished between thought and perception. This must not be taken to imply that *he* actually used the word 'perception'. The

[1] It should perhaps be said that Theophrastus is no sure guide to the actual use of certain words by earlier philosophers except when he is quoting. Moreover, like Aristotle, he tends to interpret the thought of his predecessors while expounding it—a fact which makes caution necessary.

[2] Reference to fragments of the Presocratic writings are given, as is usual, in accordance with the numbering given in Diels-Kranz, *Die Fragmente der Vorsokratiker*.

only words quoted are to the effect that animals perceive but do not understand, while man also understands. We are told also that he considered the brain to be the seat of the various senses. In much of this he may have been influenced by the Hippocratic medical writers, and it is probable that he indulged in dissection himself. It is a pity that we do not have more information about him. His influence, however, did not last. The philosophers who succeeded him differed from him in most, if not all, of his views.

Parmenides is put by Theophrastus (*De Sensu*, 1 ff.) into the class of those who thought of perception as the effect of like upon like. The reasons given for this verdict are that according to Parmenides corpses do not perceive light, heat or sound because they lack fire. The traditional Greek opposites, e.g. hot and cold, wet and dry, play a large part in the section of Parmenides' poem which is entitled 'The Way of Belief'—the section in which, despite the austere view of reality given in *The Way of Truth*, he gives his opinion concerning the composition of the sensible world. Fragment 16 of the poem, which is quoted by Theophrastus, indicates in an exceedingly brief way the role that the opposites play in the mechanisms underlying thought. But the most telling point that Theophrastus makes is that Parmenides made no distinction between perception and thought. This reads rather strangely after the rejection by Parmenides in *The Way of Truth* of the findings of sense-perception in favour of those of thought. But Parmenides must have had something to say about the physiology of sense-perception and thought, and it is evident that he made no distinction between them in doing so.

Similar remarks apply to Empedocles, of whom Theophrastus says that he also gave the same account of thought as of perception (*De Sensu*, 9; cf. frag. 109). He too is fitted by Theophrastus into the class of those who thought of perception as the effect of like upon like. In his case, however, we are given more details about the mechanism. In general, sense-perception is said to result from the passage of effluences through the pores in the sense-organs. Not all pores will admit of the passage of all effluences, with the result that the senses respond to different objects. Curiously enough, the effluences are thought of as proceeding in both directions—to the sense-organ from things outside, and also *vice versa*—so that perception occurs when an element from the sense-organ meets a similar element outside. The same theory, or one very like it, is put forward by Plato in the *Theaetetus* and the *Timaeus*, and it may be that Plato adopted it as his own. It is a curious theory, and it is scarcely to be explained in any physiological terms which make sense, even in a crude fashion. When Empedocles says that there is a fire within the eye which comes out to meet the light outside, he may have been building upon the observation that light is reflected from the pupil of the eye. He may also have thought that the light must proceed outwards, as well as inwards, if effluences are, as he maintained, given off by everything. Such an explanation does not appear sufficiently general, however, to be applicable to all the senses. How, for example, would it apply to hearing? It may be that Empedocles noted that in order to perceive things we have sometimes to concentrate and pay attention—something that might well be interpreted as a sort of outgoing from us. If that is so it is an interesting case of how something purely psychological may be forced into a physiological mould.

With Anaxagoras there is a return to a theory which is more in the spirit of Alcmaeon's. Theophrastus says (*De Sensu*, 27 ff.) that he thought of perception as the effect of unlike upon unlike, pointing to the fact that, for example, things of the same temperature as ourselves neither warm us nor cool us on their approach. But he goes on to say that Anaxagoras thought of this effect of unlike upon unlike as a kind of pain which becomes perceptible only when excessive in duration or intensity. Sense-perception is thus the result of a contact of this sort with the sense-organs, and Theophrastus comments that the supposition that all perception involves pain follows almost directly from that hypothesis. It does not in fact so follow, but it is interesting that Anaxagoras had noted that excess of stimulation in one way or another causes pain, and had inferred from this that pain is present in normal cases also.

The only Presocratics of importance that remain to be considered are the Atomists, Leucippus and Democritus. The latter is not technically a Presocratic, being a contemporary of Socrates; but his views are so inextricably involved with those of Leucippus that it is best to consider them together. Their account of sense-perception is almost entirely mechanical, since everything has to be explained in terms of the meeting and contact of atoms. In general, sense-perception is said to arise when atoms given off by bodies in the form of films or effluences (εἴδωλα—literally 'images') make contact with the atoms of the soul which pervade the whole body, including the sense-organs. Democritus (*pace* Theophrastus, *De Sensu*, 49–83) produced elaborate accounts of the details of this process, with respect to the various senses. The most complicated of these is the account of vision, in which he puts forward an elaboration of the Empedoclean theory. In his case, however, there is no doubt that the theory is meant to be a physiological one, since it is overtly intended to explain the visual 'image' in the pupil of the eye. The explanation given is that effluences from the object and from the observer meet and form a solid impression in the air; it is this which enters the pupil of the eye. Hearing is due to the mingling of the noise from the object with particles of air which affect the ear; and the details of the qualities detectable by smell and taste are attributed to the effect on the sense-organs produced by atoms of varying shape, size and texture.

It follows from this account that the so-called secondary qualities of things—their colour, temperature and so on—are by-products of the physical properties of atoms. Democritus puts this by saying that the former properties are due to convention (νόμος), while the physical properties of the atoms are there in truth. In this he was probably reacting against the sophist Protagoras, whose dictum 'Man is the measure of all things' meant in part that all the qualities which things appear to have are relative to the perceiver. Hence, Protagoras held that *all* qualities, not just the secondary ones, are due to *nomos*; that is to say, they are not due to nature. Democritus' use of the word *nomos* is in many ways unhappy, since it is not literally true that on his theory secondary qualities are a matter of convention. On the other hand they *are* relative to the perceiver, in that they are a by-product of interaction between the atoms from the external object and the atoms of the soul. This way of putting the matter has the virtue or otherwise of preserving the purely mechanical view of things which is essential to the atomist theory.

It is clear from this very brief survey of Presocratic theories about sense-perception that the interests of these philosophers were purely physiological or physical in character. They made no attempt to philosophize about the nature of the concept of sense-perception, nor did they in general raise epistemological issues, i.e. questions about the general validity of sense-perception. The word *aesthesis* was used by them only occasionally, and even then only by the later Presocratics, to mean 'sense' rather than 'perception' or 'sensation'. It was assumed, on the other hand, that the proper aim of an account of perception is to provide a theory concerning the underlying causal processes. Although the latter assumption has been made at various times in the history of thought, the Presocratic period is unique in that at that time there had been no attempt whatever to come to grips with the *concept* of sense-perception—no attempt, that is, to understand what it is to perceive things. While it is possible to say that the Presocratics were concerned primarily with the causes of *sensations*, this would strictly be incorrect, because they had no notion of a sensation as distinct from perception or *vice versa*. Attention to the concept of perception arose only as a result of epistemological inquiries—inquiries into the general validity of sense-perception. These began only with the Sophists, and especially Protagoras.

It might be objected that Parmenides and some of his successors were concerned with the validity of sense-perception. But this was not their main interest, any more than it was that of Heraclitus. Parmenides was interested in that view of the true nature of reality which he thought reason demanded; he was not concerned with knowledge for its own sake. When he cast doubt upon accounts of the sensible world it was doubt not so much whether we *know* anything about that world, but whether it is real. When Anaxagoras betrayed scepticism concerning the senses, it was only because they did not give us insight into the nature of reality as he saw it. It is sometimes difficult to separate the two issues—the one concerning the nature of reality and the other concerning the basis of our knowledge—but at this date they *can* be separated. It was the Sophists who turned their attention from the nature of the world to man, and in consequence raised the question how much of what we claim to know is part of nature and how much is due to man himself. Protagoras, as we have already seen, claimed that all the appearances of things are relative to man, indeed to each individual man. Gorgias, it would seem, claimed that there was no reality, and that even if there were it would be impossible to know or, finally, communicate anything about it. But these views did not so much of themselves cast light upon perception, as promote thought upon the part of Plato and Aristotle which did. Hence, in passing to Plato and Aristotle, one enters the period in which inquiry into the nature of perception begins.

(iii) PLATO

Socrates held that virtue is knowledge and that it was his mission in life to show men that what they took for knowledge was not in fact knowledge. Only in this way could virtue come. He was thus confronted point-blank by the Sophists, who claimed the impossibility of knowledge of reality. For this and for other reasons, such as the fact that they claimed to teach *arete*—virtue or, more specifically, an excellence at human arts of which it was presumed that living was one—he felt it necessary to refute them. On Socrates' view, the knowledge which was virtue was knowledge of quite a different kind from that to be found in the special sciences and arts. Plato's interests in knowledge, although derived from those of his master, Socrates, took him beyond the sphere of the ethical, and he sought for a general account of knowledge of reality. His answer is well known—the Forms or Ideas, with the corollary that what ordinary people call knowledge of the sensible world is only opinion (δόξα).

But what were his views on perception itself? What kind of thing did he take it to be? The main source for an answer to these questions is the comparatively late dialogue, the *Theaetetus*, but there are incidental remarks in the *Republic* which must be considered first.

At the end of Book V of the *Republic* (476e ff), Plato introduces a distinction between knowledge (γνῶσις), ignorance (ἀγνωσία) and an intermediate state, opinion (δόξα). He talks of these 'states' in such a way that they are all represented as being *of* something. They are, in other words, all forms of an awareness of or acquaintance with something. It is very difficult to apply such a notion to ignorance, as we use the word, but Plato nevertheless does so. Knowledge is said to be of that which has being, and ignorance is said to be of that which does not have being (another notion which it is difficult for us to accept). Opinion, being an intermediate state, is said to be of that which is between being and not-being.

Opinion is not formally equated with sense-perception, but its object seems to be the sensible world, and it might be inferred that Plato would have thought of sense-perception also as a form of being acquainted with something. Yet it is not knowledge, for, as he brings out at 477e, it is not free from error. And he goes on to dwell upon the reasons why error is liable to occur in connection with it. These are that the objects of opinion are relative. Any sensible thing can, for example, appear beautiful relative to one thing but ugly relative to another, and so it cannot be an object of knowledge. The implication is that, to be an object of knowledge, there must be something which is absolutely beautiful, and that this is a Form which acts as the standard of beauty. And the same applies to other relative properties.[1] It should be noted that the argument is limited by the fact that Plato confines his attention to relative properties. Not all sensible properties are relative; redness, for example, is not, and the same is true of a great number of properties. Moreover, it does not strictly follow from the fact that one cannot say of anything that it is beautiful without qualification that one would be *in error* in saying that it was beautiful.

In Books VI and VII Plato relies upon the distinction between knowledge and opinion in constructing his famous similes of the Line and the Cave. The purpose of these is to illustrate the process whereby the soul may be drawn up by education to a knowledge of reality (which consists of Forms and of the Form of the Good in particular), instead of being confined merely to the objects of opinion. At 523a ff., where Plato is beginning to talk of education and in particular of the power of arithmetic to draw the soul upwards, he has rather more explicit things to say about perception. In this passage, perhaps, a different view of the matter begins to emerge, a view which was to be consolidated in the *Theaetetus*.

In order to show the power of arithmetic in education Plato uses an illustration based upon our perception of the properties of our fingers. He says that whereas the senses can judge of themselves that they are confronted with a finger, they cannot judge whether they are confronted with, for example, something big or small. These latter properties are relative, and whether a finger is

[1] Aristotle refers to arguments for the existence of Forms both from the possibility of knowledge and from relative terms in *Metaphysics*, A.9.

big or small, rough or smooth, depends upon what it is being contrasted with. In such cases reason is brought in to make a decision. The same holds of number, on Plato's view, so that numerical predicates are thought of as relative and so presuppose the existence of Forms of numbers as standards.

In this passage Plato says that the senses make judgments and indicate the results to the soul. Reason is brought in only where the results are incompatible, and it is not brought in where the things perceived do not 'issue in the opposite perception at the same time' (523b9). Plato speaks of the senses anthropomorphically; but this is a common mistake and is far from being peculiar to him. Nevertheless, the important point that emerges is the connection of perception with judgment. In some cases that judgment is straightforward; in other cases it has to be made relative to other standards. The distinction between absolute and relative properties, which became fundamental to Academic arguments about the Forms, is a logical one. In this case, however, Plato makes the distinction by implying that the absolute properties are those which the senses are competent to judge for themselves. The relative properties, just because they are liable to give rise to incompatible judgments, require reason to be invoked, in order to provide standards. An implication might be that so far Plato had no need of Forms of non-relative properties.

At some time or other, Plato came to accept (or perhaps, apply to the present problem as something already accepted) the view put forward by Heraclitus or his disciple, Cratylus, that the whole of the sensible world is in a state of flux. It is probable that because of this he came to think that the senses never judge adequately about any sensible properties, and that the whole sensible world is imperfect, a mere imitation of the world of Forms.[1] This view is put forward in the *Timaeus* (which, there is reason to think, should be dated soon after the *Republic*)[2] and is at any rate hinted at in the *Cratylus*. Second thoughts on this matter are to be found in subsequent dialogues, beginning with the *Parmenides*, and the consequences for Plato's view of perception are to be found in the first part of the *Theaetetus*.

[1] Cf. G. E. L. Owen, 'A Proof in the Peri Ideon', *J.H.S.*, 1957, esp. pp. 108-10.

[2] See G. E. L. Owen, 'The Place of the Timaeus in Plato's Dialogues', *C.Q.*, 1953.

This part of the *Theaetetus* is concerned with the question whether *aesthesis* is knowledge.[1] The suggestion that it is knowledge is associated with the views of Protagoras in the version that everything is what it seems to a man and that therefore *aesthesis* is 'of something that is—and is infallible' (152c). This is clearly not perception in the ordinary sense of the word. The Protagorean view is then explicitly connected with the doctrine of flux, and the joint effect of the two views is to make all sensible properties relative (the theory which is implicit in the *Timaeus*). Moreover, in order to back up this view, reference is made to a physiological theory of perception (153d ff., esp. 156a ff.) which is also invoked in the *Timaeus* (67c), and which is probably derived from Empedocles. It is the causal theory that perception occurs as a result of the meeting of motions from the eye and motions from the object, the product being both perception and the perceived quality together. This causal theory is used to show that all perceived qualities are relative to the perceiver, and this conclusion is supported (157e ff.) by reference to illusions and delusions. The general outcome is the view that all perceptible properties are relative, and according to 'Protagoras' this makes perception of them infallible, since it is impossible to distinguish between what is and what appears.

In the previous dialogues, Plato had argued that the necessity of making a distinction between what is and what appears, together with the supposed fact that perceptible properties are relative, entails that reality (or that which is) must be constituted by the Forms. In the *Theaetetus* the situation is different; for Socrates' reply to Protagoras (178c ff.) involves an appeal to ordinary, everyday standards of correctness. He points to the fact that there are acknowledged experts in fields such as those of medicine or cooking and it is these experts who provide the standard of correctness in their own field. There is no appeal to the Forms, in order to provide such standards, and the knowledge of which Plato talks here is knowledge in the ordinary sense. The 'Heraclitean' view of the sensible world is in turn refuted by the consideration that, as Cratylus himself saw, it makes *any* form of discourse concerning it

[1] It is best not to translate '$αἴσθησις$' because of its ambiguity between sensation and perception. On this point and on others connected with the present discussion see my 'Eikasia in Plato's Republic', *Ph. Q.*, 1958, esp. pp. 21–2.

impossible—a conclusion which is treated as a *reductio ad absurdum*. Thus ordinary empirical judgments are vindicated, and being, not merely becoming, is attributed to objects of perception (185a ff.). This constitutes a revolution in Platonic thought, and it is connected with other developments in Platonic thought which may be discovered in the later dialogues.[1] To go into these here would take us too far afield, but it is important to note the consequences for Plato's final views on perception of the developments already noted in the *Theaetetus* itself.

As a final refutation of Protagoras, Socrates first suggests that we should talk of perceiving objects *through* the senses, but *with* the mind. This is an important step forward from the doctrine of the *Republic*, according to which the senses themselves perceive. Socrates then points out that certain properties of objects, e.g. their existence, their identity with themselves and their difference from other objects, are ascribable to them *only* as a result of the mind's judgment upon the 'impressions' which we have from those objects. According to the Protagorean thesis, *aesthesis* meant merely the having of such impressions, but now Plato implies that what we call empirical knowledge consists not merely in having these impressions, but in this with the addition of judgment or reflection upon the impressions. Elsewhere, in the *Sophist* Plato explains how such notions as existence, sameness and difference play a part in the judgments which we make about things.

Throughout this section of the *Theaetetus* Plato has used the term *aesthesis* in the special sense outlined at the beginning of the exposition of the Protagorean thesis. That is to say, to have *aesthesis* is to have an acquaintance with or an awareness of a sensible object; and the last is an impression, or what modern philosophers have called a sense-datum. He has not therefore been concerned with perception in the ordinary sense of the word. But it is noteworthy that the outcome of the discussion is that what we should ordinarily call perception involves both this kind of acquaintance with an impression and also the making of a judgment about these impressions by the mind. In the notion of an impression the notions of sensation and perception are blended

[1] Cf. my 'The Communion of Forms and the Development of Plato's Logic', *Ph. Q.*, 1955, and see also R. S. Bluck, *J.H.S.*, 1957, and J. Ackrill, *Bull. Inst. Class. London*, 1955, and *J.H.S.*, 1957.

and there is no conception on Plato's part of a need to separate them. Impressions are like sensations in so far as they are caused by things outside us; they are perceptual in so far as they afford us *knowledge* of things outside us. And the causal element in the mixture is treated, as it often has been by philosophers, as providing a reason for attributing infallibility to the knowledge which constitutes the other element.

Plato is wrong on this last point, since if a sensation is caused in us *neither* fallibility *nor* infallibility can be attributed to it; the application of the category of cause means that such considerations are ruled out—they do not make sense. This fact is obscured by the use of a term like 'impression' which is a mixture of two distinct elements. It remains true, however, that what is spoken of in the *Republic* as the object of a judgment by the sense is, in the *Theaetetus*, characterized as an impression. But there judgment is finally reintroduced; only this time (a significant and important point) it is made by the *mind*. It is this judgment which, it may be supposed, makes error possible.

The next part of the *Theaetetus* includes a discussion of how error is possible, even so. Plato takes a mistake of judgment to be a mistake of identity—the erroneous taking of one thing for another. But he finds difficulty in understanding how this is possible. Either we know the two things in question, and then no mistake is possible in taking one for the other, or we are ignorant of at least one of them, and then they cannot be compared by us or brought into the sort of relation which could lead to our being either right or wrong in identifying them. The final resolution of the problem is given in the *Sophist*, and it involves the recognition of a wider class of judgments, so that to make a mistake is not merely to take one thing for another.

In the course of the discussion in the *Theaetetus*, Plato goes through a number of cases in which mistakes are impossible, and the only one in which he allows that mistakes *are* possible is that in which a present sense-impression is fitted to the wrong memory-image. (This, it is worth noting, is not so much a mistake in identification as a mistake in detecting similarities between things.) To illustrate the process, he introduces the famous simile of the wax and the seal; the end-product of perception is literally an impression, which is wrongly assimilated to the concept which we already have. Yet even here Plato finds difficulties, and he illustrates these by the use of another simile, in which the mind is likened to an aviary and the pieces of knowledge, the concepts which we have, to birds in it. How, Plato asks, can we be mistaken concerning which bird is which? When we are called upon to fit a present sense-impression to the concept or memory which we have, it seems that mistakes are impossible if we cannot be mistaken either about the sense-impression or about the memory-image taken individually. In this discussion Plato treats both perceiving and the having of concepts (or remembering) as forms of being acquainted with an object; to perceive involves being acquainted with a sense-impression, to remember involves being acquainted with a memory-image or concept. And if they *are* treated in this way, difficulties ensue in connection with the judgment which is also necessary to empirical knowledge. Throughout the discussion, that is, perception is thought of only in the restricted sense of the *aesthesis* of the first part of the dialogue; and memory is treated analogously.

The difficulties about judgment which are raised in the second part of the *Theaetetus* are left unresolved there. In the *Sophist*, however, an attempt is made to deal with the problem by stressing the point that in making a judgment we do not equate or assimilate two separate things. Forms can interweave or overlap, and they are in consequence not separate entities at all in the strict sense. But in so far as judgment is concerned with interrelationships between Forms (and perhaps, derivatively at least, between Forms and other things) the new view of Forms makes possible the recognition of a wider class of judgments than that presented in the *Theaetetus*. In groping his way to a new view of judgment, Plato is also, I think, showing how empirical knowledge is possible. The important point remains that in so far as this empirical knowledge is what *we* should call perception (as distinct from the *aesthesis* of the *Theaetetus*), it is not merely a matter of having impressions; it involves also the making of a judgment by the mind, whatever the nature of this. In turning to Aristotle we shall find him moving in the same direction.

(iv) ARISTOTLE

Aristotle's main discussion of sense-perception, which is to be found in the *De Anima*,[1] is unlike that of Plato in that its context is not epistemological. Aristotle is not, in that work, concerned with the question whether perception brings with it knowledge or can act as the basis of knowledge. He does, it is true, make statements about the infallibility of the senses; but nothing is built upon these, and he eventually comes to the point at which he is not willing to attribute infallibility to any perception—a view which seems to be dictated purely by the empirical facts.

Aristotle's epistemological concerns were with the first principles of the sciences—how we know these and what they are; he was not similarly concerned with the reliability of the senses as a source of knowledge. In the *De Anima* he says that before perceiving the senses are nothing actual at all, and that the same is true of the relation between the intellect and thought. Moreover, he says that the soul never thinks without an image, while images depend for their existence upon previous sense-experience. On this has been built the view which St. Thomas Aquinas developed —that Aristotle was responsible for the empiricist theory of knowledge, to the effect that '*nihil est in intellectu quod non prius in sensu*'. This is not the correct interpretation of the relevant passages. They are all statements of the philosophy of mind rather than of epistemology. That is to say that they are attempts to elucidate certain mental concepts rather than to provide an account of the origins and validity of knowledge. The views noted above are all consequences of the doctrine that both sense-perception and the acquisition of intellectual knowledge are a process from potentiality to actuality. Before actualization the senses and the intellect are mere capacities; and the soul is a set of such

---

[1] I have discussed Aristotle's treatment of *aesthesis* in the *De Anima* in rather more detail in an article entitled 'Aristotle's Account of Aesthesis in the De Anima'. I am indebted to the editors for permission to reproduce material from that article. In the present discussion the references (which are to the *De Anima* unless otherwise stated) are exemplary only and further references may be found in the article.

capacities in which the higher are dependent upon the actualization of the lower. It is because human-beings use their senses that they have the capacity for thought. Hence, if the soul could think without an image, the intellect might, prior to actual thought, be more than a mere capacity for thought dependent upon the functioning of the lower faculties.

In the end, Aristotle *does* come to the view that there is a form of intellect which is more than a mere capacity—the so-called 'active intellect' as opposed to the 'passive intellect' with which we have been so far concerned. He does this because of his doctrine that in the general scheme of things what is actual is always prior to what is potential. Hence if the soul consists of a set of potentialities which require actualization, there must also be something entirely actual in it which is, so to speak, responsible for that actualization. This is the active intellect and *it has no other function in the* soul. It cannot, in particular, make possible any thinking on the part of the soul which is not composed of images provided ultimately by sense-experience. Aquinas does give the active intellect other functions in the context of the empiricist theory of knowledge which he builds upon Aristotle's theory, but it was not Aristotle's intention to produce such a theory of knowledge. He was concerned to analyse the concepts involved in an account of the soul's functioning, an analysis which he provides in terms of such general notions as those of actuality and potentiality; and these general notions are employed because they have been proved useful elsewhere.

There is one passage in the *Metaphysics* (Γ.5; cf. K.6) where epistemological interests do emerge to some extent, but this, interestingly enough, is in the context of a refutation of Protagoras. Aristotle says that each sense is more reliable concerning its own proper object than it is about the objects of another sense. Moreover, a sense never 'makes contradictory declarations' about an affection or quality (πάθος—*pathos*) either at one time or at different times, but only about the object from which the affection is derived. Hence, what a sense 'says' about the experience itself is true. Here Aristotle wishes to distinguish between the physical object and the affections which it produces.[1] This distinction,

---

[1] The difficulty here is that the word *pathos*—the same word as that which was rendered 'impression' in Plato's discussion—seems to be used to cover both the experience and the quality of the object experienced.

Aristotle maintains, Protagoras failed to make. The point made is in effect the same as that of Plato, and Aristotle echoes many of Plato's criticisms. In particular, he maintains that we have to take some standard of judgment in the case of perception, and that we must not take deviations from this, such as occur in illness, as anything else but deviations.

This passage of the *Metaphysics* contains the germs of two notions which present difficulties for Aristotle in his main discussion of perception in the *De Anima*. Firstly, perception is said to involve a *pathos*. Since this word is etymologically connected with the verb 'πάσχειν' (*paschein*—to suffer or be affected), perception may in this respect be viewed as passive.[1] Secondly, it is said that the senses make declarations about their objects. In the second book of the *De Anima* Aristotle says similarly that they judge about their objects, although in the third book he comes to talk only of ourselves or our souls making judgments. Both views, however, make perception an active process. Hence, there seem to be grounds for subsuming perception under two of the Aristotelian categories—those of passivity and activity. The Aristotelian categories—substance, quantity, quality, etc.—are, roughly, ultimate predicates or genera, such that to say that something falls under one of them precludes its falling under another. To assert that something falls under some category when it really falls under another is to make a category-mistake. Such mistakes are listed as fallacies in the *De Sophisticis Elenchis*, ch. 22. One example given in that passage is of a fallacy which arises from considering perception as active merely because the verb 'to perceive' is active in form, whereas it is in fact essentially passive.

As Aristotle comes to view the matter, the reasons for connecting perception with activity are more than grammatical, since it involves judgment. Perhaps the most explicit recognition of the connection of perception with judgment or discrimination is to be found in the *Posterior Analytics* (99b35), where Aristotle says that all animals possess a 'congenital discriminative capacity which is called sense-perception'. The persistence of sense-impressions, he says, leads to memory, and this in turn to what he calls experience—the basis of empirical knowledge but as yet unsystematized.[2] Sense-perception is not rated very highly here in the

[1] For a full-blooded espousal of this view see *Cat.* 9b5 and *Phys.*, 244b10.
[2] Cf. *Met.*, A.1.

scale of the functions of the soul, but its connection with judgment or discrimination is explicit. On the other hand, as he admits in the *De Anima* (424b16), it is a necessary though not a sufficient condition of perception that something should be receptive of something else. Hence there are grounds for connecting perception both with the category of activity and with that of passivity.

Aristotle's adherence to the view that sense-perception is a form of passivity is due not only to a respect for the obvious fact that in order to perceive something our sense-organs must be stimulated; it is also partly due to a respect for tradition. Perhaps more than most philosophers, he had a great concern for the history of his subject, despite the fact that he tried to fit the views of his predecessors into his system. The Presocratics had given causal or physiological accounts of perception and he thought it incumbent upon him to give these due credit. This general policy had the result that his views on certain subjects, of which physiology is an especially good example, were archaic and reactionary.

Aristotle held that the brain was merely the cooling system of the body, even when there was available good evidence to the contrary. In a similar way he clung with too great a readiness to the traditional four elements of which Empedocles had made so large a use. In the *De Sensu*, ch. 2, he raises difficulties about any attempt to allocate one of these elements to each sense-organ, on the grounds that whereas there are four elements there are five senses. Nevertheless, at the close of the chapter he does make an attempt to do this all the same, by treating taste as a form of touch. The considerations on which he bases his allocation of the elements vary from the empirical one that the eye contains water, to the relatively *a priori* one that the organ of smell must be connected with fire, because the object of smell is a smoky exhalation. The organ of smell is therefore appropriately situated near the brain, so that being cold as a result it is potentially hot! In the *De Anima* he gives up this neat scheme of things, maintaining that all sense-organs consist mainly of water and air, though there may be some fire present, and, in the case of touch, earth also. His physiology of the sense-organs in this work is conditioned, nevertheless, by the same presuppositions as those made in the *De Sensu*—that the sense-organs are composed of one or more of the elements, and that their objects are in consequence related to one or more of the traditional opposites which are associated with the elements; that is to say, hot, cold, moist and dry. Whatever be the exact nature of the physiology, however, sense-perception is thought of as resulting from the affection of a sense-organ by an object of a certain kind.

Aristotle uses two formulae in order to explain how this comes about. Clearly, it is not *any* kind of change produced in a sense-organ which gives rise to perception; indeed, as he notes, in certain cases, such as those where stimulation is excessive or insignificant, no perception results. The first formula is that in sense-perception the sense (424a17) or the sense-organ (425b23) receives the sensible form without the matter. Whereas, he says elsewhere, sensible knowledge is always of the particular, it is of the particular as a 'such', i.e. it is concerned with the universal, or form, *in* the particular. In this formula Aristotle uses technical vocabulary which he has evolved to deal with philosophical problems. He means that in perception the sense-organ receives a *quality* of the object without the material in which the quality inheres. A hand, for example, may become warm by coming into contact with a warm object; it receives the warmth but not the object itself. Aristotle here reveals a tendency to generalize from favourable cases without noticing possible objections. The eye does not become coloured when we perceive a coloured object. Seeing something coloured is not just a matter of being stimulated by such a coloured object.

The second formula is that in perception the sense (431b22), the faculty (418a3) or the sense-organ (422a7) is potentially what the sense-object is actually. In this case Aristotle again employs the technical distinction between actuality and potentiality. His general view is that for change to occur that which changes must first possess a potentiality for the change; although, as was previously noted, there must be something purely actual prior to all potentiality, if the process from potentiality to actuality in any particular case is to take place. In the case of the change which lies at the basis of sense-perception, the sense-organ must possess the potentiality for becoming like that which the object of perception is actually. It is again possible to see how this may be so when a hand is affected by something warm, but the formula is not applicable to all forms of perception. The two formulae are in many ways equivalent, and they have similar defects.

Nevertheless, a wider application could be given to the second formula by reference to Aristotle's physiology of the sense-organs. As we have already seen, in the *De Sensu* he assumes that the object of smell is connected with fire, while the organ of smell is cold because of its proximity to the brain and is, therefore, potentially hot. As a result, smell consists in the organ of smell becoming warm. In perceiving, therefore, the sense-organ and its object acquire the same quality, although before perception they were different.

In stating the second formula Aristotle sometimes speaks of it as applicable to the faculty of sense-perception rather than to the sense-organ. (Both formulae are also applied to the *sense*, but Aristotle's use of 'sense' is, in this case, merely ambiguous; it means either the faculty or the organ.) At 425b26 he says that the activity of the sense and of the object are one and the same, and he goes on to elucidate this with regard to hearing, saying in effect that our hearing and the sounding of the object are coincident. More than this, they *logically* involve each other. He seems to mean by this that hearing and sounding must be defined in terms of each other. There cannot be actual hearing without there being a sound to hear, and *vice versa*. That the first is so is clear, but the statement of the reverse connection would require some justification. It may well be that the most that can be said is that it would not make *sense* to talk of there being sounds in general unless it made sense to talk of hearing in general. Since, in hearing, the ear does not become like the sounding object (it does not, that is, become noisy), this is perhaps a reason for concluding that here Aristotle is talking about the faculty, not the sense-organ (an interpretation which is in any case plausible). It is, of course, true that earlier (424a25) he has said that the faculty and the organ are one and the same under different aspects—meaning by this that the faculty is the organ's capacity for functioning. But it is nevertheless important to distinguish them in just this respect.

Whatever the exact interpretation, the point made in this passage is a logical one, and it has, in consequence, no bearing upon the attempt to explain how it is that in sense-perception something in us becomes affected by the object. Aristotle gives the impression of thinking that it does have this bearing, and if so he is wrong. It is an empirical point that when put near the fire our hands become warm; it is *not* an empirical point that when someone actually hears a sound, there is something sounding. Furthermore, whereas this logical point is applicable in the case of hearing, taste and smell, since we talk of objects internal to these faculties, it is not applicable in the case of sight. There is nothing in the case of sight which corresponds to it as sound does to hearing. Aristotle supposes that the proper object of sight is colour; but there is no necessity that when someone is seeing he should see a colour, let alone that where there is a colour someone should be seeing it. It might be suggested that in fact the proper object of vision is a sight. We do use the word 'sight' as a sort of internal accusative of the verb 'to see', just as we use the word 'sound' in relation to the verb 'to hear'. But there are important differences also between the character of sights and sounds. In particular, while sounds are emitted from objects, sights are not—a sight is not something *caused* by an object. There are difficulties also in the notion that there is a special object of touch.[1] We may, of course, be said to feel the texture of physical things, and we may experience the feelings which this produces, but it is those physical things themselves which we *touch*.

The conclusions to be drawn from the discussion so far are (1) that Aristotle's attempts to explain how sense-perception may be regarded as a form of passivity are successful only in certain cases, and even then only in application to the physical or physiological processes underlying perception; (2) that his statement of the logical point that in hearing the activity of the faculty and of the sense-objects are one and the same is independent of and irrelevant to the attempt to show how sense-perception is a form of passivity; (3) that even the logical point mentioned under (2) is not applicable in the case of all the senses. In stressing the role of passivity in perception Aristotle was really emphasizing the fact that, if perception is to occur, our senses require to be stimulated (although he did not have such vocabulary at his disposal). The affection of our sense-organs is a necessary condition of perception. One might put the matter in another way by saying that Aristotle was really concerned with the conditions under which we have *sensations*. Indeed, other philosophers have used the term 'sensation' of what he calls sense-objects. But the inability to fit sights and sounds into this framework serves to indicate (*a*) that it is wrong to think of the perception of *them* as something which is

[1] Cf. G. J. Warnock, *Berkeley*, ch. 3.

purely passive, and correlatively, (*b*) that it is wrong to call *them* sensations. This does not mean that perception can occur without an affection of the sense-organ, nor does it mean that it is wrong to talk of sensations at all. It means rather that while affection of a sense-organ is a *necessary* condition of sense-perception, it is a *sufficient* condition of the having of sensations.

It has been indicated that Aristotle holds that each sense has a special object. He makes clear, however (418a7 ff.), that there are in fact *three* kinds of sense-object, two of which are essentially the objects of a sense, while the third is so only accidentally. Each individual sense has a special sense-object which is connected essentially with it; hearing has sound, smell odours, and sight, though Aristotle is wrong about this, colour. Each sense requires also a medium, such as light in the case of vision, and in a way this is also an object of sense of the same sort. There are, secondly, certain qualities of objects which are not essentially connected with any of the individual or special senses, but with what Aristotle calls the common sense. These qualities are those which later became known as the primary qualities—motion, rest, figure, size, number, unity. Particular instances of these, such as bigness or smallness, quickness or slowness, tend to be relative. Plato had indeed made constant reference to such examples when concerned with Forms of relatives.

These qualities are not essential to any special sense, for they are common to all, or at least to sight and touch. Yet they are not incidental objects of perception in general. Every coloured object, for instance, has some size. Hence, when we perceive a coloured object we do not perceive something having size merely incidentally, as would be the case if some coloured objects had a size and some did not.[1] It follows, in Aristotle's opinion, that the so-called common sensibles must be essentially connected with some sense, but not with any special sense. For this reason (as well as for others, such as the fact of self-consciousness, the fact that *all* the senses cease to function in sleep, and that we are able to discriminate between the different senses) he posits a common sense. But he denies that there is a common sense-organ, since we perceive the common sensibles *via* the special sense-organs, even if those common sensibles are incidental to the senses which go with those sense-organs. The common sensibles

[1] Cf. *De An.*, 425b4 ff. on this point.

are, therefore, essential to the common sense, but incidental to the special senses—the latter because it does not follow from the fact that, for example, we have a certain feeling when we touch something, that what we touch has a size. (I take it that this is what Aristotle intends to say, although it might well be argued that here the difficulties about the notion that there are special objects of touch and vision come to the fore. It *does* seem that if we touch something what we touch must have a size, and similarly that if we see something that too must have a size; but this is because we are normally said to see and touch *things*. Aristotle's attachment to the notion of special sensibles prevents him from seeing this.)

The third kind of sense-object recognized by Aristotle has already been mentioned implicitly; it is that which he calls incidental or accidental. It may happen that what we see or feel is, to use Aristotle's example, the son of Cleon, i.e. it may happen that what we see or feel is to be identified in a certain way. But not everything that we see or feel is to be identified in that particular way. For this reason, the son of Cleon is only an incidental object of vision; it is not essential to him that he should be seen, nor is it essential to vision that, if we see, we should see *him*. It follows on Aristotle's view that, whereas the qualities of the things which we perceive are essentially connected with some sense, the things themselves (i.e. their identity) are not.

In the passage where Aristotle first makes these distinctions (418a7 ff.) he defines a special sensible as 'that which cannot he perceived by another sense, and concerning which it is impossible to make mistakes'. The first of these criteria is similar to that given in the passage of the *Metaphysics* referred to earlier, where Aristotle is trying to refute Protagoras. The similarity between the passages is increased by the fact that in the *De Anima* he goes on to say that 'each sense judges about these things (sc. colour, sound, etc.) and is not deceived as to the fact that it is colour or sound'. Sight cannot be mistaken as to the fact that it is concerned with colour, as opposed, for example, to sound. It is noteworthy that it is the senses that are said to judge, not we ourselves. The reason why Aristotle says that sight does not make mistakes about things being coloured is, as we have already seen, that he believes that there is a necessary connection between seeing and colour. To speak of the senses making judgments merely encourages the belief that it is right to talk of incorrigibility in this context. In truth, however, the supposed necessary connection between the notions of seeing and colour is no reason for making claims to incorrigibility. There is no justification for the assumption that *because of* this necessary connection there is no possibility of making mistakes. Aristotle is seeking only to define the special sensibles, and he could well have done so merely by referring to the necessary connection between them and the relevant senses.

The thesis about the necessary connection between a sense and its objects was intended by Aristotle to explain how it is that perception is a form of passivity. If this is so, it is difficult to see how questions of being right or wrong can arise in this connection. In other words, the reference to judgment is *prima facie* incompatible with the view that perception consists in being receptive. In a later passage (430b29) he compares perception of the special sensibles with that form of the intellect which is concerned with single notions and which involves no judgment; and he says that in this case there is no falsehood. If no judgment is involved, he should in fact have said that questions of truth and falsity do not arise. But if the perception of the special sensibles is really like the form of the intellect whose function is to be receptive of intellectual forms or concepts, it must be something purely passive, something akin to the having of sensations. On this view it is impossible to make mistakes about the special sensibles because they are not the sort of thing about which one can make judgments, and hence not the sort of thing about which one can make mistakes. Nevertheless, he does feel it necessary to say that the senses make judgments, and he has in consequence two conflicting views to put forward about perception—one to the effect that it is active, the other to the effect that it is passive; and his all-over view is an uneasy compromise between these two particular views.

At 428b21, after a series of passages in which Aristotle implies that it is we who judge rather than the senses, he returns to the theme of incorrigibility, but only to say that with regard to the special sensibles error arises as little as possible. He does not now insist, that is, on absolute incorrigibility. The reason for the shift in his point of view becomes apparent when the examples which he uses are considered. He now says, not that sight makes no mistakes in being confronted with colour, but that we make mistakes as little as possible concerning whether we are confronted with something *white*. In other words, he is not now considering what is supposed to follow from a necessary connection between a sense and its object, but how far, in general, we are *in fact* mistaken about whether something is white, as opposed, say, to black. There is no necessary connection, even on Aristotle's view, between sight and whiteness. He can rightly talk of our judging whether something is white, and to the question whether we make mistakes in doing so he rightly answers, 'Seldom.'

He goes on, after this, to say that we are more likely to make mistakes over the incidental sensibles and most likely of all to do so over the common sensibles. That is to say that whereas we are not likely to make mistakes concerning whether a thing is white, we are more likely to do so concerning whether it has a certain identity. And we are most liable to error concerning whether it is big or small. On the face of it, the order of fallibility is puzzling, but the reasons for the order become evident when the examples are considered. Mistakes about common sensibles are said to be most frequent just because they are relative, and, as Plato argued, relative notions are those *par excellence* which give rise to error.

Erroneous judgments in general Aristotle tends to put down to the imagination, although many of the things that he includes under the imagination would be classified differently by us. In particular he classes illusions and delusions as facets of the imagination; and while delusions might reasonably be so classified it is much less clear that illusions can be treated in this way. A man suffering from a delusion has abnormal beliefs which may well be due to the imagination; and these beliefs need not be beliefs about that which he is perceiving. An illusion, on the other hand, is an abnormal or incorrect perception and need not be due to the imagination; some illusions arise because of the features of that which is being perceived. One reason for Aristotle's catholic treatment of the imagination is that the Greek word for the imagination (φαντασία—*phantasia*) is etymologically connected with the verb 'to appear' (φαίνεσθαι—*phainesthai*) and so covers appearances of all kinds. Hence, while Aristotle makes a general distinction between *phantasia* and *aesthesis*, much that we would call perception is attributed by him to the imagination.

The Aristotelian picture of the mind or soul differs in a well-known way from the Platonic. Whereas Plato viewed the soul as a substance responsible for the powers of movement possessed by the body and also for certain functions of its own, Aristotle thought of it as the principle of life. As such it was a substance only in the sense that it makes a person or an animal what it is—living and possessing faculties. In holding this view Aristotle was returning to an earlier and more common Greek conception of the *psyche*. For this reason he came to think that an account of the soul entailed an account of the various faculties possessed by a living animal equipped with organs. At 408b13 of the *De Anima* he says, 'It is doubtless better to avoid saying that the soul pities or learns or thinks, and rather to say that it is the man who does these with the soul.' He does not always live up to this dictum, and he often talks of the soul, or even of its faculties, doing things, but it nevertheless expresses the central aspect of his point of view.

Aristotle feels it necessary, therefore, to discuss (*a*) the nature of the sense-organs requisite for the exercise of our faculties, and (*b*) the nature of those faculties or capacities themselves. His discussion is therefore at once physiological, psychological and philosophical. But it is philosophical not in the sense that he is anxious to provide epistemological justification of the claims to knowledge which we make on the basis of perception, but in the sense that he is anxious to elucidate the nature of our psychological concepts. In its aim, therefore, Aristotle's discussion is of central importance for the whole topic under discussion.

Aristotle has, however, no conception of a distinction between sensation and perception, nor of the need to make such a distinction, despite his occasional use of a term which might be translated 'sensation'—αἴσθημα (*aisthema*). Yet much of his discussion suggests that he was on the verge of making such a distinction. This is especially evident in the compromise at which he seeks to arrive between the view of perception as passive and the view of it as active. That perception, on some occasions at any rate, involves judgment seems obvious, but it is not so obvious how this is to be squared with the fact that perception depends upon the stimulation and use of the sense-organs. A common tendency, when confronted with this problem, is to have recourse to a basic form of perception, which, while being in principle capable of being right or wrong, involves no judgment. There are suggestions of this view in Aristotle, and the view became more prevalent thereafter.

One final point: when we look at a table, for example, we may say either that we see a table or that we see something as a table (the latter perhaps suggesting doubt as to the object's actual identity). If we were called upon to say what we were doing in seeing the object as a table, we might be inclined to say that we were judging it to be one. Even if this answer is not strictly correct, as I think it is not, it has a certain plausibility. What of the case in which we say that we see a table *simpliciter*? Aristotle has no answer to this question, although in answer to Protagoras he admits that the normal case must be taken as the standard for correct perception; and this is relevant, in that, if we truly say that we see a table, the way in which we see what is there must be correct—it must be a table. But Aristotle gives no indication of realizing that an account of perception involves a consideration of 'seeing' as well as 'seeing as'. To have a sensation may well be to have a passive experience, to see something as X may have some affinity with judging it to be X; and Aristotle has some concern with both of these. But what of seeing *simpliciter*? If all seeing is a form of seeing as, if it all involves the making of judgments, what is it that we make judgments about and how do we know about it? To the first of these last-mentioned questions Aristotle's answer is ultimately, I think, *prime matter*, that which underlies all the properties ascribable to anything. Prime matter plays the role of a Kantian 'thing-in-itself' in Aristotle's system. Since it is not an object of perception it can have no perceptual properties, and must therefore be knowable in some quite different way, if at all. The view that all perception is a form of 'perceiving as' inevitably forces a philosopher who embraces it in the direction of such a notion.

In sum, Aristotle's view is that one faculty of the soul, i.e. one capacity possessed by an animal or human-being, is that of sense-perception. Each sense-organ has its own capacity for functioning and each is concerned with a specific sense modality. In addition to these there is a common sense—a general capacity for perception, which is not peculiar to any sense-organ and which is not concerned with qualities which are peculiar to any one sense modality. These capacities are elicited when the things around us affect our sense-organs, but those things themselves are incidental objects of perception only, since, unlike their qualities, perception of them is not essential to the successful functioning of the senses. (Nothing, be it noted, is said about their being *indirect* objects of perception, as is commonly supposed.) This is the biological framework which Aristotle analyses and with which he operates. The central problem which it raises is how it is to be connected with the fact that we find ourselves making perceptual *judgments* about the world around us. How, that is, can perception be a form of passivity and also, since it involves judgment, a form of activity? This is Aristotle's problem, though he can scarcely be said to have solved it.

2
HELENISTIC PHILOSOPHY

(i) INTRODUCTION

AFTER Aristotle, Greek philosophy changed its character, and a period ensued in which the main philosophical schools—the Epicureans, Stoics and Sceptics—were concerned first and foremost to present a way of life, a remedy for men's fears. (The same is true of the Academy during the period under Arcesilaus and Carneades, when it became sceptical in character.) The Epicureans and Stoics carried out this programme by prefacing their ethical views with a theory about nature and man's place in it. The Sceptics, on the other hand, sought to discourage men from speculation and maintained that only by abstaining from it could they obtain freedom from care; such speculation was, in any case, fruitless.

The concept which was of central importance for their views about perception was that of *phantasia* (the word is that which Aristotle used for imagination and appearances in general). The so-called dogmatic schools—the Epicureans and Stoics—claimed that *phantasiae* were both true and also clear and distinct (to use the later Cartesian terminology which affords an appropriate translation of the Greek 'ἐναργής'). Both schools opposed *phantasiae* to *phantasmata*, i.e. delusions, dreams and appearances in the literal sense, so making clear that they thought it possible to distinguish between veridical perception and delusive experiences. There are also other similarities between their positions, but there are fundamental differences as well, and their philosophies of mind are radically opposed to each other.

In contrast with the dogmatic schools, the Sceptics sought to show, by means of a series of arguments which are forms of what has since become known as the argument from illusion, that *phantasiae* conflict and are generally unreliable. Our perceptions, they claimed, continually conflict with each other and are always relative; hence it is important to go only by the momentary perception and not to speculate about what lies behind—not, that is, to use *phantasiae* as signs of some hidden truth. All these schools, therefore, had epistemological issues in mind when they discussed perception. They were interested in the question whether and how perception provides knowledge. We find such issues discussed by Sextus Empiricus—the Sceptic philosopher and doctor, to whom we owe much of our knowledge of the views of all the schools—under the heading of the 'Criterion of Truth'. Problems about the criterion of truth are problems about the source of the certainty which, it is commonly supposed, is necessary to knowledge.

(ii) EPICURUS

Epicurus took atomism to the extreme. Literally everything— material things, souls and gods—was, in his view, composed of atoms, and besides the atoms there was only the void. The movements of the atoms and hence of everything else were completely mechanical. The soul, as Democritus had also thought, consisted of small, smooth atoms held together by and distributed throughout the body. Its main constituents were 'particles resembling breath and heat' to which the doxographer Aëtius (iv. 3, 11) added air and a nameless element—the 'fourth nature'—which was responsible for sensation and consciousness in general. Because of the nature of the soul, death consisted only of the dispersal of its atoms. Hence, as Epicurus says, death is nothing to us.

According to the Epicurean theory, all sense-perception is the result of a direct contact with the atoms of the soul which permeate the sense-organs on the part of atoms which are emitted from objects. All objects give off atoms continually and these may affect the senses. Vision, for example, is due to the fact that objects give off films of atoms (εἴδωλα or *simulacra*) and these produce *phantasiae* when, in the mass, they stir the particles of the soul in the eyes. So far the process is entirely passive and mechanical.

The *phantasia* is the outcome of a strictly causal process, and one might justly suppose that it is a mere sensation. It is clear, however, that Epicurus supposes, firstly, that to have a *phantasia* is to *perceive* something and, secondly, that all *phantasiae* are veridical. Moreover, in his *Fundamental Tenets* (23 and 24) he stresses that our sensations (αἰσθήσεις—the same ambiguity between sensation and perception attaches to the word as in its use by earlier philosophers) are the ultimate standard to which we must refer all our judgments; and Diogenes Laertius (X. 31–2) quotes him as saying that they are the standard of truth and that they admit of no other check. These remarks belong to his *Canonice*, that part of his philosophy which was concerned with the foundations of knowledge, i.e. with his epistemology. Its purpose was to show that there is no other source of knowledge, except sense-perception, on which a metaphysical theory may be based.

In saying that sensations admit of no other check, Epicurus' position is similar to that of Aristotle, when he claimed incorrigibility for the perception of the special sensibles. Our sensations admit of no other check because there is no other information which is relevant to that 'given' in each sensation. But whereas Aristotle says this because he thinks that the senses judge about their objects, Epicurus' view is a full-blown causal theory of perception: that is to say that he thinks that the result of the causal process involved in the stimulation of the sense-organs is a perception *of* something. And because such a perception is *caused* he thought that it must be incorrigible; it is, so to speak, guaranteed. But in truth, if something is caused, it is not the sort of thing which *can* be right or wrong—a point which was noted in connection with Aristotle's comparison between perception of the special sensibles and the intellect which merely receives intelligible forms.[1] Epicurus admits that every sensation is *alogos*, i.e. unconnected with reason or judgment, but he nevertheless draws the conclusion that it is proper to speak of sensations as incorrigible.

Indeed he goes further than this. Diogenes Laertius (X. 32) records him as saying that even the *phantasmata* of the madman or the dreamer are true, since they produce effects in the mind. The reason given for the dogma is not very cogent if 'true' be given its

[1] See page 26 of this book.

usual sense, but it seems that Epicurus supposes dreams to be veridical for the same reason as *phantasiae*: they are both results of causal processes. Yet the possibility of our making mistakes about *things* is not precluded; for what *we* should call perception of things is more than *phantasiae* or *phantasmata*. To perceive things *phantasiae* have to be fitted in with already existing general conceptions (προλήψεις), which are a sort of composite photograph built up from successive sensations. These again are in general thought of in an entirely passive way. They are the source of opinion, and it is opinion that is the main cause of illusions, in that the incoming *simulacrum* is fitted to the wrong concept (Diog. Laert., X. 50).

Not all illusions, however, can be explained in this way. In some cases, e.g. when a square tower in the distance looks round, or a stick in water looks bent, it would seem that, in Epicurus' terms, the *simulacra* themselves must be misleading.[1] Epicurus is not very coherent on this point. There is a suggestion (Diog. Laert., X. 50; cf. Lucretius, iv. 353 ff.) that sometimes the *simulacra* become distorted, torn or decreased in size in their passage through the air. If this is so, even greater confirmation is given to the view that the only sense to be attached to the saying that all *phantasiae* are true is that they represent the effect which the *simulacra* have on the sense-organs. Even so, this explanation will hardly account for all illusions. Without further justification it is not very plausible to explain in this way the fact that sticks in water look bent. In sum, Epicurus explains perceptual errors, in so far as he can, (*a*) by reference to the distortion suffered by *simulacra* and (*b*) by reference to the effect of opinion or judgment. In the latter respect he follows Plato and Aristotle, except that he conceives of an opinion not as something *formed by us*, but as a process produced in our mind in a mechanical way. How this is possible is not at all clear even in Epicurean terms.

The *phantasiae* themselves are, like the sense-data of modern philosophy, a cross between sensations in the strict sense and forms of perception. But because of the purely causal and mechanical nature of Epicurus' view of the world, the passive features of perception are stressed to such an extent that there is left only a residue of the active aspects of perception, to account for which

[1] Cf. Sextus Empiricus, *Adv. Math.*, VIII. 9.

Plato and Aristotle had invoked judgment. Epicurus gave an elaborate account of the ways in which different forms of perception are produced, but the details add little to our picture of the way in which he regarded perception. In some of the details he follows Democritus, e.g. in attributing hearing to the effects of vibrations of the air set up by movements of atoms. Like Democritus too he distinguishes between what were later to be called primary and secondary qualities, i.e. properties like size and shape on the one hand and properties like colour on the other. But he shows less scepticism than Democritus about the latter; for he makes the primary qualities the properties of the atoms themselves, while the secondary qualities are properties of compounds only and are thus, so to speak, emergent.

It is perhaps worthy of note that in the case of vision he remarks that the brightness of objects has an effect upon our impression of their distance and size.[1] Lucretius adds also an explanation of distance-perception in terms of the length of the interval between the arrival at the eye of a puff of air produced by the *simulacrum*, when it leaves the object, and the subsequent arrival of the *simulacrum* itself.[2] Such explanations are intended to provide the mechanism whereby an impression of distance is set up; they are not meant, as they might be if they were fact, to indicate the features on which we rely in *estimating* distances. Epicurus' account of perception is, therefore, all of one piece.

(iii) THE STOA

The Stoics were opposed to the school of Epicurus in nearly every way. Where he despised logic, they studied it eagerly; where he put forward a mechanical conception of the universe, they put forward an organic conception designed to show that it was throughout rational; where he sought to show that man was merely a complex of atoms which split up at death, they sought

---

[1] It is for this reason that he says that the sun is of about the same size as it appears to be—for being bright it cannot be far away and therefore cannot be much bigger than it appears (Diog. Laert., X. 91). See Lucretius, *De Rer. Nat.*, Bk. iv, for other details.

[2] Lucretius, *De Rer. Nat.*, iv. 244 ff.

to show that man was the exemplification of reason and had at any rate a chance of survival. In their psychology, the Stoics emphasized the part played by reason and judgment; the passions, for example, were put down to false judgment—a view for which something is to be said, since only a rational creature, and hence a creature capable of being irrational, could experience passions. Nevertheless, they took such views to extremes.

The Stoics maintained that everything which either acts or is acted upon is corporeal (σῶμα). The soul, which is the unifying principle of living things, both acts and is acted upon; it is therefore corporeal, consisting of *pneuma* (πνεῦμα—breath or spirit). It has eight parts or faculties, organized under the 'ruling part', reason, and it has its seat in the heart (Diog. Laert., VII. 159). The view that the soul is corporeal might be thought to entail that they were no less materialist than Epicurus in this respect. Yet it is not clear that much turns upon the use of the word 'corporeal', since to call something this was to contrast it with such things as time, the void, and propositions. Hence, to call something a body is close to calling it a substance, or, perhaps, to calling it real.

In the field of perception, the central concept was, as in the case of Epicurus, that of *phantasia*, and this was similarly opposed to that of *phantasma*. It seems, however, that they may have used the first term quite generally, to cover any mental event as long as it has some connection with external phenomena, i.e. as long as it was not a *phantasma*—a dream-image or a delusion. The definition of a *phantasia* given by Zeno, the founder of the school, was 'an impression (τύπωσις) in the soul'. Chrysippus, the most important figure in the Stoa, seems to have used the term 'affection' (πάθος) instead. He denied that the word 'impression' should be understood as signifying a literal imprinting on the soul by a seal. It would be absurd, he thought, that a number of such impressions should be at the same place at the same time; and this would be necessary if the phenomena of perception were to be accounted for in this way. For this reason, he asserted that Zeno had meant by 'impression' only a change in the soul—a *pathos* induced by an object in such a way as to indicate the nature of that object.[1] According to Sextus Empiricus,[2] other Stoics insisted on

[1] Diog. Laert., VII. 50; *Plac.*, iv. 12,1.; Sext. Emp., *A.M.*, VII. 228 ff.
[2] Sextus Empiricus, *loc. cit.*

adding that the change was in the 'ruling part' of the soul; others again that it was a change not *in* the 'ruling part' but *of* or *about* it. Finally others insisted on adding that it was a change in respect of passivity and not activity. The Stoics clearly enjoyed such refinements.

Phantasiae themselves were classified in various ways. According to Sextus Empiricus (*A.M.*, VII. 241 ff.) they might be, in the first place, credible or the reverse (or, Sextus adds, neither or both of these!). If credible, they might be true or false (and, Sextus adds again, neither or both); and if true, then apprehensive (καταληπτίκος) or the reverse. The word *aesthesis* might be used of either (1) the activity of the soul—the issue of *pneuma* into the senses, (2) the sense-organ, or (3) the resulting apprehension.

The Stoics made no claim that *phantasiae* were in any sense *necessarily* veridical; they were merely 'images' produced by stimulation of the senses, and as such they might well be distorted (Sext. Emp., *A.M.*, VIII. 67). Little is known about Stoic views concerning the actual details of the way in which the senses are stimulated. Stoic physics, in contrast with that of Epicurus, stressed the notion of continuity. Hence it was thought that in vision the air in the form of a cone with its basis on the object seen and its apex on the eye conveys the impression to the eye; in hearing, the air strikes the ear in waves.[1] But it is clear from the definitions of *aesthesis* noted above that they thought of perception as involving more than mere stimulation of the sense-organ; for the soul itself responds with an extension of *pneuma* to the sense-organ. Psychologically, the latter corresponds to what they called 'assent' (συγκατάθεσις). On receipt of an impression a person can, if he so chooses, assent to it. The receipt of the impression is a passive affair, but the assent to it is an active one, and Chrysippus referred to this in his discussion of free-will, in order to indicate that our assent to an impression is the primary cause of perception and hence is in our power. The receipt of the impression is only a subsidiary cause; if it is a necessary condition, it is not a sufficient condition of perception. To assent to the impression is, so to speak, to register it; it is not in itself to vouch

---

[1] On the Stoic physics and its connection with their theory of sense-perception see S. Sambursky, *The Physics of the Stoics* (cf. the same author's *The Physical World of the Greeks*); cf. also Diog. Laert., VII. 157-8.

for its validity. Only when an impression is apprehensive can its validity be vouched for and the resulting state of mind is then apprehension. To be apprehensive the impression must be clear and distinct (ἐναργής)—intuitively certain.

Zeno used a simile to illustrate these processes. An impression, he said, is like the open hand; assent is like the hand with the fingers slightly contracted; apprehension is like the hand fully closed into a fist (Cicero, *Acad.*, ii. 145). The point of this simile is not at first sight obvious, but its intention is probably the following. It is meant to show that an impression by itself makes no claim upon the mind, but that with assent on our part the hand begins to close and the mind is lightly held, while finally, when we have apprehension the mind is gripped. (The word 'καταληπτικός' means literally 'gripping'.) The simile was completed by the assertion that when one fist is enclosed and gripped in the other this is knowledge.

The Stoics, then, believed that there were forms of perception that were intuitively certain, such that our assent is demanded and such that the soul is gripped. Nevertheless, a necessary condition of having this experience is the giving of assent to the initial *phantasia*. For this reason error can arise not only from the distortion of the impression itself but also because of erroneous assent. To this extent, since assent is in principle in our power, error depends, as Descartes was to say later, on the will. The Stoic concept of assent corresponds in some ways to that of judgment as used by Plato and Aristotle, and to that of opinion as used by Epicurus. The Stoics differed from Epicurus in making assent or opinion something manifestly active, something for which we are responsible. Their view of apprehension, however, placed them in a somewhat ambiguous position, since it involved the existence of impressions such that, although assent to them is still theoretically in our power, they nevertheless grip us in such a way that assent cannot be witheld. What is there, it might be asked, about the experience that makes it *impossible* for assent to be withheld, and what sort of impossibility is this? The difficulties in this view are common to all those which presuppose intuition or incorrigible experiences; they can be met in modern discussions of sense-data. The sceptical critics of the Stoa seem to have fastened on this point, for Sextus Empiricus (*A.M.*, VII. 253) records that later Stoics asserted that apprehensive impressions were a guarantee of truth *as long as there was no obstacle*. In other words, the very fact that something seems intuitively certain is only a guarantee of its validity if nothing else in the surrounding circumstances gives a contrary indication.

As already indicated, the Sceptics, and the New Academy in its sceptical phase under Arcesilaus and Carneades, discussed *phantasiae* only in order to show that they tended to give conflicting views about the nature of reality and hence that there was no point in treating them as signs of a hidden truth. They thus tended to accept the current view of *phantasiae*, and therefore of perception, without producing any fresh account of it. Indeed, any account of this sort would have been for them speculative and hence to be eschewed.

No other school had anything new to say on the matter until the resuscitation of Platonism by Plotinus in the 3rd century A.D. in the form which became known as Neo-Platonism. There had been forms of Platonism current before this in the 2nd century A.D.—the so-called Middle Platonism—but it was only by Plotinus that a comprehensive system was expounded.

(iv) PLOTINUS AND NEO-PLATONISM

Plotinus is a Platonist only in a certain sense. He relies most heavily upon the more mystical passages in Plato's dialogues, especially those which suggest a transcendent world. But he also owes a great deal to Aristotle and the Stoics. He often employs Aristotelian notions and distinctions, but he tends either to restrict their application or to alter their use in such a way as to make them more compatible with Platonism. In particular, while he uses the Aristotelian distinction between potentiality ($\delta\acute{u}\nu\alpha\mu\iota\varsigma$) and actuality ($\dot{\epsilon}\nu\acute{\epsilon}\rho\gamma\epsilon\iota\alpha$), he interprets the former notion, in Platonic fashion, as *power* rather than potentiality, and the latter notion as the former's exercise. Plotinus thinks of the world as a continuum with a centre—the One—which is transcendent and unknowable, but whose power extends outwards and downwards in such a way that it grows less as it reaches the outer and lower extremes. The exemplifications of the different degrees of power form a hierarchy of three kinds of being, or 'primary hypostases', as Plotinus calls them. These are the One, the Intellect and the

Soul. The One, while not a person, is divine. The Intellect is, roughly, the world of Forms in the Platonic sense—a perfect replica of everything in the sensible world—though Plotinus takes this notion further than Plato did. The Soul corresponds to the world-soul of Plato's *Timaeus*; it makes everything alive and it includes within itself, as a sort of lower stage, Nature. At the lowest extreme is bare matter, which is known only by way of negation. Because Nature and all that it comprises, including human bodies, is included in Soul, the latter is more powerful than it, even though it depends upon bodies and material things for its exercise. Analogously, the human soul has more power than the body, although the former depends upon the latter.

The human soul extends, in its powers, into the different bodily organs; they participate in it. Each power or faculty of the soul is exercised where it is most fitting. While the powers of the soul have their physical source-point in the brain, they are really drawn from elsewhere, since each soul is part of Soul and the latter participates in the realm of Intellect above it. According to Plotinus, therefore (*Ennead*, iv. 6; cf. 3 and 5), the soul functions actively in perception; it does not merely receive impressions passively. In fact, things do not leave an impression on the soul itself and cannot do so; they can only affect the body. Since perception is concerned with things outside it, a body is necessary if the soul is to perceive. But perceiving itself is a function of the soul. If objects left an impression directly on the soul, Plotinus says (*Enn.*, iv. 6, 1), we should never see objects themselves, but only their vestiges, their shadows. The soul, that is, would be concerned only with itself and its contents.

For confirmation of the view that perception is an active process he points to the fact that in using sight we direct our gaze directly towards the object. This is a point which, it was previously suggested, may have led Empedocles and Plato to think of perception as the result of two movements—one from the object and one from the sense-organ. For Plotinus it provides confirmation of the view that in perception the soul looks outwards; it reads, as it were, the impressions and uses the organs of sense as instruments. Hence perception is indirect, although in a peculiar way. Memory, of course, plays a part in our knowledge of sensible things, in that the soul's reading of a present impression must be fitted to a memory image, as Plato maintained in the *Theaetetus*.

But again, memory itself does not depend upon the body directly. The soul remembers its own activities, not what happens to the body. Memory has a link with the body only through the initial impressions which were the occasion for the soul's activity.

In one passage (*Enn.*, ii. 8) Plotinus discusses distance-perception. As Berkeley was to maintain later, Plotinus asserts that touch provides vision with the standard for our estimation of the size of objects; that is to say that *the* size possessed by objects is that discoverable by touch. He rejects the view that the perception of the distance of objects by sight depends upon the 'visual angle' which they subtend at the eye (the farther away an object is the smaller the angle which it subtends at the eye). He does so because this would be too passive a matter, and he seeks for more positive information that the soul can 'read'. He finds it in the fact that, on his view as on Aristotle's, the primary object of vision is colour. Colours are less distinguishable and fainter at a distance and the apparent magnitude of objects at a distance is, he thinks, decreased in proportion.

Despite his emphasis upon the soul's exercise of its powers in perception, Plotinus also insists upon the fact that the body is necessary—for how else could perception be distinguished from other mental functions? Yet Plotinus brings into sharp focus a problem which already existed for Plato, Aristotle and their successors: What is the connection between the physical processes which take place when our sense-organs are stimulated and the judgments etc. which we ourselves or our souls make when we perceive? This question is still with us, whatever be the terms in which it is raised, but the problem emerges in a sharply-focussed manner in Plotinus, because of the pre-eminent position which he gives to the soul as opposed to the body. While the problem was there for Aristotle, the issue was less clear-cut because of his view that the soul is the form of the body.

Plotinus serves as the link by which Greek thought passed into the Middle Ages. Just as a remark of Porphyry, the chief disciple of Plotinus, set off the mediaeval dispute about universals, so Plotinus' views about perception and their opposition to that strand of Aristotle's teaching which spoke of perception as the reception of sensible form without the matter gave rise to a lesser dispute about perception and empirical knowledge. St. Augustine derived his position on this matter directly from Plotinus. At the revival of Aristotelianism in the 13th century, predominantly at the hands of St. Thomas Aquinas, a rival view was put forward, and despite certain attempts at compromise the issue was handed on to the philosophers of the 17th and 18th centuries in very much the same form.

3
MEDIAEVAL THOUGHT

(i) INTRODUCTION

THE mediaeval philosophers were mainly concerned with matters other than the nature of perception, since philosophy was for them closely entwined with theology. Nevertheless, some philosophers of this period *were* concerned with perception, chiefly from an epistemological point of view, their aim being to show the relation of our knowledge of the sensible world to other forms of knowledge. It is not necessary to conduct a specialized and detailed review of *all* the theories put forward, since the main issue that developed was that between the views of St. Augustine and St. Thomas Aquinas—between 'Platonism' and 'Aristotelianism'. Besides these main views it is necessary to mention only the reaction by the Augustinian tradition to the rise of 'Aristotelianism' in, for example, the person of St. Bonaventure, and finally the rise of a somewhat new tradition in William of Ockham.

(ii) AUGUSTINE

Augustine's philosophical upbringing was in the philosophical writings of Cicero, and through him he became acquainted with Scepticism (in Cicero's *Academics*). His salvation from both Scepticism and Manicheism he owed to Neo-Platonism. This came from a reading of Plotinus, probably, since Augustine knew little Greek, in the Latin translation of Marius Victorinus. The result was that Augustine's philosophy is Neo-Platonism poured into the mould of Christianity. The Platonic or Neo-Platonic Forms become thoughts in the mind of God, and the move of the soul towards God is interpreted as an ascent from forms of knowledge which are of less importance to those which are of greater importance and value. Like Plotinus, Augustine had no doubt concerning the existence of the sensible world, although he thought it of little importance in comparison with the objects of intellectual knowledge and spiritual aspiration. Although he anticipated Descartes in his reaction to scepticism by the declaration, *Si fallor, sum.*, his aim was not primarily to justify *empirical* knowledge, but to provide a road to knowledge of a higher kind. It is perhaps not without significance that it was *Neo-Platonism* that provided his conversion from Scepticism; for that philosophy is a full-blooded metaphysical system, to be accepted as a whole if at all.

Augustine's account of perception is typically Neo-Platonic, and, if anything, the superior position given to the soul or mind over the body is even more obvious in his theory than in Neo-Platonism. The clearest statement of his position is to be found in the *De Musica* (vi. v. 9–10), where he says that the mind controls and attends to the body as a result of the will. The mind, that is, works purposively. Sometimes, objects which affect the body thereby cause the mind's control to be more difficult or its attention to be heightened. From this result sensations, pleasant when the body's functions are promoted, unpleasant when they are hindered. The mind directs the body, therefore, by means of the will, and perception is an activity of the mind which ensues when the body receives impressions. But the mind receives no impressions itself; it forms its own images and impressions, which are not those of the body.

Augustine is sufficiently influenced by Aristotle to postulate an inner sense with the functions of Aristotle's *sensus communis* (*De Lib. Arbitr.*, ii. 7–8). But in most respects he follows Plotinus. Like him he stresses the role performed by memory in perceiving things and he treats memory in a way similar to that in which Plotinus treated it. He also points to the difficulties which arise for his view of perception from considerations such as that we can perceive the distance of things from us and that we can identify the precise nature of what we see (cf. *De Quant. Anim.*, 23 ff.). Perception is more than the apprehension by the mind of what happens to the body; it is necessary that the mind should take note of the details and make inferences. Thus the role of judgment begins to emerge and with it the question of the validity of perception. On Augustine's view, the fact that the senses reproduce the form of the object of perception needs no questioning, and he gives no explanation why they should do so. The question which Aristotle or Epicurus, for example, raised, whether what the senses tell us is true or false, does not arise at all, on the Augustinian theory. Truth and falsity, he maintains, are properties of judgments, and a judgment is made only when a sense-impression formed by the mind is fitted under a concept. Truth and falsity are not properties of sense-impressions themselves at all.

It may be said that this is a refusal to face the issue squarely. Even if sense-impressions cannot be said to be true or false, there remains the question whether they correspond to the objects of perception. This is a fair objection, but Augustine was not really interested in the sceptical questioning of the validity of the senses; he took it for granted that sense-impressions corresponded to their objects, just as Locke was later to take for granted the correspondence between ideas of primary qualities and those qualities themselves. We shall see later that Aquinas adopted a compromise position here; while he followed Aristotle in saying that the judgments of the senses may be true or false, he insisted that truth and falsity belong in the primary sense to judgments made by the mind.

Granted that on the Augustinian view experience results from the fitting of the sense-impressions to a concept, it must not be supposed that those concepts themselves are derived from experience or are a result of the functioning of the senses. The concepts of which Augustine speaks are in no way abstract ideas in a Lockean sense. They are, as one might expect from a Neo-Platonist tradition, Forms which the mind directly apprehends. Sense-impressions are the lowest stage on the way to knowledge of God, in whose mind the Forms exist.

The position which Augustine adopts on this issue in so clear-cut a way was not that of Plato himself. While, therefore, it may sometimes be convenient to refer to it as Platonist, in that it depends upon a conception of the soul which is Platonist in being opposed to that of Aristotle, it is more correct to describe it as Neo-Platonist in its essentials. It must be remembered that from this time and for many centuries to come (the exact date at which the period ended is not easy to determine) Plato was seen through

Neo-Platonist spectacles, despite the obvious differences. In many ways a similar caveat must be uttered about the relation between Aristotle and Thomism.

(iii) AQUINAS

Aquinas accepted in its main essentials the Aristotelian view of the soul as the form of the body. Hence, on his view, that which is responsible for perception is neither the body nor the soul by themselves, but the composite of both. It follows that for Aquinas there did not exist the same problem as that which confronted Augustine, namely how the soul can have perceptions. If both their theories of perception may be regarded as causal or representative, the problem of justifying the claim that our perceptions are truly representative of the objects of perception is not so difficult for Aquinas as for Augustine.

In his account of the nature of perception, Aquinas follows Aristotle to some extent, but not altogether. He views sense-perception primarily as a form of change in which the sense-organ is altered. But this cannot be all that is involved, for along with the physical change there goes the reception of a sensible form without the matter. The latter Aquinas takes to be not something that happens to the sense-organ, but something that happens to the faculty of the soul or mind. It is, in his words, a spiritual change. In this he differs from Aristotle, since, as I indicated earlier, it is the sense-organ which, on Aristotle's view, receives the sensible form. Aquinas sees that the eye cannot be said to receive the colour of the object of vision, and in consequence he puts a refinement upon Aristotle's doctrine. In a similar way, he treats Aristotle's dictum that in perception the sense and the object become assimilated as a truth about what happens to the *mind* in perception, not the sense-organ. In Aristotle, as I indicated, the position is ambiguous. Aquinas views the reception of the form as an apprehension (*intentio*) of the object, and he goes into some detail concerning the way in which that apprehension is arrived at. These details constitute part of the Thomist theory of knowledge. Finally, Aquinas follows Aristotle in saying that in perception the activity of the sense and the activity of the object are one and the same: for, he says, in perception the faculty actualizes its potentiality in response to the change in bodily conditions.

Before going into the details of the process, it is worth noting that Aquinas increases the number of 'inner senses' from the one *sensus communis* recognized by Aristotle to five (Avicenna, the Arabic 'Aristotelian' philosopher, had already postulated five; cf. Aquinas, *Summ. Theol.*, 1a, 78, 4). To the *sensus communis* he adds: (*a*) a *vis aestimativa*—a capacity for an intuitive apprehension of something, possessed by animals, e.g. a sense that something is useful or hostile, (*b*) *imaginatio*—the power of conserving sensory images or *phantasmata*, (*c*) a *vis memorativa*—the power of conserving ideas, whether those possessed by animals as a result of the *vis aestimativa* or those possessed by men as a result of the capacity which they have corresponding to the *vis aestimativa*, namely (*d*) the *vis cogitativa*. It is, of course, misleading to call these 'senses'. All that Aquinas means is that they are non-rational capacities.

Granted that in response to the stimulation of the sense-organ by an object the faculty actualizes its potentiality or power in perception, how does this occur? The first state consists in the production of the sensory images or *phantasmata* already mentioned. Aquinas here comes very near to the making of an explicit distinction between perceiving and the having of sensations. The *phantasmata* or sensory images are like sensations in being passive, but like images in being reproductions of the objects of perception. They are produced in all the senses, but are not directly known as such. They can be detected only when isolated artificially. Like images in the true sense, they are particular in their nature, but to function in perception they have to become, to use Hume's words, general in their representation. The problem is how this can be so.

In all this Aquinas goes far beyond Aristotle. The latter used the term *phantasma* to refer to images in the ordinary sense, and there are also a few suggestions of its use by him to cover appearances in general. Aristotle also used on occasion the term *aesthema* ($\alpha\ddot{\iota}\sigma\theta\eta\mu\alpha$) to refer to a sensation, but he made no systematic use of it in order to outline an apparatus for sense-perception. It does not appear that Aristotle saw the necessity for such an apparatus. The Thomist theory looks like a combination of the Aristotelian point of view with one such as that put forward by the Atomists. Aquinas makes frequent reference to Democritus.

Aquinas believes, therefore, that corresponding to the physical change in the sense-organ there is a spiritual change resulting in a *phantasma*, which is a particular mental entity. Perception of an object as white demands that the universal quality, whiteness, should be abstracted from the particular *phantasma* in order that it may be attributed to the object in the making of a judgment. This in turn demands that there should be some connection between the senses and the intellect. Aquinas accuses Augustine of separating the two faculties, while he himself wishes to establish their connection, and so produce something like an empiricist theory of knowledge which is supposedly coincident with Aristotelianism—the doctrine that *nihil est in intellectu quod non prius in sensu*. The link between the two faculties is made possible for Aquinas by the active reason (*intellectus agens*), which illumines (*illustrat*) the *phantasmata* (*Summ. Theol.*, 1a, 79, 4). This is the so-called *conversio ad phantasmata*.

According to both Aristotle and Aquinas, it is the passive reason which is the source of intellectual conceptions, or, as they would put it, of the knowledge of intelligible forms or species. But the passive reason cannot function without the active reason, since the acquisition of intelligible form is, like the acquisition of sensible form, a process from potentiality to actuality. The active reason, being pure actuality, makes that process possible. Because we are tied to our senses, Aquinas maintains, we cannot altogether, as God can, divorce our conceptions from their material conditions, but without the active reason we could do nothing at all in this direction (*Summ. Theol.*, 1a, 84, 2). The process whereby the active reason illumines the *phantasmata* is that it *abstracts* from them the form or *species impressa*.[1] This is then imposed upon the passive reason, which produces the *species expressa* or *verbum*. Thus the final concept issues in a verbal form, even if expressed internally, and it is applied to the object of perception in judgment. To judgment questions of truth and falsity are applicable, and through it our perceptions may be veridical or the reverse.

In this account of the functions performed by the different parts of the soul, Aquinas is a long way from Aristotle's dictum that it is better to say that *we* do such things with the soul. The

---

[1] That this is Aquinas' view has recently been denied by P. Geach, *Mental Acts*, p. 130. He points to the fact that Aquinas says that the active reason *illumines* the *phantasmata*, and maintains that Aquinas means that the active reason *forms* the species. Nevertheless the 'abstraction' view is the one generally held.

difference between Aquinas' account and Aristotle's is a good illustration of the meaning of 'Scholasticism'. While Aristotle's account is not altogether consistent, and while it may be inadequate in other ways, it is designed not so much to give a psychological explanation of the processes involved in sense-perception as to give a philosophical analysis of the *concepts* involved in thinking about sense-perception. On the other hand, Aquinas' account is an attempt to say something of those psychological processes in abstract philosophical terms derived for the most part from those which Aristotle employed for a quite different purpose.

This is no more apparent than in the account of the functions ascribed by Aquinas to *phantasmata* and the active reason. As I have indicated, Aristotle makes scarcely any reference to *phantasmata* in connection with perception; for in our talk about perception we ordinarily make no reference to sensory-images. We should feel the need to talk of those, if at all, only as a result of reflection upon how sense-perception could possibly result from an affection of the mind by objects. The concept of a sensory-image is thus linked with a causal theory of perception. On the Thomist view the *phantasmata* set up are mental entities and for this reason are like the sensations which are produced by stimulation of our bodily organs; yet, being somehow representative of the objects which produce them, they are more than mere sensations. They are indeed more like the ideas or impressions of the British Empiricists, Locke, Berkeley and Hume, except that Aquinas holds that we are not ordinarily aware of them.

Phantasmata, then, are postulated as the mental products of the stimulation of our senses. They are introduced to fill a gap in a causal theory of perception, even if they are not thought of as perceptions themselves. Once it is admitted that the mind can be affected by external objects through the reception of species, a link must be found between the physical stimulation of the sense-organ and the final judgment about those objects. This role the *phantasmata* play. There is no need for such a concept in Aristotle, since he is not concerned to specify all the steps, psychologically speaking, between the stimulation of the sense-organs and the final judgment. Nor indeed does Aristotle in fact say that the mind receives the sensible form or species; he says, as we have seen, that the sense-organ does so.

The same sort of considerations are relevant to Aquinas' treatment of the active reason (and he is not alone among mediaeval philosophers in this). He uses the active reason to fill another gap in the account of the processes involved in the acquisition of empirical knowledge. All the processes so far discussed have been passive. The outcome of the changes produced by stimulation of a sense-organ is particular in its nature, because the cause, the external object, is particular. Since judgment involves the fitting of a thing under a concept or universal, it is necessary, if we are to be able to make a judgment of perception, that something should *abstract* the relevant general information from the *phantasma*, or apply a general notion to it. But, as we have seen, Aquinas denies that we are normally consciously aware of the *phantasmata* which we have. For this reason it cannot be the case that *we* abstract the universal from the *phantasma*, although something else may do so. In consequence some active agency must be postulated to do the work; and this work is ascribed to the active reason, which, therefore, functions like another person within us.

Aristotle had no need to postulate such an agency to do this work, since he was not concerned to explain how it is that the universal is abstracted from whatever it is that is the mental product of the stimulation of our sense-organs. If he had no need to postulate *phantasmata*, still less did he require to postulate an agency to abstract information from them. Aristotle's active reason is merely a logical requisite of his system, since any transition from potentiality to actuality demands a prior pure actuality. If the active reason plays in Aristotle's theory the part of a para-mechanical cause (to use the terminology of Ryle's *Concept of Mind*), postulated to explain how human beings can, ultimately, be active, it is given little else in the way of functions to perform. Despite the reference which Aristotle makes to faculties, he is not really a faculty-psychologist. The references to faculties are not meant to *explain*, psychologically, our various functions; they are meant merely to sum up the various capacities which we possess.

Moreover, while it is doubtful whether Aristotle can be called, without qualification, an empiricist, there is no doubt that Aquinas was one. He was anxious, that is, to show that all the materials for knowledge—including, in the end, theological knowledge—are to be derived from sense experience. The precedents for such a view, if any are needed, are to be found in Epicurus rather than

Aristotle. Aquinas combines an atomist epistemology with an Aristotelian (or almost Aristotelian) view of the soul. He adds to these, and resulting from the combination of them, an explanation of his own of the way in which our perception that, for example, the table is brown can arise from a purely mechanical stimulation of the sense-organs. His intricately involved attempts to deal with this problem lead, as a necessary consequence, to the assumption of agencies in the mind which can operate upon the rest of it. But it is the combination of these three theories—atomist epistemology, Aristotelian theory of the mind, and Thomist psychology—in one apparatus, which leads to the involution of his theory and a justified accusation of 'Scholasticism' in a pejorative sense of that word. Most philosophers have been willing to give up at least one of the aims which Aquinas pursued.

(iv) BONAVENTURE

Bonaventure was a contemporary of Aquinas, and like him he was influenced by the rediscovery of Aristotle. But, *qua* philosopher, he was in the Augustinian tradition. He reacted to the influence of Aristotle only by attempting something of a compromise, by giving up certain elements of Augustinianism. In particular, he accepted the Aristotelian definition of the soul as the form of the body, but nevertheless maintained that it was a spiritual substance as well, possessing spiritual form and spiritual matter.

Bonaventure agrees with Aquinas in espousing empiricism, but differs from him in not separating so clearly the active and passive intellects. These work together, he thinks, in abstracting the species. But for present purposes it is the compromise at which he arrives over perception which is the most important. He is willing to abandon Augustine to the extent of allowing that a sensible object can act upon the mind, but he also treats the mind as active in the Augustinian fashion. In fact he considers that perception involves three elements. Firstly, there is the effect of the sensible object upon the sense-organ, with the result that a sensible species is produced in it; that is to say that, as Aristotle maintained, the organ receives the form of the object. Secondly, there is the consequent effect upon the *faculty* of sense-perception, so that the faculty too receives the species. It is in this second respect that the

Thomist point of view influences the Augustinian. Thirdly, there is the judgment about the object made by the mind; here the soul acts upon the body *qua* its power of activity, and in this last respect the Augustinian point of view is re-affirmed. It is difficult to see how these three views can be reconciled. Indeed Bonaventure's position strikes one as a very unhappy compromise between two quite incompatible points of view—that of Augustine and that of Aquinas.

(v) WILLIAM OF OCKHAM

If the precedent for Aquinas' theory of knowledge is that of the Atomists, the precedent for the theory of knowledge of the 14th-century thinker, William of Ockham, is that of the Stoics; for Ockham bases knowledge on intuition. But he broke away from the main scholastic tradition in other ways also—in particular away from realism towards nominalism, and away from the view that the mind is concerned with the universal towards the view that it can be concerned with the particular. Indeed Ockham's central view is that the objects of the mind's intuitions are always particular. His main interests, however, are logical in character; they are concerned with the theory of meaning or supposition and the logic of propositions. In this, too, although there are mediaeval precedents, the tradition stems from the Stoics.

Because of the nature of Ockham's interests, his views on perception are incidental in character, but they are worthy of mention just because they are so different from the main line of mediaeval thought hitherto followed. It might be pointed out, however, that Duns Scotus seems to have allowed that an intuition of a single thing is possible, and even necessary, if the abstraction of the universal is to follow. But Scotus also holds that such an intuition can, in this life, only be confused. Ockham differed from him greatly on this point. In other respects Scotus was closer to Aquinas, differing from him mainly in the primacy which the will may have over the intellect.

On Ockham's view, intuition gives us knowledge whether a thing exists or not (*Sent. Prol.*, qu. 1). Intuitive cognition is thus distinguished from abstractive cognition, which is concerned with a thing as abstracted from questions of its existence or non-existence; abstractive cognition is the thinking of something, whether particular or general, apart from the conditions of its existence. Under the heading of intuitive cognition, an intuition is said to be perfect when it is constituted by an immediate experience; it is said to be imperfect if past experience has to be brought in also. Within an intuitive notion it is possible to distinguish both a sensory and an intellectual element (compare the Stoic theory that apprehension involves both a sense-impression and assent). A sensation can tell us *that* a thing exists, but the intellect is required if we are to know *what* it is. Sensations are to be found in the sensitive soul, which can be distinguished from the intellectual soul, since the former is spread out through the body while the latter is not. Although these can be distinguished they still form a unity (*Quodlibet*, ii. 10).

The functioning of the intellect is not different in kind from that of the senses; for its function too is to provide an intuition. Intellectual intuitions may be of various kinds, including those known as intuitions of 'second intentions', i.e. intuitions of the meanings of terms. In perception, however, the function of the intellect is to provide an intuition of the nature of a particular object. Such an intuition will not generally be perfect. Nevertheless, Ockham thinks, the possibility of a direct acquaintance with things is presupposed by the fact that we apply to our immediate experience ideas drawn from past experience. In other words, judgment must be founded upon an initial direct apprehension of the nature of particular things.

The most striking feature of this theory is the rejection of any representative or indirect theory of perception. Such theories have been characteristic of mediaeval thought hitherto. Ockham, that is to say, completely rejects the notion of a species being transmitted from an object to the mind. It must be admitted, however, that one reason why it is easy for Ockham to take up this position is his lack of interest in how perception comes about. He does speak of sensations or intuitions being *caused* by things (*Quodlibet*, vi. 6; cf. ii. 10), but this is not explained in any way. There was a similar lack of interest and failure to go into details on the part of the Stoics.

There are also manifest difficulties in squaring the possibility of illusions with the notion of intuition (and the Stoics too had difficulties on this very point). Ockham resorts to the notion of judgment in this matter, saying that error must be due to judgment, since the senses present us with a direct acquaintance with things. In the case of after-images, he says that a man sees not, for example, the sun, but the 'light impressed on his eyes' (*Quodlibet*, vi. 6). It is the last with which we have a direct acquaintance, and if we seem nevertheless to see an object, the error is due to the judgment which we make concerning what we directly see. Error thus depends ultimately on the fact that some intuitions are imperfect. How this comes to be so is not explained. Ockham's account is primarily descriptive or interpretative in terms of a certain conceptual scheme; it is not meant to be explanatory.

Finally, it may be noted that Ockham follows Augustine and anticipates Descartes in the claim that while all experience is simple and direct, it is not all equally clear. Our inner experiences are more clearly intuited than experiences of external objects. Hence knowledge of the self is more immediate than knowledge of objects.

Few important advances in the understanding of this subject were made between Ockham in the 14th century and Descartes in the 17th century, and Ockham provides a fitting transition to the views of the modern philosophers. Between him and Descartes other advances and developments did take place, however—notably the rise of modern science—and these did influence the course of philosophical thinking in a profound way. Nevertheless, there are points in common between the philosophy of the 14th century and that of the 17th, so that the transition is not too abrupt.

4

THE 17th CENTURY—
AN INTRODUCTION

IT is a common opinion that Descartes ushered in a new era of philosophical thought. It is also clear that he had a close connection with mediaeval philosophy. He continually uses scholastic terminology and sometimes scholastic doctrines without question or argument, e.g. the notion of substance and the doctrine that each kind of substance has an essential attribute or attributes.[1] At the same time, there are manifest differences between him and the scholastics. One of the most pertinent is constituted by his belief that it is possible to devise a *method* by means of which truth can be attained. It is a common presupposition of the philosophers of the 17th and 18th centuries that philosophy requires a method. It is to be found not only in the Rationalists, Descartes, Spinoza and Leibniz, but also in the Empiricists, Locke, Berkeley and Hume. The two great schools of philosophy differed, if in nothing else, in that they had different opinions about the nature of that method. That Descartes believed in the method of geometry, even if he was not very ready to apply it to philosophy in all its details, was due in large part to his own researches into the subject. The British Empiricists were similarly influenced by the results of Newton's inquiries.

The initial stimulus to the new self-consciousness about method lies farther back, in the rise of experimental science, which was so largely due to Galileo. The emergence of the new experimental science of physics encouraged thinkers in the belief that it provided the key to the system of the universe. This is noticeable in

[1] Cf. Descartes, *Principles of Philosophy*, I. 51-3.

two ways in particular. Firstly, the rise of science encouraged the belief that the methods of experimental science on the one hand and of mathematics on the other were those to be followed in pursuing *any* inquiry. Together with this went a vehement attack upon Aristotelianism in its scholastic form—a rejection of final causes and of the notion of forms or species as in any sense explanatory. The writings of Francis Bacon express this view most clearly. Bacon believed firmly both in the method of eliminating possible but false hypotheses as the supreme method for a solution of all problems, and in his mission to reveal prejudices as such.[1]

Secondly, the success of physics encouraged the belief that its subject-matter was reality itself. Not only was its method supreme, but its subject-matter was the essential nature of the universe. The fact that physics was unable to deal with colours, for example, and in general those properties of things to which measurement is not really applicable, gave rise to a reintroduction of the distinction between primary and secondary qualities; secondary qualities, it was thought, were somehow not part of the nature of things.

This last belief had been characteristic of Atomism both in its Democritean and its Epicurean form, and it is therefore no surprise to find a recrudescence of Atomism in the 17th century. Of this the main philosophical exponents were Gassendi in France and Hobbes in England; and the latter was the more forthright. Gassendi excepted the soul from the principles applicable to physical bodies, and, while he likened sensations to motions, he did not attempt an outright reduction of the one to the other. Hobbes, on the other hand, says (*Leviathan*, ch. 1[2]) that bodies press the sense-organs and that the pressure is mediated by the nerves to the brain and heart, so that there is caused there 'a resistance or counter-pressure, or endeavour of the heart to deliver itself, which endeavour, because outward, seemeth to be some matter without. And this seeming, or fancy, is that which men call sense'. And he goes on to say that, just as all the qualities of objects are merely kinds of motion, so their effects in us are motions only; it is the endeavour outwards which gives the impression of externality.

[1] Bacon thought that the object of science was the search for forms of natures, but he did not treat the notion of 'form' as the scholastics did.
[2] Cf. R. S. Peters, *Hobbes*, p. 103.

THE 17TH CENTURY—AN INTRODUCTION

In the same chapter, Hobbes criticizes as unintelligible the traditional scholastic view concerning the transmission of species. Yet when all is said and done, his theory is only the scholastic theory translated into mechanical terms. For 'transmission of species' is substituted 'transmission of atoms'.[1] Hobbes thinks that sense-perception involves the use of 'phantasms' which linger as a result of past experience; in other words, as Epicurus thought, perception involves not only present impressions but also notions derived from past experience. This is a mechanical version of the view that perception involves judgment. Hobbes' forthrightness, however, leads to little in the way of subtlety, and he shows no sign of appreciating the fact that there are vast problems in the translation of the phenomena of perception into completely mechanical terms.

The revival of Atomism, therefore, brought with it no real attempt to come to grips with the phenomena of perception, let alone to gain an understanding of the concepts involved. Yet the existence of the movement is illustrative of a general point—that no rigorous distinction was made at this time between what was scientific and what was philosophical. Philosophers incorporated scientific discoveries and speculations in their works. Harvey's discovery of the circulation of the blood, for example, led Descartes (cf. *Discourse on Method*, ch. 5) to speculate about neural transmission; and for this purpose he used the common 17th-century notion of 'animal spirits' carried by particles in the blood. Reference to animal spirits became part of the stock-in-trade of philosophers in discussing the senses.

At the same time, many issues which might *prima facie* be considered scientific were discussed in philosophical terms, e.g. the question of the existence of atoms or a vacuum. Purely scientific questions concerning these matters were rarely distinguished from more philosophical questions. Descartes' refutation of the idea of the vacuum, for example, was really a refutation of the postulation of the void by philosophical atomists, despite its superficial appearance of being concerned with genuine scientific issues. Descartes' general refutation makes this clear, since it depends

[1] There is some evidence that Hobbes initially thought of species as substances in a literal sense, and in consequence the identification of them with atoms was easy. Cf. F. Brandt, *Hobbes' Mechanical Conception of Nature*, ch. 1, 'The Little Treatise'.

THE 17TH CENTURY—AN INTRODUCTION

upon an appeal to the view that extension is an essential attribute of bodies—'As regards a vacuum in the philosophical sense of the word, i.e. a space in which there is no substance, it is evident that such cannot exist, because the extension of space or internal place is not different from that of body' (*Princ.*, II. 16).[1] Similar considerations apply to his treatment of the idea of the existence of atoms. To an atomic view Descartes opposes a view of physics in which the notion of continuity plays a large part. There are indeed elements of Stoicism in Descartes' thinking (cf. the notion of animal *spirits* with the Stoic *pneuma*).

To return to the considerations of method—. The problems which confront a scientist or mathematician are not the same as those which confront a metaphysician or an epistemologist. A scientist may be asked how we know, for example, the value of the gravitational constant, and he should be able to give an account of the method by which the answer may be arrived at. But the question 'How do we know anything at all?' does not admit of an answer of the same sort. Yet this latter question, among others such as 'What do we know at all?', has been asked by epistemologists—that is to say, by philosophers interested in the theory of knowledge. One answer which has commonly been given to these questions, though an erroneous one, is based upon the view that only that which is indubitable can be known. An answer of this sort has been commonly given because it has been thought that only such an answer can meet general scepticism. The notion that indubitability is the hall-mark of knowledge is as old as Plato.[2] Hence, the attempt to identify that of which we have indubitable knowledge has traditionally been part of any theory of knowledge.

Yet there is another, though connected, sense to the phrase 'theory of knowledge'. Aquinas, for example, presented a theory of knowledge of an empiricist kind in that he tried to show that

---

[1] Although elsewhere he does adduce evidence of a quasi-scientific kind. Cf. the passage from the *Traité de la Lumière* quoted by N. Kemp Smith, *New Studies in the Philosophy of Descartes*, p. 110.

[2] See Plato, *Rep.*, 477e, and page 11 of this book. Although there were not in his time any adherents of general scepticism for Plato to meet (unless one counts the Sophists), the arguments which led him to the Forms—the existence of relative terms and the possibility of universal flux—were such that they could play a part (as they later did in fact) in sceptical arguments concerning the reliability of the senses.

THE 17TH CENTURY—AN INTRODUCTION

all the *materials* for knowledge—all the notions, etc.—are to be derived from experience. He was not so much interested in the thesis that the knowledge which we have possesses an indubitable guarantee. But in Descartes, and perhaps more particularly in Locke, these two strands become united. These philosophers wish to show that knowledge is possible because some truths are indubitable. They also wish to show what is the source of the notions or ideas on which such knowledge is to be based. And this is combined with the conception that there is a method by which human knowledge can be shown to be guaranteed.

The 17th-century Rationalists and Empiricists shared the belief that knowledge requires justification and that its justification is to be provided by showing that some truths are certain. Locke, for example, says of his inquiry that he is to set down 'some measure of the certainty of our knowledge'. These philosophers shared, therefore, a belief in what has become known as the search for certainty. They differed about how certainty was to be attained. They differed also in their conception of the extent to which the ideas in terms of which knowledge is to be formulated are derived from the use of our senses, as opposed to the use of our reason. It should be added, however, that these differences are differences of *tendency* only. In a sense, to talk of opposing *schools* of philosophy in this context is misleading. There is much in Descartes, for example, that would by certain criteria make him an Empiricist, and there is similarly much in Locke that would make him a Rationalist. But they exhibit tendencies in opposite directions. Rationalists tended to espouse geometrical method, Empiricists a method much more like that of chemistry. Rationalists tended to appeal to reason as the source of knowledge and of some ideas at least, Empiricists tended to depreciate reason as a source of knowledge and insist that all ideas come from experience. Finally, the Rationalist view of the mind tended to be that of a substance engaging in cognitive activity, while the Empiricists tended to take a passive view of the mind and to eschew the notion of substance. In assessing these tendencies, it is helpful to oppose the most extreme Rationalist, Spinoza, to the most extreme Empiricist, Hume.

Today, as many philosophers would agree, Descartes can be seen to be wrong or confused on each of the three issues which were his prime concern—the justification of claims to knowledge, the question of philosophical method and the problem concerning the source of our ideas.

In the first place, human knowledge does not require the sort of justification which Descartes supposed necessary. The way to deal with scepticism is not to seek for truths which, because indubitable, are immune to sceptical arguments, but to tackle those arguments themselves in the way which Plato and Aristotle called dialectical. It may be argued, for example, that the very possibility of scepticism demands at least the possibility that something should be known. Moreover, if anyone claims that much of what we ordinarily call knowledge is not so, he must have a standard of his own for the application of the word 'knowledge'. And it is as well that we should know what this standard is and why it is different from that normally accepted. It is impossible to go into the complexities of the issue here, but it must be emphasized that it is by argument rather than by indubitable truths that the sceptic is to be answered.

Secondly, it is a mistake to suppose that philosophy can take over the methods appropriate to particular disciplines like science and mathematics, since its problems are different from theirs. Moreover, the difference does not lie merely in the fact that philosophy is more general than they are (although in a sense it is so). The truth is that a great part at least of the aim of philosophy is to arrive at understanding—understanding of concepts such as that of knowledge. It is a clear mistake to suppose that methods appropriate to the discovery of truths belonging to a particular field can be relevant to the attainment of this sort of understanding. This is not to say that there are not methods by which philosophical investigation may be pursued. These, however, are autonomous, not drawn from other disciplines.

Finally, the issue between Empiricists and Rationalists over the genesis of our ideas can be said to be misplaced. In so far as it is strictly a question about the *genesis* of those ideas, it belongs to the province of psychology. In so far as it is a question about the logical character of those ideas—whether they are applicable in any simple way to things around us and if so how—it is too complex a question to be dealt with by a simple-minded espousal of Rationalism or Empiricism. Clearly, not all the ideas which we have are like that of redness, for example. But how the different kinds of ideas which we have differ from each other is an extremely complex question and one which is essentially philosophical in nature.

That many contemporary philosophers feel out of sympathy with Descartes and his immediate successors casts no discredit upon him. Had he not said what he did and established the view of philosophy which, through him, became prevalent, we should not be where we are today. Credit is due to him for reintroducing the spirit of dispassionate inquiry into philosophy, and for being the fountain-head of a new stream of thought.

5
THE RATIONALISTS

(i) DESCARTES

THE Cartesian method, as Descartes makes clear in the second chapter of the *Discourse on Method*, is (1) not to accept as true anything of which we have not a clear and distinct idea, (2) to analyse the problem, (3) to start from more simple and more certain thoughts and proceed to the more complex, and (4) to review the field so thoroughly as not to omit any consideration. These rules are given in an amplified form in an earlier work, the *Regulae*. In sum, the method is to start from simple and axiomatic data and proceed by deductive steps to that which is more complex. Which ideas are clear and distinct, however, remains a problem, as Descartes admits in chapter 4 of the *Discourse*. To deal with this problem, Descartes employs the method of doubt, so setting on one side anything that can be supposed to be false and arriving finally at the conclusion that there is one thing that cannot be supposed to be false—namely the proposition 'I am'. In other words, *Cogito ergo sum*. From this again Descartes concludes that I have certain knowledge of myself as a thinking, non-extended substance, since he takes it to follow from the *Cogito* that I have a clear and distinct idea of my mind.

The following points may be made about the *Cogito*:—

(1) It is possible to argue for the indubitability of the proposition 'I think', and still more cogently for that of the proposition 'I am', on the grounds that the contradictories of such propositions cannot be asserted without absurdity.[1] This view, which, as

---

[1] Cf. A. J. Ayer, *The Problem of Knowledge*, ch. 2, sect. iii, and P. Geach, *Mental Acts*, sect. 26.

it stands, is manifestly true, is generally backed up by the consideration that the word 'I' is not a name with a special reference, but an expression which serves in its use to draw the attention of others to the speaker. Hence, to say 'I do not exist' is to indicate one's existence and at the same time to deny it. Correspondingly, but more indirectly, to say 'I do not think' is to exhibit a manifestation of intelligence and at the same time to deny its possibility. This kind of indubitability, however, would not be sufficient for Descartes, since nothing further can be built upon it. It is important for his programme that the word 'I' should be taken, though wrongly, as the name of a mental substance. The reasons for this supposition are largely that, in the case of first person, psychological assertions such as 'I think', the word 'I' cannot be taken as referring to any thoughts, let alone any bodily manifestations. (If the word 'I' refers to a thought, the proposition 'I think' would be analytic or logically true, and one cannot build a system about the world merely on analytic truths.) It is therefore concluded that the word 'I' must be the name of a special substance which can have manifestations in forms of thought. But an important premise in this argument is that the word 'I' is the name of *something*.

(2) While the official Cartesian view is that the whole *Cogito ergo sum* is an intuitive truth, there are also indications that it is taken to rest on the further point that whereas I can doubt all else, I cannot doubt that I am doubting and hence having thoughts. In other words, if I am supposing something to be false, I cannot also suppose it to be false that I am doing so. This, however, is not true; or at least no contradiction arises from denying it, so that it is at the most a contingent psychological truth. But if the *Cogito* is to do its work it must rest on premises which are *necessarily* true. On the other hand, if I am supposing something to be false, I cannot be in doubt that I am; for to suppose something to be false presupposes that I know what I am doing. Descartes, however, cannot rely on this fact, since he has to show, not that I cannot be in doubt about something, but that I cannot suppose something to be false. From the fact that when I am thinking I cannot be in doubt that I am it does not follow that it is necessarily true that I think. In other words, this line of argument for the conclusion that it is an indubitable truth that I think or have thoughts rests upon an equivocation between two senses

of 'doubt'. Cartesian doubt is, as it has sometimes been called, 'methodological doubt', not doubt in the ordinary sense.

(3) Even if it were allowed that it might be an indubitable truth that I think, there is still a very large gap between this and the conclusion that there necessarily exists a thinking, non-extended substance.[1]

Other things might well be said about the *Cogito*. It is sufficient to note that it certainly does not *prove* that we have direct knowledge of a mental substance. Knowledge of the second kind of substance—extended, non-thinking substance, or body—is, Descartes thinks, less clear. While, on Descartes' view, we know of extension by intuition (*inspectio mentis*—extension was in the *Regulae* listed as one of the 'simple natures' known by the natural light), this intuition is indirect in comparison with our knowledge of the mind. Indeed, the demonstration of the existence of material substance in the Cartesian system depends not only on the primary knowledge of the mind but also on knowledge of God. For it is only on the premises that God exists and that he is not a deceiver that Descartes takes the existence of a material world to be demonstrable.

There are many points of similarity between Descartes and Augustine. The latter anticipated Descartes in his use of the *Cogito*, although he did not have the same aim in mind. There is also the consequent similarity that they both thought of knowledge of the mind as more direct than that of material things. Malebranche, a later Cartesian, assimilated Descartes' views even further to those of Augustine. In general Descartes' view of the mind is in the Neo-Platonic tradition. Indeed, Leibniz remarked that Descartes was more like Plato while he himself was more like Aristotle. One might expect, therefore, that Descartes would find difficulty in explaining how it is that we can perceive things, how it is that the mind can be influenced by physical objects. For Augustine the answer, as we have seen, was obvious—the mind is *not* influenced by physical objects; and he did not feel obliged

[1] It has been suggested to me by Mr. A. P. Griffiths that in effect the knowledge of the essence of the self (along with knowledge of other essences) was a *presupposition* of the argument, not its conclusion. The argument is then directed to the conclusion that something has that essence, namely we ourselves. It turns on the point that no reason can be given for doubt concerning the existence of that particular thing which has the essence which is consistent with that doubt.

to answer the question how in that case we can know about them. Descartes, however, was confronted directly with the sceptical problem because of his adoption of the method of doubt, and he therefore *had* to answer that question. His answer leaves much to be desired.

On Descartes' view there are two distinct kinds of substance (and that they are distinct is one of the main points of the *Meditations*). But (cf. *Principles*, I. 53) every substance has some essential attribute—that of mind being thinking (*cogitatio*, *pensée*) and that of body extension. It is important to note, in this connection, that Descartes' terminology, especially with regard to the mind, is somewhat unsystematic. He often uses the term 'thinking' for anything which is an activity of the mind. Thus at *Principles*, I. 9, he says that by thought 'I understand all that which so takes place in us that we of ourselves are consciously aware of it; and accordingly not only to understand (*intellegere*, *entendre*), to will (*velle*), to imagine (*imaginari*) but even to perceive (*sentire*, *sentir*) are the same as to think'.

At other times 'thinking' is used in a narrower sense so as to be coincident with 'understanding' only. Thus in the 2nd *Meditation*, when Descartes tries to answer the question 'What am I?', he answers that I am a thinking thing, but excludes perceiving from the faculties of that thinking thing on the grounds that perceiving is dependent on the body (K.S., p. 205).[1] Later, in the 6th *Meditation*, he calls both perception in the specific sense and also sensations like those of pain *modes of thinking* (the latter being *confused* modes of thinking—see K.S., p. 257, and *Principles*, I. 46). They are, he says, faculties of thinking which are special modes distinct from myself—'I can clearly and distinctly apprehend myself as complete without them, but not them without the self, i.e. without an intelligent substance in which they reside. For in the notion which we have of them, or (to use the language of the schools) in their formal concept, they include some sort of intellection' (K.S., p. 255). The meaning of the term 'mode' in Rationalist parlance is here specified. Perceiving is a mode of thinking because it depends upon the mind, although the mind can be conceived without it.

[1] Page-references to Descartes' writings are given to the convenient collection of translations by N. Kemp Smith, *Descartes' Philosophical Writings*. This will be referred to as K.S.

The words of which 'perceive' is a translation are the French *sentir*, and the Latin *sentire*. These and connected words like *sensus* are used to cover both perception, in the sense in which we should talk of people perceiving something, and the having of sensations like those of pain. Descartes makes no distinction between the two in his terminology, and he thinks of them both as *caused* in the mind by the stimulation of our sense-organs. The words *perception* and *perceptio*, on the other hand, have a very much wider use. They are used to cover any form of cognition, whether intellectual or sensory. They are applied to all those things which Descartes, in the *Passions de l'âme*, calls the 'passions' as opposed to the activities of the soul.[1]

Another word used in this context is 'idea'. Ideas Descartes defines in the 3rd *Meditation* (K.S., p. 215) as thoughts which are 'as it were images of things', and he opposes them to volitions, affections and judgments (cf. *Principles*, I. 32, where he talks of judging as a mode of willing). He goes on to say that ideas, when 'considered only in themselves and not as representative of another thing', cannot strictly speaking be false. Falsity arises from the will, i.e. from the use of judgment. God guarantees our ideas, but not the use to which we put them. The exact nature of an idea is not clear from this; it is like an image in being representative, but it is more than just an image. We have ideas both in perceiving and understanding. Whichever of these we are engaged in, our soul is confronted with an idea. In perception we have a spontaneous impulse to believe that our ideas are veridical, but that they are so can be demonstrated only by reference to God.

Descartes thinks of sense-perception as something akin to sensation in the strict sense, although there is added to this our use of judgment; and if the ideas which we receive are clear and distinct we are not liable to fall into error in the judgments which we subsequently make. In so imposing judgment upon an initial passive sensation Descartes follows the mediaeval tradition which he had inherited. Nevertheless his concept of sensation is ambiguous between sensation in the strict sense and perception, and this is indicated by his terminology, his use of the terms *sentir* and *sentire*. There is perhaps something to be gained by trans-

[1] It is perhaps worth noting that Descartes uses *l'âme* or *animus* when concerned with the mind's union with the body, *l'esprit* or *mens* when concerned with its separation. The distinction may often be ignored.

lating the terms by the English 'to sense', as Kemp Smith does. But if one does so translate them it is important to add that Descartes would say 'to sense' both where we should say 'to perceive' and also where, as in the case of feelings, we should not.

The ideas which we are said to have in perception are passive, like sensations, but unlike them in being representative; and to that extent they are like Aquinas' *phantasmata*. According to Aquinas, we are not directly aware of the *phantasmata*; it is *reason* which turns to them in perception, not we ourselves. Cartesian ideas, on the other hand, are by definition such that we are immediately aware of them, since our minds are constituted essentially by our thoughts, of which ideas are a sub-class. There cannot be ideas of which we are not aware. In the second place, according to Aquinas, *phantasmata* are the means whereby the mind receives sensible species; they are the spiritual correlate of the change in the sense-organ. Descartes is very definite that nothing of the sort is transmitted to the mind in perception. What then does happen? For an answer it is necessary to turn to the *Dioptric* (cf. also the 6th *Meditation* and *Principles*, Bk. 4).

Descartes was opposed not only to the suggestion that perception arises from the transmission of species, but also to the atomist theory of moving particles. In the *Dioptric*, pt. I, he compares vision to the use of a stick by a blind man. On his view, the transmission of light consists in the fact that movements are set up in a medium and these more or less instantaneously affect the sense-organ. As a result movements are set up in the nerves and these proceed to the brain. These movements may have a pattern corresponding in respect of figure, magnitude and motion—but in no other respect—to the object seen (cf. *Principles*, IV. 11). In the case of secondary qualities, the movements set up in the brain determine the mind to have the relevant sensations, but there is no correspondence between the sensations and the movements. (Although, in the earlier *Regulae* (Rule 12) he had attempted to explain the impression of colour by reference to variations in the shape of the impression in the sense-organ, which is then transmitted to the brain.)

Descartes thinks that the primary qualities are more clearly and distinctly perceived than the secondary qualities, as witness the success of mathematics and physics. Only the fact that God is not a deceiver guarantees that objects can be said to possess secondary qualities at all, and we can have no guarantee that these properties of objects are in any case exactly as we suppose, considering the indistinctness of our ideas of them. Descartes expresses the lack of correspondence between the movements in the brain and the subsequent ideas by saying that no images are dispatched to the brain for the soul there to contemplate (*Dioptric*, 4). This is his rejection of the species theory. The movements determine or are the occasion for the soul's having of ideas, but they are not themselves images for the soul to see. The ideas produced by the movements in the brain are more or less representative of the objects which we see. That they are so is, in the last resort, guaranteed only by God, although the clearness and distinctness of certain ideas may suggest that there is an external world. Granted that this is Descartes' main view, it must be admitted that he sometimes argues as if the fact that the movements in the brain have figure, magnitude and motion is in itself a warrant for the supposal that our ideas are veridical in representing objects as possessing the same properties. This is doubly wrong, since, on his own terms, it can provide no such warrant, and also because the evidence for the physics and neurology can ultimately come only from our ideas. (Cf. *Principles*, IV. 11, and *Dioptric*, 6.)

While Descartes' physiology is rudimentary, it is at least on the right lines. He grasps firmly the point that whatever may be the nature of the pattern of neural activity, it need bear no resemblance to how we perceive things. He makes many other useful points, too, in connection with the psychology and physiology of perception. He discusses, for example, the working of the eyes and the part that accommodation and binocular convergence play in enabling us to see the distance of things from us. He points out also that the view that the apparent size of objects is proportional to the angle of vision subtended by them is not universally true. The sun and moon, for example, do not appear of the same size when at the zenith as at the horizon (the so-called 'zenith-horizon illusion'). The reason for this, he says, is that when they are at the horizon we gain a better impression of their distance from us. He is acquainted also with the possibility of other illusions and the need for their explanation in terms of the context of stimulation. These matters are the concern of optics.

Whatever may be the nature of the physical and physiological processes underlying perception the result is that the mind has ideas;

and it would not have those ideas were it not for a link between the mind and the body. But what is the nature of that link? It is not part of the essential nature of the mind that it should perceive; it is the intellect alone which is essential to the mind. While perception depends upon the mind as a mode or modification of it, the mind can be conceived of itself without reference to perception. Perception must therefore depend on some sort of connection between the mind or soul and the body. There are some suggestions in Descartes' writings of the view called 'Occasionalism'—the view that the body's movements are mere occasions for the activity of the soul. In the *Dioptric*, pt. 4, for example, he talks of the physical movements in the brain giving occasion to the soul to sense different qualities. Occasionalism in the full-blooded sense, i.e. the view that God expresses himself in such a way that the bodily movements and the ideas coincide on any given occasion, was accepted by other Cartesians, notably Geulincx and Malebranche, but it is doubtful whether Descartes ever meant to put forward such a view himself. On the other hand, he is quite definite that the connection between the soul and the body is not an accidental one, or at least, as he said in the letter to Regius in 1641 (K.S., pp. 269–70), it is accidental only *quodam modo*, in that the soul is separable from the body after death. During life there is a union between them by their very nature.

Yet the union between soul and body cannot strictly be by their very nature, since it has already been established that their natures are different. Descartes is anything but clear on this point, as the Princess Elizabeth indicated in correspondence with him. In the 6th *Meditation* he says categorically, 'I am not lodged in my body merely as a pilot in a ship, but I am so clearly conjoined and mixed with it that I form a unitary whole with it.' For this reason, the union between soul and body is in a sense substantial. Nevertheless, as he says in the correspondence with the Princess Elizabeth, we can have no clear and distinct idea of the union, it being available to the senses only. It is for the last reason, he says, that everyone, when not philosophizing, is aware of the connection. The difficulty lies in conceiving its nature; it is especially difficult to conceive both the distinction between soul and body and the union between them. In fact, Descartes says (K.S., p. 275), the human mind is not capable of it. Such a conclusion is scarcely encouraging.

Descartes is in no doubt that perception does take place. What we take to be perceptions are not merely products of the mind alone. But it still remains true that, given the initial rigorous distinction between soul and body on 'Platonic' lines, it is most obscure how perception can take place. The problem existed for Augustine, but he did not feel the need to deal with it. Descartes had to deal with it, because he felt that otherwise claims to empirical knowledge would not be valid; and he was right in this. Such is the crux for a philosopher who thinks of perception as the having of ideas which must, at any rate sometimes, represent reality.

It is well known that Descartes sometimes puts forward another account of the link between soul and body—a physiological account. In the *Dioptric* and elsewhere he maintains that the movements in the brain finally reach a 'certain small gland', which is the seat of the *sensus communis*. This is the pineal gland, and perhaps the clearest account of its functioning is given in the *Passions de l'âme*, Articles 30 ff. There he says that while the soul is really joined to the whole body, the latter being somehow indivisible, the pineal gland has a more specific function than any other part of the body. In it the soul has its seat, for the immediate exercise of its functions. The animal spirits which reach the gland affect it and so influence the soul; contrariwise, the soul, through it, irradiates through the rest of the body. It is not clear whether Descartes *thinks* that in this account he is dealing with the same point as that with which he is concerned in insisting on the substantial union of soul and body. It *is* clear that if he does so think he is wrong. The difficulties concerning the union of soul and body are not of a factual nature, and so not to be resolved by a theory which purports to be factual itself. The difficulties are conceptual; they arise from problems concerning the *concepts* of soul and body, when treated as they are by Descartes. If soul and body are independent substances they cannot also be interdependent. The theory concerning the pineal gland is perfectly consistent with the view that the connection between the soul and the body is accidental only.

To show that perception is possible, it is necessary, in the first place, to show that, in Cartesian terms, some of our ideas are objectively valid. If an idea has reality objectively in it, it must have a cause which has that reality formally or eminently in it (cf. the

3rd *Meditation* and *Principles*, I. 17). Descartes explains these terms by saying that if a man has the idea of a machine, he may have it, in the first place, because he has seen an actually existing machine. In this case, the machine is formally the cause of his idea; the latter is an actual copy of the machine and is produced by it (the term 'formally' stems from the scholastic use of the term 'form'). Alternatively, the man may have the idea because he has conceived of the machine himself, because he has produced the idea without there being anything initially for it to be a copy of; in this case his mind is the cause of the idea eminently.

To say that an idea has objective reality, is, therefore, to say merely that it *could* represent something, or that it would represent something if that something existed. It is not to say that the thing in question *does* exist. Indeed in the 3rd *Meditation* Descartes goes out of his way to argue that all our ideas of physical things could have their causes either formally or eminently in ourselves. Their causes would be formally in us if something corresponding to them existed in the mind (e.g. duration and number are actual or formal properties of mental events and for this reason our ideas of these properties, which also belong to physical objects, could be derived from the mind alone). Their causes would be eminently in us if the ideas were such that we ourselves could make them up. It still remains possible, therefore, that our ideas of physical things may be objectively real only in the sense that it is we or God who is their cause, and not that physical things are their cause either eminently or formally.

If the first stage in the demonstration that perception is possible was constituted by the proof that our ideas of physical objects are objectively real, the second stage necessarily consists of showing that those ideas are not caused by God or our minds alone, but by physical objects themselves. In the course of his argument in the 3rd *Meditation* for the view that our ideas of corporeal things *might* be derived from ourselves, Descartes points to the natural disposition which we have to believe in the existence of objects and also to the fact that perceptions and sensations do not depend upon the will. He rejects these considerations as *sufficient* to show that the causes of our ideas of physical objects are those objects themselves. In the 6th *Meditation*, however, he returns to the subject, and in his argument there he adduces those very same considerations. It should be added, however, that in the latter passage he is also concerned with the point that perception and other faculties which are mediated by the body are not part of the essence of the mind, but of the *mind plus body*.

In consequence he maintains, 'I cannot doubt that there is in me a certain passive faculty of perception (*de sentir*), that is to say of receiving and recognising the ideas of sensible things; but it would be useless to me, and I could not profit myself by it, if there were not also in me, or in some other thing, another active faculty, capable of forming and producing those ideas. But, this active faculty cannot be in me in so far as I am a thing that thinks, considering that it does not in the least presuppose my thinking, and considering also that those ideas often present themselves without my contributing to them in any way, and often even against my will.' He concludes that this faculty must be in something which contains either formally (corporeal things) or eminently (God) all the reality which is objectively in the ideas. It would seem, therefore, that Descartes rejects the supposition that we ourselves might be the cause of our ideas of physical objects on the grounds that perception, being dependent on the body, is passive and quite distinct from the active thinking which constitutes our real nature. It would be difficult to see in this argument more than a flat contradiction of the views put forward in the 3rd *Meditation*, if it were not for the fact that the whole section is set in a context in which Descartes is anxious to stress the union between the soul and the body, with the accompanying conclusion that it is only on the basis of that union that perception is possible at all. The final alternative to the view that physical objects themselves are the causes of our ideas of them—the alternative that God is the cause of them—is dismissed by means of the assertion that God is no deceiver, and hence that our natural disposition to believe in what our ideas suggest is justified. Descartes offers no argument for this view; he seems to take it as true by definition.

Descartes believes himself to have shown, therefore, that neither we ourselves nor God can be the cause of our ideas of physical objects and that, in consequence, their cause must be the physical objects themselves. The crucial point lies in his elimination of the hypothesis that we ourselves might be the cause of our ideas of physical objects, on the grounds that we are able to distinguish between those psychological functions which are essential to the mind and those which are not so essential but which are nevertheless clearly perceived to exist. This distinction is in turn dependent on the view that there is a union between the mind and the body. This union, however, Descartes believes to be recognizable only by the senses. There is in consequence a gap in the argument which cannot be filled on Descartes' terms. Indeed if we begin with the view that we are directly acquainted with, and only with, the contents of our minds, it is impossible to justify the belief that anything lies outside them. The remedy is not to treat perception as if it consisted only in the having of ideas, but to attempt a different analysis.

If Descartes' argument had been valid he would have shown that all our ideas of physical things are in some sense representative. But this would mean only that all the reality in the ideas must be in the objects which cause them. It would not necessarily mean that the ideas *exactly* correspond to their causes. We could know this only if we had some independent knowledge of the reality lying behind our ideas, and since this independent knowledge cannot be provided by the senses, it must be provided, if at all, by the intellect. We have this knowledge, Descartes thinks, to the degree that our ideas are not only clear but also distinct. Our ideas may be said to be clear in so far as they are directly open to the mind, but they are distinct only if we have a full knowledge of their nature and the means whereby they may be distinguished from other things. Descartes thinks that we have clear and distinct ideas of primary qualities because of the part which they play in mathematical knowledge. In mathematics, therefore, the intellect has knowledge of reality. This is not to say that we cannot make mistakes in attributing particular primary qualities to particular sensible objects. Descartes points out that we *can* be subject to such illusions. But since the ideas of primary qualities, *qua intelligible*, are clear and distinct, we cannot be mistaken on the general principle that objects possess qualities of the same sort as is represented by our ideas of primary qualities.

Our ideas of secondary qualities are not distinct because mathematics cannot deal with those qualities. For this reason we have no way of telling whether our ideas of colour, etc., do exactly correspond to the qualities which objects possess, apart from the weak consideration that God is not a deceiver. We may have a clear, though not distinct, idea of the so-called 'sensation of colour', but we have no apprehension whatever of the properties of the objects which produce it (cf. *Principles*, I. 69–71). In any case, our senses were provided for the conservation of life rather than for the acquisition of knowledge, and if our ideas of secondary qualities do not exactly correspond to the qualities of objects themselves this does not matter very much.

It has been noted above that in *Principles*, IV. 11 and *Dioptric*, 6, Descartes argues that, since the effects in the brain caused by the stimulation of our sense-organs possess the properties of motion, figure and magnitude only, there is no means by which we could attain a direct apprehension of any other properties of objects. It would appear from this that Descartes supposed the argument to show that we *do* have a direct apprehension of the primary qualities, motion, figure and magnitude. It cannot, however, do this, since all ideas, considered as the effects of physical processes, are in the same position. Sense-perception is always indirect. Hence the preference for primary qualities must rest only on the consideration that the intellect can provide a knowledge of them, *via* mathematics. But it is clear that mathematics does not in fact provide an *independent* means of knowing these qualities, since it is a formal discipline, and if it *is* applicable to physical objects this is not because it has an insight of its own into them, but because physical objects *happen* to possess properties which are similar in structure to the subject-matter of mathematics. That physical objects do happen to have these properties is not something that mathematics can discover of itself. It may be that there is a genuine distinction to be made between primary and secondary qualities in terms of the measurability of the former, but a distinction in these terms affords no reason for saying that ideas of primary qualities give a more adequate picture of reality than do those of secondary qualities.

To sum up: There is an inevitable problem for any philosopher who adopts a 'Platonic' view of the mind, especially if he adds that we are immediately aware of the mind's contents or activities, but not of the things around us. Descartes' somewhat uncomfortable and certainly untenable position is the result of the attempt by a philosopher whose view of the mind is essentially 'Platonic' to deal with a world which he thinks should be shown to exist on a level with human minds. Perception is a special problem, since, on this view, the nature of the mind is to be active, to indulge in intellectual activities, while perception seems to involve passivity. Descartes attempts a resolution of the problem by reference to the union of the soul with the body. But the nature of that union, and indeed the grounds for belief in the existence of the body at all, are left obscure. To deny the existence of the body or to view the mind as quite separated from it would be to assimilate perception to the other activities which are peculiar to the mind itself. There is always a tendency on the part of Rationalists to assimilate the senses to the activities of reason, just as the Empiricists had the opposite tendency. Descartes represents an honest but unsuccessful attempt not to give way to the tendency to which Rationalists in general are prone. This tendency will become more obvious in considering the other 17th-century Rationalists.

(ii) MALEBRANCHE

Malebranche was a theologian whose prime interest was in Augustine, but he was influenced by Descartes when he read the latter's work on *Man*. As a result Malebranche's philosophical views were largely Cartesian, but with leanings towards Augustinianism in the pure sense, especially in its more mystical aspects. But even as a Cartesian he differed from Descartes in some respects, especially in his Occasionalism. Geulincx had made the move to Occasionalism by saying that God puts into our minds the ideas of objects by means of the bodily processes. Malebranche said that God acts directly on the mind, putting ideas there on the occasion of the corresponding bodily occurrences. From this he drew the conclusion that in all our ideas we have knowledge of God; we know all things in God. Malebranche thought that he had Augustinian authority for this view, but whether this is so or not does not for present purposes matter very much. Of more importance is the view that we have in consequence no direct knowledge of physical objects, but only of such ideas of them as God has given us. For this reason he maintains that, if we think that we actually perceive things as they are, we are subject to error. Freedom from error can be attained only by relying on that of which we have clear and distinct ideas.

A second respect in which Malebranche differed from Descartes was in the view that we have no clear and distinct idea of our soul. We know of it only by a *sentiment intérieur*. That is to say that we know of it only by a sort of inner sense; we have no adequate representative ideas of it in itself. Yet we do know that it is a thinking thing and that its nature is, in consequence, to be active. This is clearly of importance when it is considered that bodies are said to exert no real influence upon the soul. (Although it must be admitted that Malebranche often talks incidentally as if they do.)

Like Descartes, Malebranche thinks that we can have clear and distinct ideas of extension, figure and movement, in that these qualities are intelligible. His reasons for this view are the same as those of Descartes, namely that they are rationally conceivable in mathematical terms. The only gloss on this on Malebranche's part is the previously mentioned view, that we know all things in God. Because of that view, Malebranche maintains that we know of extension, figure and movement only in God (it is difficult, of course, to see exactly what this means). But he follows Descartes (and perhaps expresses himself even more forthrightly on this point) in holding that the senses tell us nothing about these properties in themselves, nor about any other properties which we tend (though, on his view, wrongly) to ascribe to things. The grounds for this view are given clearly by him in the *Recherche de la Vérité*, I. 5, 3: 'They (sc. the senses) were not given to us in order that we might know about things in themselves, but only for the conservation of the body.' This point is vital, and while it is Cartesian in tendency it is given far more emphasis than Descartes gave it. For this reason, Malebranche maintains, we must 'never judge by the senses what things are in themselves, but only the relationship (*rapport*) which they have with our body'. Yet even here we must not expect exactness, for, he says (*Rech. de la Vér.*, I. 6, 3), 'Exactitude and precision are not essential to those forms of sensible knowledge which should contribute only to the conservation of life.' Perception of things which are distant from us is always inexact, for they have less direct relationship with our body. On the other hand, perception of things which are close to us, especially if held in the hands (note the importance attributed to touch) is 'sufficiently exact', though even in this case there is no guarantee of correctness.

Malebranche is here in a rather ambiguous position. On the one hand he wishes to say that the senses provide *no* knowledge of things in themselves. If this were so, to talk of the exactitude or otherwise of that knowledge would be out of place. On the other hand, he wishes to deny that our perception of things is exact, as if it made sense to say that it might be so. Yet in the case of things which are near to us, so that their relationship with the body is important, he says that our perception of them is exact enough. His real view seems to be that if we use our senses in the belief that they do provide us with knowledge of things we are bound to be mistaken. Any kind of judgment whatever about sensible things is liable to be erroneous. We are directly acquainted only with sensations. 'When you see light,' he says (op. cit., I. 5, 2.), 'it is very certain that you see light; when you feel heat, you are not at all deceived in believing that you feel it. . . . But you are deceived when you judge that the heat which you feel is outside the soul which feels it.' In other words, we can be quite certain of the effects which objects have on the soul as a result of their relationship with the body (or rather, in view of the Occasionalism, of what would be effects if the body could have any real connection with the body). We can have no knowledge of objects themselves by means of the senses. Malebranche spends some considerable time in pointing out the mistakes which arise from the failure to keep this in mind. 'Our eyes,' he says (op. cit., I. 6, init.), 'generally deceive us in all that they represent to us.'

While our senses are said to be generally deceptive concerning objects themselves, they are also said to be more deceptive in some respects than in others. Malebranche is anything but clear on this point, but what he must mean is that the senses vary in deceptiveness concerning the relationship which things have with the body. It is this relationship which is the concern of the senses in their function of conserving life, and they can be more or less efficient in carrying out that function. Nevertheless, if the senses ensure only that the soul has certain sensations on the occasion of a certain relationship between things and the body, error, if it exists, must strictly speaking be the result of subsequent *judgment* concerning that relationship. Malebranche reveals a constant ambiguity on this point.

He maintains that it is not certain that there are even as many as two men who have the same sensation of the same object (op. cit., I. 6, 1 and I. 13, 5); for their sense-organs vary and God puts into our minds sensations corresponding to the effects in the sense-organs which are caused by objects. He admits that all men may see an object as having the same size in the sense that they see it as having the same boundaries or as being included within the same angle of vision. He thinks, however, that in another sense 'the sensible idea' which men have in this case may differ in size, and this is bound to differ for men who are of different sizes themselves. The sensation which we have in any given case corresponds to the 'image' on the sense-organ; and the sense-organs themselves are designed for the conservation of life. In consequence, things which produce sensations which are small to us will produce sensations which seem big to people who are much smaller than us. In this thesis Malebranche appears to run two different points together—(1) that size is relative in itself, and (2) that the size of our sensations may be relative to the size of our apparatus for perception. These points are not essentially connected. An object may appear big to one man and small to another because size is relative and depends upon the standard of comparison, whether or not the men's sense-organs are different.

It is presumably because the senses are said to be concerned with the relations of things to the body, that relativity plays a large part in Malebranche's account of sense-perception. He tries to show that our estimates of size, figure, movement and distance are all partially relative at least. Yet he thinks that our estimates of figure are less liable to error than those of the other properties because 'figure is nothing absolute in itself, but its nature consists in the relationship (*rapport*) between the parts which delimit some space and a certain straight line or a point which one conceives in that space, and which one can call, as in a circle, the centre of the figure' (op. cit., I. 7, 1). Nevertheless we can be deceived even here 'in a thousand ways'. It is difficult to follow the exact trend of this argument.

Malebranche thinks that the essence of perception consists in the having of sensations which, while not strictly representative of the objects which have 'caused' them, are representative of the effects that these objects have on the body, at any rate in the case of primary qualities. He thus follows the Cartesian tradition in thinking of sensations as representative, and in consequence runs together on the one hand sensations in the strict sense, e.g. pains, and on the other hand our perception of the qualities of things. (cf. op. cit., I. 13). This is mitigated only by the fact that, strictly speaking, Malebranche should say that we never perceive the qualities of things, but only the effects which they have on the body. But this is no real mitigation since, in the first place, to perceive those effects is still on his view merely to have sensations which are representative of them, and in the second place, we do ordinarily think that we perceive things around us and not merely the effects which they have upon us.

So far we have been concerned chiefly with Malebranche's views on our liability to error in perception. But he is also concerned with how we manage to attain knowledge of things which is 'exact enough'—how, for example, we manage to perceive how far things are from us. Descartes had attempted to explain distance-perception by reference to the mechanism of the eye and the pattern of stimulation upon it. Malebranche takes the same course but in an interesting way (op. cit., I. 9, 3). Like Descartes he points out that the convergence and accommodation of the eyes, and the size of the retinal image, have little efficacy in enabling us to perceive how far very distant objects are from us. In consequence he adduces also the facts that the retinal image loses detail as the object recedes from us, that we generally obtain as a result of experience some idea of the comparative size of objects and that we always see objects in a context which gives us a clue to their distance (and this last fact he considers the most important). Malebranche agrees with Descartes that there is no question of our perceiving the retinal image and then on its basis, making judgments about the objects which produced it. If variations in the nature of the retinal image play a part in distance perception it is as parts of the mechanics not as a basis for judgment. On the other hand, some of the other factors adduced by Malebranche, e.g. experience of comparative size and perceived context, do seem to be the sort of thing which could be used as a basis for judgment. Yet we are not always conscious of making any judgments when we perceive the distance of things.

Because the view that perceiving is in some ways like judging is so plausible, despite the fact that we are not always conscious of making any judgments, Malebranche introduces the notion of *natural judgments* or *judgments of sense* as opposed to *free judgments*. He first introduces the notion (op. cit., I. 7, 3) to deal with the phenomenon which is now known as shape-constancy—the fact that we tend to see things as of more or less their right shape even when they are not at right angles to the direction of vision. He says that since painters are obliged 'to paint, for example, circles as ovals, this is an unmistakeable mark of the errors in our vision in the case of objects which are not painted'. (The premise in this argument is of course that the sensations which we have must correspond to the pattern of stimulation on the retina of the eye—a thesis which the Gestalt Psychologists later called the 'Constancy Hypothesis'.) Malebranche goes on, 'These errors are corrected by new sensations, which should be regarded as a kind of natural judgment and which could be called judgments of sense. When, for example, we look at a cube, it is certain that all the sides which we see hardly ever produce a projection or image of equal size in the fundus of the eye, since the image of each of the sides which is painted on the retina or optic nerve is very like a cube painted in perspective, and in consequence the sensation which we have of them should represent the faces of the cube as unequal, since they are unequal in a cube in perspective. Nevertheless we see them all equal, and are not at all deceived.'

But, he goes on to say a little later, 'Since the senses, properly speaking, only sense and never judge, it is certain that this natural judgment is only a complex sensation (*sensation composée*), which can in consequence sometimes be false.' He explains that by a complex sensation he means that the sensation depends upon two or more impressions at the same time. For instance, when I see a man coming towards me he appears of the same size throughout because there are two kinds of impression in the retina, (1) an impression of size and (2) an impression of distance. The outcome of both is that as the impression of size increases the impression of distance diminishes, or *vice versa*, so that we actually see the man as of the same size.

It is evident that Malebranche's main position is that perceiving consists merely in the having of sensations, even if we go on to make definite, 'free' judgments about the objects in question. But he thinks at the same time that there is something in the having of sensations which is more akin to judgment. For how can one sensation correct another unless it is *used* to that end? Yet that judgment is not a free judgment, depending on our will. In consequence he says that God excites in us a kind of judgment which we cannot help making—though it is really a sensation! Malebranche had to clarify and even alter some aspects of this view in reply to

Régis, who criticized him for saying that it is our mind that makes these judgments (a thing which would seem to be impossible if we are not aware of them). His final statement on the matter is to be found at the end of the *Recherche*, I. 9, 3. There he denies explicitly that it is our mind that makes these judgments; instead he says that God makes them in us in consequence of the laws of the union of soul and body. God puts into our mind *via* the body judgments which we should make of ourselves did we but know 'optics, geometry, and all that happens at the moment in our eyes and in our brain'. These judgments are not due to us, and they sometimes are made in spite of us; that is why from our point of view they are sensations. If they were sensations in the strict sense, however, they could not be false, since falsity belongs to judgments. For this reason they must be said to contain a judgment which is induced in us for the conservation of life. Indeed every 'sensation of external objects' includes at least one false judgment, to wit that we are seeing an external object in itself (op. cit., I. 14, 1).

Natural judgments can lead to error also, e.g. in the zenith-horizon illusion of the moon, when the moon looks bigger at the horizon than at the zenith (cf. op. cit., I. 7, 5; I. 9, 3; I. 14). This illusion Malebranche explains by saying that the moon looks farther away at the horizon than at the zenith because of the intervening objects. Since the retinal image is of the same size in each case the moon appears larger when at the horizon. He rejects any explanations in terms of vapours arising from the earth between us and the moon when it is at the horizon (an explanation with which Berkeley toyed), and in the 12th *Dialogue on Metaphysics* he maintains that the illusion disappears when the sun or moon is looked at through smoked glass. The explanation is ingenious and forthright. It follows that natural judgments can be responsible either for illusion or for freedom from it. But since they often lead to a corresponding free judgment the possibilities of error are in that case so much the greater.

In referring to complex sensations Malebranche is at least pointing to the fact that the impressions on the retina must be considered as a whole and not in isolation. Yet there is something clearly unsatisfactory in treating the notion as he does in general. In seeing something, we usually see it in a context, and the object of perception is to that extent complex, as is the consequent effect upon the sense-organ. But to call the perception itself a complex sensation is to follow up the implications of a causal theory of perception and is subject to all the previously noted objections. On the other hand, one result of assimilating perception to sensation is that in a complex sensation one factor must be taken to counteract or correct another. And how can one sensation correct another? Malebranche in a sense takes it that since sensations are representative we are given information in each perception. Sometimes, therefore, one piece of information can correct another. But the making of corrections looks very much like the making of judgments, only they are in this case judgments which we cannot help making. Whichever way we look at the situation, Malebranche's position reveals difficulties. There are objections to the assimilation of perception to either the having of sensations or the making of judgments. Malebranche's difficulties at least bring this out.

(iii) SPINOZA

Spinoza's philosophy can be dealt with adequately only if considered as a whole. In so far as it is valid, it hangs together, and it it impossible to elucidate fully one part of it without considering the rest. Spinoza's remarks about perception are incidental only, but they are interesting to the extent that they show that for a consistent Rationalist perception must be assimilated to thinking. Nevertheless, an adequate understanding of those remarks presupposes a reasonably full account of Spinoza's system; and since that is impossible here, the following account must be considered incomplete.

In effect Spinoza took seriously Descartes' passing remark (*Princ.*, I. 51) that in the proper sense the concept of substance belongs only to God. He concluded that everything else but God is a mode or modification of him, depending on him, that is to say, for existence. God is infinite and has infinite attributes; he may be considered as God or nature, and nature possesses the all-pervasive attributes of extension and thought. Bodies are therefore modifications of God *qua* extended (*Ethics*, II. Def. 1). Mind is not defined as such in Pt. II of the *Ethics*, although one aim of that section is to elucidate what minds are. Spinoza does, however, give an explicit definition of an idea: 'By idea I understand a conception of the Mind, which the Mind forms because it is a thinking thing'. And he adds, 'I say conception rather than perception, since the word "perception" seems to indicate that the Mind is affected by an object; whereas "conception" seems to express an activity of the mind.' Because God is both a thinking and an extended thing, 'the order and connexion of ideas is the same as the order and connexion of things'. (*Ethics*, II. 7). Indeed the relation between ideas and bodies is that between ideas and their objects or *ideata*.

What then is the human mind? Spinoza takes it as axiomatic that human beings think, that we each perceive the affections of one particular body, and that apart from modes of thought the only single things which we perceive are bodies (*Ethics*, II. Axioms, 2, 4, 5). He concludes that the human mind is constituted by an idea whose object is the body. Given that the relation between the mind and the body is that between an idea and its object, the order of events in the mind and in the body must necessarily be parallel. But an idea has been defined as a conception, not a perception (even allowing for the broad sense given to 'perception' in Rationalist thought). It would seem to follow that our body is merely what we *conceive* to exist. But Spinoza explains (*Ethics*, II. 11, Coroll), 'It follows that the human Mind is part of the infinite intellect of God; and hence when we say that the human Mind perceives (*percipere*) this or that, we say nothing else than that God, not in so far as he is infinite, but in so far as he is explained through the nature of the human Mind, or in so far as he constitutes the essence of the human mind, has this or that idea'. Hence it is permissible to say that our mind perceives things, i.e. is in a passive relation to things, only in so far as the ideas constituting our mind express the nature of God in a certain way. We can be said to perceive the body and other things by means of it, only because our minds are constituted by God's thinking in a certain way which is parallel to the order of things.

The closer our thoughts approximate to those of God the more active they are. It is quite impossible that our thoughts should ever coincide with those of God, for his are infinite and ours are mere modifications of his *qua* finite. But some of our ideas may be what Spinoza calls adequate ideas. An adequate idea is one 'which, in so far as it is considered in itself without relation to an object, has all the properties or intrinsic marks of a true idea'. (*Ethics*,

II. Def. 4). Hence Spinoza says (*Ethics*, III. 1), 'Our mind is active in respect of certain things, and passive in respect of others; that is to say, in so far as it has adequate ideas, so far is it necessarily active in respect of certain things, and in so far as it has inadequate ideas, so far is it necessarily passive in respect of certain things.' It follows that what we call perceiving is the having of inadequate ideas. Spinoza maintains (*Ethics*, II. 24 ff) that the human mind has therefore no adequate knowledge of the body or of the things which are perceived by its means. Sense-experience (*experientia vaga*) is the lowest of the three grades of knowledge distinguished in the *Ethics* (II. 40, note 2). It covers not only the direct receipt of sensations but also any knowledge derived ultimately from the senses and hence dependent on the body. Spinoza calls it also 'opinion' and 'imagination', and since both memory and imagination depend on the body his conception of experience presupposes these. It is thus in line with the Greek conception of experience.

Anything that might be called 'experiential knowledge' is considered by Spinoza, in true Rationalist manner, very much inferior to knowledge which is derived from the use of our reason, let alone to that knowledge which he calls 'intuition'. Knowledge derived from reason or intuition is necessarily true, while experience is 'the only cause of falsity'. There is more to this than a mere disparagement of that knowledge which is to be derived from the senses. While Spinoza takes it as axiomatic that we do in a sense perceive things, however inadequately, he in effect does away with the idea that we are thereby in a passive relation to independent objects. What we call perceiving is really God having this or that idea, and things are the objects of those ideas. *Sub specie aeternitatis*, we are, when we perceive, merely having inadequate ideas. What we call passivity is really inadequacy, and what we call activity is, conversely, adequacy.

Furthermore, there is no room in Spinoza's system for the Cartesian suggestion that we can distinguish between the having of ideas (perception in the general sense) and the making of judgments. The latter would depend upon the will, and Spinoza in effect denies that this can be so. The will and the intellect are the same (*Ethics*, II. 49, Coroll). The having of an idea and what would otherwise be called judgment are therefore one and the same. For this reason, ideas can be said to be true or false. Suspension and affirmation of judgment are likewise termed by Spinoza 'perceptions'; they are not additional to perceptions.

Spinoza recognizes the existence of images or 'imaginations of mind' (*Ethics*, II. 17, note, and 49, note), and he says that they in themselves contain no error. But he is somewhat ambiguous as to their status. In the first passage he uses the term 'image' to refer to the affections of the body, 'the ideas of which represent to us external bodies as if they were present'. And he adds, 'The Mind does not err from what it images, but only in so far as it is considered to lack the idea which excludes the existence of those things which it imagines to itself as present'. Hence, in imagination we have images of bodily modifications, and no error arises in this respect unless we 'affirm' the existence of entities corresponding to the images. In the second passage he distinguishes between ideas and images, insisting that images, like words, are such that their essence is 'constituted solely by corporeal movements, which least involve the conception of thought'. The last phrase reveals an ambiguity. Either images are bodily movements (and the Cartesians had used the word of neural excitations in the retina) or they are modes of thought. There is no room for a half-way stage in Spinoza's system. And this remark holds good for all Spinoza's discussions of these topics.

(iv) LEIBNIZ

Perhaps the most noteworthy aspect of Leibniz's thought is the fact that he had a multiplicity of reasons for most of the views which he put forward. His view, for example, that the world consists of an infinite number of monads—simple spiritual substances, similar in some ways but not in others to the so-called 'ego' in human-beings—was based by him partly on logical considerations, partly on considerations derived from his dynamics, partly on empirical observation backed by theorizing, partly on inference from scientific discoveries about minute organisms seen through the newly invented microscope, and partly on general scientific theories, such as the biological theory of the preformation of the organism in the germ-plasm. It is in consequence difficult to expound his view on any one matter in a simple way. But some points concerning his views may be brought out by contrasting his views with those of the other Rationalists.

Spinoza's views were in general anathema to Leibniz, especially the view that there exists one single substance with modes such that everything is rigorously determined. Leibniz was very anxious to preserve free-will, which he thought of as axiomatic. He thought that common-sense was sufficient to justify belief in a plurality of substances, and that the reasons noted above justified the belief that there were in fact an infinity of them. At the same time, Leibniz's conception of each one of these substances was in many ways similar to Spinoza's conception of his single substance. In particular, he thought that all the properties of a substance, and indeed anything that could or might be attributed to it, was internal to it. He maintained as axiomatic (e.g. in the *Discourse on Metaphysics*, 13) that in every true proposition the predicate is contained in the subject. Hence, all the properties, past, present and future, of a substance are part of its nature, and every substance is 'big with the future' (*Nouveaux Essais*, Pref., W., p. 376).[1] Every substance is in fact a microcosm of the macrocosm in that all the relations between it and every other thing are internal to that substance. Every monad is, he says, a mirror of the universe. In order that a substance should be both simple and capable of representing the universe at large in this way, its nature must be peculiar, and Leibniz thought that only a spiritual substance could fulfil the qualifications. Only something like the soul or ego could be both simple and yet infinitely varied in its powers of representing other objects.

Leibniz came to see that his view entailed that the relations between each substance and every other were only ideal; no substance had any real effect on any other. Russell maintains (*The Philosophy of Leibniz*, p. 132) that this was, in effect, an extension of the doctrine of Occasionalism to an infinite number of substances. This statement, however, requires qualification. While Leibniz's theory is like Occasionalism in that there is no real causal relationship between any two monads, including the monad which constitutes any given soul and the other monads which constitute its body, the ideas which the soul has on any occasion are not put there by God on that occasion. Leibniz replaced Occasionalism in the technical sense by a view which he

[1] References to Leibniz's works are, wherever possible, made to the volume of selections edited by P. Wiener (Scribner). This will be referred to as W.

called that of the 'pre-established harmony'. In his correspondence with Leibniz, Arnauld criticized this view, that God has pre-established a harmony between what goes on in the soul and what goes on outside it, in such a way that we think that we perceive something independent of ourselves, saying that it was in fact equivalent to Occasionalism. Leibniz replied that Occasionalism amounted to belief in a continual miracle, while his view did not.

In *his* correspondence with Leibniz, Samuel Clarke made the same criticisms, and Leibniz's reply sums up his beliefs (*Letter* 5, 84, W., p. 266): 'I do not assent to the vulgar notions that the *images of things are conveyed* by the *organs* (of sense) to the *soul*. For, it is not conceivable by what passage, or by what means of conveyance, these images can be carried from the organ to the soul. This vulgar notion in philosophy is not intelligible, as the new *Cartesians* have sufficiently shown. It cannot be explained, how *immaterial* substance is affected by *matter*; and to maintain an unintelligible notion thereupon, is having recourse to the scholastic chimerical notion of I know not what inexplicable *species intentionales*, passing from the organs to the soul. Those *Cartesians* saw the difficulty; but they could not explain it. They had recourse to a (certain wholly special) concourse of God, which would really be miraculous. But, I think, *I have given* the *true solution* of that *enigma*.'

A little later (sect. 87) he goes on, 'In truth and reality, this way of perception is wholly chimerical, and has no place even in *human souls*. They prehend what happens *outside* them, by what happens *within* them answering to the things without; in virtue of the *harmony*, which God has pre-established by the most beautiful and the most admirable of all his products; whereby *every simple substance* is by its nature (if one may so say) a *concentration* and a *living mirror* of the *whole universe*, according to its *point of view*.'

It may be objected (cf. Russell, op. cit., p. 135) that, since Leibniz believed that everything consisted of monads, perception ought not in any case to be a question of the influence of matter on the soul but of the influence of one monad on another. Nevertheless, the main point remains—one monad does not *really* influence another. Leibniz's position is in the end similar to that of Spinoza; activity and passivity are really only a matter of the distinctness or otherwise of the perceptions of a monad. '*Action* is attributed to the monad in so far as it has distinct perceptions, and *passivity* in so far as it has confused perceptions.' (*Monadology*, 49, W., p. 543.) A perception or an idea is obscure, Leibniz says (*Reflections on Knowledge, Truth and Ideas*, W., p. 283), 'when it is not sufficient for the recognition of things after they have been experienced'. It is clear when it is sufficient for the recognition of a new instance of the thing in question. But ideas or perceptions may, while being clear, be indistinct rather than distinct. They are so when we are unable to list the characteristics required to distinguish the thing in question from others. To have a distinct perception requires some self-consciousness about our awareness of objects, so that we may know what it is that enables us to distinguish and recognize things.

At this stage it is necessary to note an important distinction which Leibniz makes—that between perception and apperception. To have a perception is to have an idea which corresponds in some way to an object, although it is not caused by that object. 'Perception' is merely a general term for the representation of other things in a monad—the expression of plurality in a unity, as Leibniz puts it. Each monad perceives all other things in that it is, as it were, a reflection of them. While, then, to have a perception of an object is to have an idea of it, an idea is not, Leibniz says, 'a certain act of thinking, but a power or faculty'. (*What is an Idea?* W., 281). We can have an idea of a thing when not actually thinking about it, provided that there is in fact a means of expressing the power which is constituted by that idea. The fact that we have a perception of something does not entail that we are aware of actually perceiving it. When we are so aware we have apperception, and this entails that our perceptions must be distinct. That is to say that in order to have apperception we must be conscious of what is involved in our perceptions, and this necessarily requires that those perceptions should be distinct.

Leibniz's contemporary, Locke, held that the soul does not always think, and that there is nothing in it of which we are not conscious. Leibniz objected to both of these views, as well as to others.[1] On the first point, he said that Locke was right only if he meant that the soul does not always have apperceptions, since it always has perceptions. His reply to the second point is connected

---

[1] Since he believed in innate truths and ideas he particularly objected, of course, to Locke's view that the mind is initially a *tabula rasa*.

with his answer to the first—that while we are always conscious of our apperceptions, we are not always conscious of our perceptions. He thought that the existence of unconscious mental states, in a general sense, was shown by the fact that, if there is not to be an infinite regress, reflection upon our thoughts must stop at some point, so that there is no further reflection upon reflection. And if this is so there must be thoughts of which there is no further consciousness. This argument fails to take into account the possibility that there may be self-conscious thoughts which do not involve actual reflection upon those thoughts. But Leibniz's second line of argument is, *prima facie* at any rate, rather better. This is to the effect that since a perception must reflect all the complexity of its object, there must exist in the perception parts corresponding to the parts of the object. If this is so, our perception of, for example, the noise produced by the waves of the sea must have parts corresponding to the noise produced by each ripple. But we are not conscious of all these little noises (*Nouveaux Essais*, Pref. W., p. 376). Hence there must be perceptions of which we are not conscious. These Leibniz calls *petites perceptions*. Confused perceptions in general have parts which are either *petites* or unconscious in some other way (cf. *Monadology*, 21 ff., W., p. 537).

It seems to follow from this that perceptions do not become conscious until they reach a certain magnitude or intensity. This is often represented as an important psychological advance. But it is important to notice that the whole argument turns on the premise that every perception must be completely representative of its object. That is to say that Leibniz's argument presupposes the representative theory of perception which is common to Rationalist thought. In so far as Locke also held this theory he could not validly deny what Leibniz said. But if the representative theory of perception is rejected Leibniz's argument loses it force. To perceive an object is not a matter of there occurring in the mind an event which corresponds to events in the external world. When we hear the noise produced by the waves of the sea, we hear the noises produced by each ripple only in the sense that these contribute to the total noise. We do not hear them in the sense that we can distinguish them.

Another point is that if the existence of *petites perceptions* were a psychological discovery the use to which Leibniz actually put the notion would be paradoxical. He uses it as the foundation of certain metaphysical views, in particular that each monad is a mirror of the universe (i.e. it represents the whole universe within itself) and that it is big with its future (*Nouveaux Essais*, Pref. W., p. 376). Leibniz's main theory about the relation of soul to body is that the body consists of monads which are made into an organic unity by a dominant monad which is the soul. Indeed every monad has an organic body, this being made possible by the fact that the number of monads is infinite. The highest monad of all is God, and under him there is a hierarchy of monads *ad infinitum*. The dominance of one monad over those which constitute its body is determined by its power of activity and hence by the clarity of its perceptions. In human-beings the monad which constitutes the soul has clearer perceptions than those which constitute the body. But we are not aware of the fact that our soul represents the whole universe within itself; we have not apperceptions to this effect, for our apperceptions of things are limited in number and the universe is infinite. For this reason, Leibniz maintains that since each monad is a mirror of the universe, it must have perceptions which are *petites* and therefore unconscious. Only in this way too is it possible for us to be unaware of our own futures, since each monad is big with its future, in the sense that it contains within itself all the possibilities for its future development. The existence of unconscious perceptions is not, therefore, a psychological discovery; it is primarily a logical demand of the metaphysical system, even if Leibniz thought that psychological considerations had bearings on the matter.

Monads not only have perceptions; they also have appetitions. Appetition is the tendency to pass from one perception to another and is due to the intrinsic activity of the monad. All monads share in this, and for this reason the fact that a monad has appetitions has nothing to do with whether it is active or passive *relative to other monads*. Appetition is an intrinsic property of a monad, not something that determines its relations to other monads. The activity or passivity of a monad with respect to other monads is, as we have seen, considered by Leibniz to be a question of the distinctness or indistinctness of its perceptions. Since to be active is thus to have distinct perceptions, Leibniz cannot give any function to judgment, as something active, independently of the having of perceptions. Error cannot be put down by him, as it was by

Descartes, to judgment or the will; it consists merely in the having of confused ideas. In this Leibniz agrees with Spinoza. In what we ordinarily call perception, when we suppose ourselves to be affected by external things, we are really having confused perceptions (in the Leibnizian sense of 'perception'). We are mistaken in thinking that our perceptions are *due to* external things. While our perceptions may correspond to a greater or less extent to things around us they are certainly not due to them.

Like Spinoza, therefore, Leibniz is an example of a philosopher who pays lip service to our ordinary ways of talking about perception, while maintaining the general view that everything in the mind is due to that mind alone. According to Leibniz, it is appetition which ensures the passage of a monad from one perception to another, but the correspondence of those perceptions with their objects is due to the pre-established harmony. Thinking and perceiving are to be distinguished, not by saying that the first is an activity of the mind and the second something passive, if activity is taken to imply an exercise of volition. The distinction between the two is merely a question of the distinctness or indistinctness of what is in the mind. The final test of distinctness lies in the ability to give a definition of what is thought. Leibniz and Spinoza are supreme Rationalists in the sense that they make everything that has to do with the mind a function of the mind alone. They give no account of our *ordinary* conception of perception.

Christian Wolff, Leibniz's main disciple, gave up the monads and limited the doctrine of the pre-established harmony so that it was a doctrine about the parallelism between the mind and the body alone. Despite a distinction between *psychologia rationalis*, a deductive systematization of the concepts related to the mind starting from first principles, and *psychologia empirica*, a study of the same notions based on observation, his view of perception differed little from that of Leibniz. Wolff maintained that what was fundamental to the mind was a *vis representativa*, the power of representation of the complex in the simple, and he developed a view of the hierarchy of ways in which this could come about. This in turn resulted in a kind of faculty psychology. While he stressed the bodily concomitants which are parallel to perception, he could, because of his Leibnizian views, offer no further insight into the nature of perception itself. Wolff systematized Leibniz's thought, with respect to the functions of the soul, but he added little to it.

In sum, the Rationalists in general tended to think of the mind as something active, its activity being thought. This brought with it manifest difficulties concerning perception, and Descartes at least made an honest if abortive attempt to deal with the difficulties within the terms of reference. The other Rationalists tended to assimilate perception more and more to a species of thinking, while sometimes, as in the case of Leibniz, paying lip service to ordinary notions on the matter. The Empiricists tended in the opposite direction, but met with difficulties there also.

6

THE EMPIRICISTS

(i) INTRODUCTION

I HAVE already insisted that the so-called British Empiricists were opposed to the Rationalists only in tendency. In their theory of knowledge they tended towards the view that sense-experience is the sole source of that certainty which was supposed to constitute knowledge. They also looked to sense-experience as the sole source of our ideas. Perhaps because of this last view, they tended to conceive of the having of ideas as a passive affair. Locke held that ideas are produced in our minds by things outside us; Berkeley held that they are caused by spirits; and while Hume denied the existence of things which could be the causes of our ideas, he used a terminology which suggests the contrary view, i.e. the terminology of 'impressions' which suggests the model of the wax and seal.

Many of the writings of the Empiricists were critical in tone (and this is especially true of Berkeley and Hume). The view that all the materials for knowledge are derived from experience was made the basis of criticisms of claims to certain kinds of non-empirical knowledge on the part of the Rationalists. That is to say that one of the main purposes of the empiricist philosophy was to delimit the understanding. To achieve this end Hume proposed to use the 'experimental method'—the putting of philosophical claims to the test of experience, by seeing whether the ideas on which they were based could themselves be derived from experience. Berkeley in effect adopted the same procedure, at any rate in the critical parts of his philosophy. As a result he rejected certain metaphysical notions, like that of 'substance', which

Locke had retained; although he also put forward a rival metaphysics, to the effect that there are no things independent of our ideas and that the only causes of those ideas are spirits. In Hume's case, the result was the adoption of views which have often been looked upon as those of a sceptic, although they may at the same time be regarded as attempts to analyse notions like those of 'material things' and the 'self' in terms of the contents of experience alone.

In Locke, the orginator of the 'new way of ideas', there is less criticism and more of an attempt to delimit the understanding for its own sake. At the same time, it must be admitted that his writings contain far more in the way of irrelevance, incoherence and, indeed, inconsistency. He is by no means a philosopher with a systematic and elegant mode of thought. But he was the pioneer in the attempt to see whether from experience alone can be built up all the materials for knowledge.[1] By his insistence, in however incoherent a fashion, that knowledge is always a matter of having ideas, he set the scene for the subsequent discussions by Berkeley and Hume.

(ii) LOCKE

Locke sets down as his purpose (*Essay Concerning Human Understanding*, I. 1, 2),[2] 'to inquire into the original, certainty, and extent of human knowledge, together with the grounds and degrees of belief, opinion, and assent'. He proposes not to 'meddle with the physical consideration of the mind', and he wishes in general to eschew consideration of the physiological conditions under which perception takes place. Instead he sets out to use the 'historical, plain method', i.e. to pay attention to how we come to acquire knowledge. This last point is somewhat deceptive, for one might be forgiven for thinking that Locke proposes to discuss psychology. His procedure is in fact logical or epistemological. He sets out, that is, not to describe the processes whereby people actually do acquire knowledge, but to give an account of the logical presuppositions of our claims to knowledge. This is given a psychological dress.

[1] Aquinas maintained this as a truth, but he scarcely set out to justify it in detail.
[2] All future references to Locke will be to the *Essay*, and the references to the title will therefore be omitted.

He thus sets out to show that all our ideas are built up from simple ideas, and that knowledge is 'the perception of the connection of and agreement, or disagreement and repugnancy, of any of our ideas' (IV. 1, 2). In the last respect he is not fully consistent. He claims that there are three degrees of knowledge—(1) intuitive, (2) demonstrative and (3) sensitive. The first two at any rate may be concerned with the relations between our ideas, but it appears that, like (3), they may also be concerned with 'particular existences'. Locke claims that we have intuitive knowledge of our own existence, demonstrative knowledge of God's existence, and sensitive knowledge of the existence of particular finite things (IV. 3, 21; IV. 9. ff.). Sometimes he appears to say that these forms of knowledge consist in the perception of the agreement between the ideas of these things and the idea of existence. At other times he suggests that more is required than this, and in certain passages (IV. 4, 4; IV. 11, 2 ff.) he attempts to justify our knowledge of particular existences by justifying in turn the view that our ideas conform to the things which cause them.

Locke is here in the difficulty which besets all philosophers who adopt a representational theory of perception without providing an independent means of coming to know about those things which our ideas represent. Like Descartes, he treats ideas—that which the mind is 'applied about whilst thinking'—as at the best representative of things outside the mind. And his main theory admits of no way of finding out about those things independently of ideas of sense. As an empiricist, Locke should insist that knowledge can come only through ideas of sense. To the extent that he claims to know about the causes of our ideas at all, let alone about the degree to which our ideas are truly representative of their objects, he is inconsistent.

As already indicated, Locke defines an idea as that which the mind is applied about whilst thinking. Ideas may be either of sensation or reflection, and they may be simple or complex (although in the 4th edition of the *Essay* the scheme breaks down somewhat, and ideas of reflections and general ideas are admitted as separate categories). The use of the term 'idea' to cover the object of any 'mental operation' is, of course, not without its ambiguities. It has frequently been noted that Locke gives notions such as *whiteness* as examples of simple ideas of sense. It seems, therefore, that to have a simple idea of whiteness in perception is to perceive something as white (it is not of course to have a general or abstract idea of whiteness). It is, that is, to perceive the quality which something possesses. But the idea-terminology by no means brings this out.

Ideas come into the mind in the first place as the result of 'an impression or motion made in some part of the body, as produces some perception in the understanding' (II. 1, 23). Despite the declared policy of eschewing physiological considerations, he hints at such matters, making the usual reference to animal spirits (e.g. II. 8, 12 ff.). The motion set up in the sense-organ is conveyed to the brain—the 'mind's presence-room' (II. 3, 1) or the 'seat of sensation' as he calls it—and so, in some unspecified way, produces an idea in the mind. Having ideas, and perception, he says, are the same thing. In saying this he is using the term 'perception' in the general way in which, as we have already seen, it was used by the Rationalists. In this use, a perception is any representative function of the mind. But Locke is not very precise in his terminology, and he also uses the term 'perception' in a more restricted sense, in which it is coincident with 'sense-perception' (e.g. II, 9). The term is also used either of the idea in the mind or of the having of it (Locke is sometimes accused of a similar ambiguity in his use of the term 'idea' itself). For example, he says (II. 1, 3), 'First, our Senses, conversant about particular sensible objects, do convey into the mind several distinct perceptions of things, according to those various ways wherein those objects do affect them'. Here the word 'perception' clearly means an idea. On the other hand, at II. 6, 1 he speaks of perception as an *action* of the mind, and at II. 9, 1 he speaks of it as a faculty exercised about our ideas. No doubt our ordinary use of the word is equally slipshod.

The same considerations apply to his use of the term 'sensation'. He uses the term (1) of the process by which we come to have ideas of sense; (2) as an equivalent to 'sense-perception'; (3) of the physiological effect which objects have on the sense-organs and brain; and (4) of the consequent ideas. He also uses the term 'impression' (e.g. II. 9, 3) in an ambiguous way—mainly to account for the effects which objects have on our sense-organs, but also to account for the effects on the mind.

This ambiguity of terminology is not without significance; it reflects also an ambiguity of thought. Locke is never clear whether perception is to be considered as active or as passive. Sensation, if it may be distinguished from perception, is passive. There are passages in which Locke appears not to make the distinction, although there are equally passages in which he does. As already noted, he refers to perception in the general sense (II. 6, 2) as one of the 'great and principal actions of the mind' of which there may be various modes. Later (II. 19, 1) he refers to sensation as the mode of thought 'which actually accompanies, and is annexed to, any impression on the body, made by an external object, being distinct from all other modifications of thinking'. In such passages Locke follows the Cartesian line of making perception a mode of thought. In II. 21, 5 he classifies different kinds of perception: (1) the perception of ideas in our minds; (2) the perception of the signification of signs; (3) the perception of the agreement or disagreement that there is between any of our ideas—and he calls perception an act of the Understanding. The passage suggests that perception, while an act, brings with it in all cases some form of awareness—though Locke does not explicitly say this.

There are, however, many passages which give a contrary indication. At II. 1, 25 he insists that in having ideas of sense the understanding is merely passive—'For the objects of our senses do, many of them, obtrude their particular ideas upon our minds whether we will or not'. It will be remembered that Descartes adduced similar considerations in seeking to distinguish perception from the having of ideas in general. In the same passage Locke likens the mind to a mirror, saying that a mirror cannot 'refuse, alter, or obliterate the images or ideas which the objects set before it do therein produce'. He is speaking here of simple ideas of sense, but he thinks that what he says does not preclude the possibility that ideas may in fact be altered by the mind when set in a certain context. He explains what he means at II. 9, 8, saying that 'the ideas we receive by sensation are often altered by the judgment, without our taking notice of it'. By way of example, he asserts that a globe of uniform colour 'imprints' on our mind the idea of a 'flat circle, variously shadowed, with several degrees of light and brightness coming to our eyes. But we having, by use, been accustomed to perceive what kind of appearance convex bodies are wont to make in us; ... the judgment presently, by an habitual custom alters the appearances into their causes.' He does not explicitly explain how we know the nature of the causes, but it would appear from the succeeding discussion that we judge the visual appearance of objects by what we know of them through the other senses, especially touch. It must be emphasized, however, that the resulting idea is one 'formed by our judgment'.

Despite what might be taken as a creditable observance of the empirical facts, it is difficult to see how Locke's account fits into his general scheme of things. It cannot strictly be the case that the original idea is altered by the judgment, but at the most that another idea is substituted for that which we should have had if we had allowed our minds to be influenced solely by the object before us. But even this is quite inconsistent with the view that the mind is a mirror which must record what is set before it. At II. 30, 3 he again maintains that the mind is passive in respect of simple ideas, but goes on to maintain that it has some kind of liberty in forming complex ideas. He seems to have in mind here that we have some freedom in deciding what combinations of simple ideas shall be formed into complex ideas, but this does not seem applicable to the example of perception discussed in the earlier passage.

The truth is that Locke does not always regard the mind solely as a mirror. In II. 9, 1, at the beginning of his chapter entitled 'Of Perception', he distinguishes perception in the narrower sense from thinking by saying that in the former the mind is 'for the most part only passive'. But he goes on to say (II. 9, 3), 'This is certain, that whatever alterations are made in the body, if they reach not the mind; whatever impressions are made on the outward parts, if they are not taken notice of within, there is no perception' (cf. II. 8, 1). This is the crux. While caused by the effects of things upon our bodies, perception is still an activity of the mind, at least to the extent that the mind must pay attention. But to what? The passage in question suggests that it is the bodily impressions to which attention is paid, but this can hardly be so in all cases. On the other hand, it is not clear how it is possible to have an idea which is not attended to, if having an idea and perceiving are the same. This point is vital for Locke's theory of perception. The causal theory of perception conflicts with the view that perception involves an activity of the mind, and Locke can never completely decide whether to think of perception as purely passive, or as in some respects active.

Locke supports his view that the mind must attend to the bodily impressions if there is to be perception by reference to the undoubted facts that sometimes, for example, fire may burn our body without our feeling any pain. This is an interesting point, for it brings out the extent to which he is inclined to assimilate perception to sensation. To feel a pain is to have a sensation: it is not in itself to perceive anything. The causal theory of perception applies to perception what may be true of *sensation*, to wit that certain effects which things have on our bodies produce an experience which we call a sensation or feeling. Even so, to have the experience our attention must be directed towards it, or at any rate not directed away from it. We sometimes have aches which we cease to notice when we are absorbed in other things, so that it seems a *sine qua non* of feeling the ache that we should not be absorbed in other things. Some aches and pains are so severe that it is physically impossible to become absorbed in other things; they *demand* our attention. It seems, therefore, that Locke is right in connecting the feeling of pain with attention. We may sometimes be said to *have* a pain when we have ceased to notice it, e.g. we may have a prolonged toothache which we feel or notice intermittently; but we cannot *feel* a pain without noticing it. Just as it is possible for us not to feel a pain because we are not attending to it, so we may sometimes fail to see something through not paying attention. But in the latter case it is not our sensations to which we fail to pay attention but the things or events in question. Because Locke does not notice this important difference he takes the undoubted facts about the having of sensations to hold also in the case of sense-perception in general. If by 'bodily impressions' he means the physical stimulation of our sense-organs, he is in a worse position still. How, on his view, can the mind attend to something which is not one of its contents but only the cause of such?

Similar considerations apply to Locke's use of the distinction between primary and secondary qualities (II. 8, 9 ff). He asserts that there are certain qualities of a body 'such as are utterly inseparable from the body, in what state soever it be', namely 'solidity, extension, figure, motion or rest, and number.' As opposed to these there are 'such qualities which in truth are nothing in the objects themselves but powers to produce various sensations in us by their primary qualities—as colours, sounds, tastes, etc.' These are the primary and secondary qualities of bodies respectively. Locke believes that our ideas of primary qualities resemble those qualities, while our ideas of secondary qualities do not. The latter are produced in the mind by reason of powers which objects possess and which are themselves dependent on the primary qualities of those objects; there is nothing in the objects for the ideas of secondary qualities to resemble, and the term 'secondary quality' is to that extent a misnomer. Locke's general argument for this conclusion is that our perception of secondary qualities varies with the circumstances. The temperature which we feel objects to have varies with their distance from us, porphyry has colours only when light falls on it, and almonds change their colour and taste when pounded in a pestle. Berkeley was later to add that the same considerations apply equally to primary qualities.

Locke, it will be noticed, calls the ideas of secondary qualities sensations, and he goes on to assimilate them explicitly to pains, which undoubtedly can be the effects of certain qualities of objects. When he points out that our feelings of the temperature of objects vary with the distance of those objects from us, he also indicates that when a fire is very near to us it may produce sensations of pain. He adds that anyone who admits this 'ought to bethink himself what reason he has to say—that this idea of warmth, which was produced in him by the fire, is *actually in the fire*; and his idea of pain, which the same fire produced in the same way, is *not* in the fire' (II. 8, 16). It is true that any feelings or sensations that the fire may produce in us will be akin to pain, but to feel the fire as warm or to feel its warmth is not just to have those feelings. Or rather, pain and similar feelings fall under the concept of sensation, but when we talk of feeling the warmth of the fire we talk of what we *perceive* by feeling, and hence we invoke the concept of perception. The idea-terminology again obscures this distinction.[1] Locke also points out that men are willing to admit that manna produces sickness and pain and that these are not in the manna

[1] There are other distinctions to be made here. When I feel the warmth of an object I perceive one of its qualities. The object may also cause my body to be warm, in which case I may perceive the warmth of my body by feeling. It may also make me warm. The last is a very difficult notion to analyse but it is certainly not a matter of having 'warm sensations'. (I owe these points to discussion with Mr. G. N. A. Vesey; cf. his 'Berkeley and Sensations of Heat', *Ph. Rev.*, 1960.)

itself, but they are not willing to admit that the sweetness and whiteness of manna are not in it (II. 8, 18). Warmth, sweetness and whiteness may differ from each other in certain respects (e.g. warmth can be emitted from objects while whiteness cannot), but they can all be properties of objects which can be perceived. Locke wishes to assimilate them all to pains, since he considers the ideas of them to be sensations. The causal theory of perception inevitably results in the running together of the concepts of sensation and perception.

If this is so, why does Locke think that our ideas of primary qualities resemble qualities existing in objects themselves? Implicitly it may be that his views were determined by the common 17th-century belief in the power of physics and measurement to give an account of the nature of reality. But his explicit reasons are not clear. There is the negative point that he thought that ideas of primary qualities are not variable in the same way as those of secondary qualities, and on this Berkeley was to prove him wrong. But that bodies do have primary qualities Locke tends to make a matter of definition; for he says that the mind finds primary qualities inseparable from every particle of matter. Nothing would count as a body if it did not possess those qualities. Unlike Descartes, Locke cannot say that it is through the intellect that we have ideas of primary qualities, for this would be to give up empiricism. He does, however, follow Descartes, though not perhaps in a very clear-cut manner, in having recourse to theories about the physics and physiology of sense-perception; for he maintains that imperceptible bodies affect the sense-organs, setting up motions in the animal spirits in the nerves. Whereas the Cartesian theory revealed aspects of Stoicism, Locke's theory here follows Epicurus.[1] But both Locke and Descartes agree that the only properties which can be possessed by the elements in this process are the primary qualities. Hence they maintain that we have a justification for the belief that our ideas of primary qualities do in fact correspond to the properties of things. But the argument is invalid. The considerations which apply to our ideas of the qualities of objects in general apply equally to our ideas of the qualities possessed by the constituents of physical and physiological processes, even if these are imperceptible. A repre-

[1] That Locke had many points of connection with Gassendi has been argued by R. I. Aaron in his book on Locke.

sentative theory of perception cannot, without further access to the objects of which our ideas are said to be representative, distinguish between the ideas of those things; all ideas should be treated alike.

One final point in this connection is that when Locke comes to consider the certainty to be attached to our knowledge, he argues (IV. 4, 4) that whereas complex ideas may not correspond to things, since the mind can play a part in putting their constituents together, simple ideas must do so. In Descartes' case the justification of the general view that our ideas are representative was ultimately that God is not a deceiver. Locke has no such resort, and claims only that simple ideas must conform to things because they are caused by them. The problem is now not that of *which* ideas correspond to the qualities of things but that of whether any ideas at all do so. Locke adduces the fact or supposed fact that simple ideas are caused in the mind to support the view that at least some of them must be representational. But even if we grant the premises, the argument shows only that simple ideas, being passively received in the mind, cannot be 'fictions of our fancies'. Locke might be taken as saying that the question of being wrong arises only when we make judgments, but the conclusion which should be drawn from this is that it makes no sense to ask whether simple ideas are veridical or otherwise (a point that has been noted before in analogous cases). Locke does not draw this conclusion; he concludes that if an idea is not the product of the imagination it must be veridical. But no such conclusion follows; even if delusions can be put down to the imagination, not all illusions can be explained in that way.[1]

In *Essay* IV. 4 Locke is concerned with the general validity of our ideas: in IV. 11 he concerns himself with the extent to which we can, as a result of sense-perception, justifiably claim knowledge of particular existences. On the original theory that the mind is employed about ideas alone, neither question should arise; but the second question in particular definitely presupposes that we know of things independently of our ideas. While the earlier section starts from ideas and asks how we can know that they are veridical, the latter starts from things and asks how we can know that ideas correspond to them. The two sections are complementary, but the second brings out more strongly the incon-

[1] For the distinction see page 27 of this book.

sistency with the main view. In this second passage Locke adduces as relevant considerations (1) that 'perceptions are produced in us by exterior causes affecting our senses', (2) that sometimes we find that we cannot avoid having ideas produced in our mind, (3) that many ideas are produced in us with pleasure or pain, and (4) that 'our *senses* in many cases *bear witness to the truth of each other's report* concerning the existence of sensible things without us'. Locke admits that these considerations do not amount to demonstration, but he maintains that they produce as much certainty as our condition needs.[1] In fact, while they might be relevant to the question whether we are *in any particular case* really perceiving something, rather than being subject to a delusion or a 'fiction of the imagination', they cannot be relevant to the question whether our ideas are *in general* veridical.

The fourth consideration might also be relevant to the question whether we are subject to *illusion with respect to any one sense*, as well as whether we are subject to delusion. We might, for example, use touch to check what vision tells us, as well as to ensure that we are not being led away by our imagination. This presupposes the belief, very plausible in itself, that our senses are adjusted to each other, so that they can work together in perception—that we might perceive an object as round equally by sight and by touch, for example. As Locke indicates in II. 9, 8, William Molyneux, who wrote a contemporary work on optics, set Locke the problem whether a man born blind, who had learned to distinguish by touch a cube and a sphere, could distinguish them by sight alone, should this be restored. Molyneux himself answered 'No' to this question, and Locke agreed. In II. 9, 9, he explains that light and colours are the proper objects of vision, and that we tend to make judgments concerning space, figure, etc., the ideas of which we also receive by vision, in terms of those of light and colour. This happens as a result of experience, but the connection is made so constantly that we are not usually aware of having made a judgment. Locke does not deny that we do receive ideas of figure etc. by vision, as Berkeley was to do. Having made the distinction between primary and secondary qualities he had to admit that one feature of the former is that they are perceptible by more than one sense. Berkeley's denial of the distinction entailed the denial of the consequence. Leibniz also discussed Molyneux's

[1] Cf. Malebranche on sensations and the conservation of life.

problem in the corresponding section of the *Nouveaux Essais*, and insisted, in accordance with Rationalist principles, that a sphere and a cube are so different in structure that if the blind man were told that these were the figures in front of him he would, on gaining his sight, be able to distinguish them 'by the principles of reason'.

On the face of it the problem appears to be an empirical one, although it is difficult of solution in empirical terms, because blind men become so attached to the use of touch in distinguishing and identifying objects that they would be loath to adopt other means when available. But, as discussed by Locke, Berkeley and Leibniz, the problem is treated in very *a priori* terms. The position of the Empiricists is especially interesting, because it stands on the notion that the senses have proper objects. Once this is admitted, the only way in which these objects can be correlated or identified is by experience. But it may be disputed whether it is legitimate to suppose that there are such proper objects, and the question becomes crucial in connection with Berkeley.

In effect, Berkeley attempted to take Locke's view further by ridding it of its inconsistencies—attacking in particular the views that there are material substances acting as the causes of our ideas, and that these substances possess primary qualities. In Locke, the causal theory of perception was meant to provide a justification for the belief that our ideas are veridical (an aim which we have seen to be logically unattainable), but it entailed that we must have some knowledge of the causes of our ideas. Berkeley denies that there are material substances to act as the causes of our ideas: the only causes are spirits—in particular, God. Nevertheless, the basic notions of Locke's 'system'—the 'new way of ideas' with all its difficulties—was handed down by Locke to his successors.

(iii) BERKELEY

Berkeley's philosophy, as I have already said, results in large part from an attempt to rid Locke's view of inconsistencies—in particular to dispense with notions which are inconsistent with the general empiricist doctrine that all ideas are derived from sense-experience. Hume's view in turn is in large part the result of dissatisfaction with Berkeley's conclusions. But that dissatisfaction was largely due to the fact that Berkeley's views are also metaphysical throughout. Berkeley gives us a new picture of the world in terms which might be called those of a 'purified Locke'. But the purification led him to views which have often seemed far more paradoxical than any that Locke produced. Berkeley is consistently metaphysical in a way that Locke never was; he employs in a rigorous way a neat and systematic set of concepts into which everything has to be fitted. I have not stressed to any great extent this metaphysical scheme in what follows, but it must not be forgotten.

Berkeley took over from Locke the terminology of 'ideas' and used it in an equally uncritical way. In his earliest work, *The New Theory of Vision*, 45, he defines an idea as 'any the immediate object of sense or understanding'. He does not, however, indicate what he means by the understanding, although the *Principles of Human Knowledge*, 27, shows that he was later to use the word in such a way that it could be coincident with 'perception'. In this latter work (*Princ.*, 7) he says that 'to have an idea is all one as to to perceive', and he often uses the terms 'idea' and 'sensation' as alternatives. At the very outset of the *Principles* he is more careful, classifying ideas as (1) 'imprinted on the senses', (2) 'perceiv'd by attending to the passions and operations of the mind' and (3) 'formed by help of memory and imagination; either compounding, dividing, or barely representing those originally perceiv'd in the aforesaid ways'. Ideas which are in any sense ideas of perception do not depend upon the will, while those of memory or the imagination do, and hence imply activity on our part. These may also be distinguished from each other (and here he anticipates Hume) in that the ideas of the imagination are less regular, vivid, constant and distinct than those of sense (*Princ.*, 29, 33; *Dialogues* (Everyman Ed.), III. pp. 271 ff).[1] While the ideas of the imagination imply activity on our part, Berkeley is careful to point out that the ideas themselves are 'visibly inactive'; and he adds, 'A little attention will discover to us that the very being of an idea implies passiveness and inertness in it' (*Princ.*, 25; cf. *Dialogues*, I. pp. 226 ff). The ideas which we have in perception are therefore utterly passive, for perception is an entirely passive affair.

[1] References to the *New Theory of Vision* and the *Principles of Human Knowledge* will be given by the relevant sections: references to the *Three Dialogues between Hylas and Philonous* will be given by the page-number of the Everyman Edition.

So far Berkeley agrees to a large extent with Locke. But the latter had asserted that these ideas were produced in the mind by the things which we are said to perceive. Berkeley agrees that ideas must be in a mind, but he denies that they can be produced there by material things. We can have no knowledge of any physical things except by way of idea, and hence we can have no independent knowledge of things apart from ideas. Since by perception we can have reason to believe only in what we perceive, and since all perception consists in the having of ideas, we can justifiably believe in their existence. But we have no justification for believing in a material substance lying behind those ideas. The existence of ideas, Berkeley thinks, is a matter of their being perceived—their *esse* is *percipi*; it is indeed true by definition that if an idea exists it must be perceived and *vice versa*. But, on the same principles, there can be no such things as material substances.

Nevertheless, Berkeley thinks that ideas must be due to something. We note that some ideas, namely those of the imagination, are subject to our will, and hence may be said to be produced by us. We can therefore conclude, Berkeley thinks, that they are produced by a mind or spirit—that spirit by which we are constituted. Ideas of perception, not being produced by ourselves, must be produced in our mind by some other spirit, namely God. Spirits are the only source of ideas, for they are the only things which are active (ideas, as already noted, being passive by definition). We cannot have ideas of spirits, but we have some notion of them, in that we can understand what we mean by the word 'spirit' and because we can know that we are the source of some ideas (*Princ.*, 140).

Berkeley substitutes for the Lockean view that matter can cause the ideas which are to be found in our minds the view that only spirits can do this. Our perceptions in particular are caused by God. Perceiving is merely a matter of having such ideas, not, as Locke supposed, the having of ideas which may in certain cases resemble things 'without the mind'. In Berkeley's theory ideas cease to be representative in any sense, and although they are produced in the mind they are not produced by material things (*Princ.*, 26 ff.). What we should call perceiving a thing Berkeley would interpret as the having of a certain bundle of ideas. To the objection that we do not generally believe that things go out of existence when we cease to perceive them he replies that when we no longer have the relevant ideas God still does so. (Although at *Princ.* 3 he plays momentarily with the view—the phenomenalism familiar to modern philosophers—that what we mean when we say, for example, that there is a table in our study when we are not there, is that *if we were there* we should perceive it. But this is not a suggestion that he develops, except to the extent that he insists upon the fact that the order of nature demands regularities in the sequence of our ideas—regularities which we can presume because God has the ideas too.)

Locke had made a distinction between primary and secondary qualities, such that the former exist in things, while the latter are not really qualities at all, but only powers to produce ideas in our mind. It was noted in the discussion of Locke that he tended to assimilate ideas of secondary qualities to sensations in the literal sense. Berkeley does the same, but because he refuses to recognize the distinction between primary qualities and secondary qualities he assimilates all qualities to sensations. In the 1st *Dialogue* (pp. 203 ff.) he produces a series of arguments, firstly for the position that secondary qualities are only sensations in the mind, and secondly for the position that there is no distinction to be made between primary and secondary qualities. The arguments for the first view are similar to those of Locke. Berkeley, like him, assimilates the warmth of a fire to the painful feelings which it may produce in us when it is too hot. He points out that a feeling of intense heat is indistinguishable from a feeling of pain, and he draws the invalid conclusion that the heat of the fire itself is only a sensation in the mind. Whether or not feelings of intense heat and feelings of pain are distinguishable is a debatable point, but *qua* feelings they are both to be distinguished in fact from the heat which causes them. The argument is thus to the effect that since an object which possesses a quality to an extreme degree can cause an experience which is undoubtedly subjective, that quality must be subjective. The conclusion manifestly fails to follow. He points also to a variety of cases in which the qualities of objects appear different to different people or under different conditions; how we perceive those qualities is thus dependent on the conditions of perception. From this he draws the conclusion that it is impossible to say that any of the qualities as perceived are the real properties of the objects. This conclusion is invalid, since it does not follow from the fact that we perceive things in different ways that none of the ways is the right way. Indeed, there is a presumption that the real qualities of things are those perceived under normal conditions. It is against this presumption that we talk of things appearing otherwise. Berkeley, however, concludes that, because of their variability, the apparent qualities of things must really be sensations in the mind.

In all this Berkeley follows Locke, but he goes further than him, in that he extends the arguments to primary qualities, indicating that size, shape, etc., are also perceived differently under different conditions.[1] He draws the conclusion that all perceived qualities are really 'sensible things', i.e. sensations in the mind. Because he operates within the terms provided by the relics of the representative theory of perception—because, that is, he thinks in terms of ideas and sensations—it does not occur to him to take the fact that there is no fundamental difference in the relevant respects between primary and secondary qualities to show that they are both qualities of independent objects. Because there cannot be a quality which is not a quality of something, Berkeley's view that there are no objects to possess qualities means that the notion of a sensible quality in effect ceases to have application in his theory. Sensations, on the other hand, do not have to be sensations of anything—a pain is not a pain *of* anything. This fact reveals yet again the difference between a perceived quality and a sensation. A perceived quality must be attributable to an object; a sensation is an experience which a subject may have.

Berkeley's final view that we perceive nothing but collections of sensations has, justifiably, an air of paradox. His repeated claim that his views are completely in accord with common-sense depends on the point that the statement that we perceive nothing but sensations *can*, given his view, be interpreted as equivalent to the statement that we perceive nothing but qualities. Even this last notion has an air of oddity, in that we should normally suppose that we also perceive the things which have the qualities, but it is at any rate considerably more plausible than the view that we perceive *sensations* only. The view that we perceive qualities only is wrong but plausible to the extent that in order to identify a thing we need to describe it, and in doing so we shall mention

[1] He has one argument to the effect that apparent size must be relative to the size of the perceiver—an argument which is similar to one of those employed by Malebranche for a rather different purpose (*Dialogues*, I. p. 219).

only qualities—there is nothing else to mention. Hence it seems plausible to say that things are only bundles of qualities. The view is wrong, if only for the reason that a quality must be a quality of something: we need expressions to *refer* to things as well as to describe them (and we merely describe them when we list their properties).[1] To be able to ascribe properties to a thing we need also to be able to refer to it. The view that we perceive only sensations (or ideas, if these are the same as sensations) is a worse error, since it depends on the mistaken assimilation of perceived qualities to sensations. Berkeley's view is in this respect a consistent application of what Locke had said about ideas of secondary qualities.

The sensible qualities, the perception of which Berkeley equates with the having of sensations, are not the qualities which we *know* an object to possess—for some of his arguments, as we have seen, are designed to show that we cannot know this—but the qualities which the object *seems* to possess on any given occasion. In common with a number of philosophers since his day, Berkeley maintains that these qualities are such that they 'are immediately perceived by sense' (*Dialogues*, I. p. 203): that is to say that they are qualities the perception of which is direct or without inference. He sums up his position at the conclusion of the 3rd *Dialogue* by saying, 'I do not pretend to be a setter-up of *new notions*. My endeavours tend only to unite and place in a clearer light that truth, which was before shared between the vulgar and the philosophers: the former being of the opinion, that *those things they immediately perceive are the real things*: and the latter, that *the things immediately perceived are ideas which exist only in the mind*. Which two notions put together, do in effect constitute the substance of what I advance.' It is possible to use the phrase 'immediately perceive' in such a way that the thesis that we immediately perceive only our ideas becomes true by definition; and in effect this is what Berkeley does. But in the ordinary sense of the word it is false to say that we perceive only ideas, and the thesis remains false if we add 'immediately' to 'perceive', in any ordinary sense of the word 'immediately'.[2]

On Berkeley's use of the words 'immediately perceive' we cannot be mistaken about that which we perceive; for immediate perception is direct and free from the inference or judgment which

---

[1] See G. J. Warnock, *Berkeley*, pp. 105–9.
[2] See G. J. Warnock, op. cit., pp. 161–2.

could give rise to error. For this reason Berkeley suggests (*Princ.*, 86 ff.) that his view prevents scepticism and 'gives certainty to knowledge'. Thus Berkeley accepts Empiricism not only in the sense that all the materials for knowledge are to be found in sense-experience but also in the sense that the source of the certainty which knowledge supposedly requires is sense-experience too. Because ideas are the only real things, and because these are immediately perceived, we can have real knowledge. But while, on his view, we immediately perceive only ideas, not all ideas are the objects of immediate perception; some may be ideas of the imagination. The latter may, as we have already seen, be distinguished from ideas of sense, because they are less regular, vivid and constant, and because they are more 'dependent on the spirit'. Hence the distinction between veridical and illusory perception turns on the regularity of the ideas constituting the former—a regularity which is due to laws of nature which are themselves due to God. The distinction between perception and imagination, on the other hand, ultimately turns on the fact that the latter is dependent on our spirit or will. Because our spirit is active in imagining, in a way in which it is not when we perceive, we must by our very nature be aware of which is going on in any particular case. How else could the objects of immediate perception be clearly distinguished from other ideas? They cannot be distinguished by their internal character.

When Berkeley introduces the notion of immediate perception in the 1st *Dialogue* (p. 203), he says, 'You will further inform me, whether we immediately perceive by sight any thing beside light, and colours, and figures: or by hearing any thing but sounds: by the palate, any thing besides tastes: by the smell, besides odours: or by the touch, more than tangible qualities.' Here Berkeley appears to be listing what Aristotle called the special objects of the senses, and what Locke, and elsewhere Berkeley himself, called the proper objects of the senses. Aristotle thought that colour was the special object of sight because the two were connected essentially; in his opinion, the notion of seeing entails the notion of a colour to see. He drew the conclusion that when we see we cannot be mistaken in thinking that what we see is a colour. But Aristotle did not say that we directly or immediately see colour, whereas Berkeley does say this. The difference between them is due to Berkeley's epistemological interests—his concern to refute scepticism; but they are mistaken in what they have in common.

It does not follow from the fact or supposed fact that sight deals with colour, light and figures only that we cannot be mistaken over any instance of these (as Aristotle himself came to see). Moreover, when we see that something is, for example, white, our perception is not necessarily inference-free; for sometimes the circumstances may be such that we have to interpret what we see in order to see it as white. Hence, by this criterion, not every perception of the colour of an object is immediate. The criteria of being proper to a sense and of being inference-free or immediate are quite distinct and need not coincide in all cases. Berkeley thinks that they do coincide because he likens the perception of a colour, or any other object of sense, to the having of a sensation, and he attributes error to the inferences made on the basis of that sensation (*Dialogues*, III. p. 275). Sensations are the immediate objects of perception; any further ideas are not. But while sensations are certainly inference-free, this is because in having them we do not, strictly speaking, perceive at all. For this reason questions of corrigibility or the reverse ought not to arise in connection with them. Berkeley is wrong in his identification of the proper objects of the senses with the objects of immediate perception, and also in his identification of these with sensations. In attempting to specify instances of immediate perception in this way Berkeley only undermines his case, for the instances do not conform to the formal definition of immediate perception. We are left only with that purely formal definition, the notion that immediate perceptions, whatever they are, are inference-free, not subject to the will. The Berkeleian thesis thus turns on the fundamental point that there are active spirits as well as passive ideas; and spirits are the source of the will.

It remains to consider the notion of proper objects of the senses for its own sake, independently of the notion that these proper objects are things which we immediately perceive in an epistemological sense. Berkeley's *New Theory of Vision* is *based upon* the conception of proper objects of the senses, a conception which Berkeley took over from Locke and tried to apply in a more consistent way. Locke had maintained on the basis of his distinction between primary and secondary qualities that some qualities were proper to particular senses, while others, the primary qualities, were common to more than one sense. In rejecting the distinction, Berkeley gave systematic consideration to the idea that there were no qualities common to the different senses, with the corollary that seen size, for example, could not be taken as the same as felt size. *The New Theory of Vision* is both a treatment of these philosophical issues and a treatment of optics, and this gives the work an ambiguous status.

After stating his purpose in writing the work, Berkeley says (*N.T.V.*, 2), 'It is, I think, agreed by all, that *distance* of itself, and immediately, cannot be seen. For *distance* being a line directed endwise to the eye, it projects only one point in the fund of the eye. Which point remains invariably the same, whether the distance be longer or shorter.' It might be objected that in saying this Berkeley flies in the face of what is obvious; for it is manifest that we do see things at a distance from us, even if the way in which we do so is not the same as that by which we see the distance of one thing from another. But such an objection misfires, since Berkeley says that it is distance *in itself and immediately* that cannot be seen, and in one sense this may be a truism. It is things at a distance that we see, not distance itself. It is equally a truism, as Berkeley says, that the third dimension cannot be recorded on a two-dimensional surface. (Although the projections upon a two-dimensional surface of things at varying distances may show interesting differences.[1] Berkeley does not consider this point, but given the terms of his argument he had no reason to do so.) If distance itself cannot be seen, the problem is *how* things can be seen *at a* distance, and on this question Berkeley has criticism to make of contemporary optics.

It was generally agreed at the time that the perception of the distance of things must come as a result of experience. The contemporary writers on optics had pointed to facts such as that the visual angle subtended by an object at the eye decreases as its distance increases. Berkeley rightly pointed out that we have no experience of such facts when we do see things at a distance from us. It may be true that the visual angle decreases as the distance of the object increases, but we are not aware of this in perceiving the object. In other words, this cannot be *how* we see things at a distance; we do not estimate the distances of things in this way.[2]

[1] Cf. J. J. Gibson, *The Perception of the Visual World*.
[2] Berkeley's criticisms are equally applicable to any theory which merely provides more facts of the same sort connected with the stimulation of the eye in visual perception, e.g. to that of J. J. Gibson, op. cit.

In giving his own answer Berkeley points to experiences such as the sensations derived from the convergence of the eyes, the distortion of the appearance of the object due to failure of accommodation of the eyes when the object is brought near to us, and the straining of the eyes in accommodation. These are all experiences on which we might rely in telling the distance of an object. There are clearly other factors also, but at least Berkeley is on the right lines. Malebranche had already pointed to additional factors of the same sort.

Berkeley, however, does not say that these experiences are ones *on which we rely in telling the distance of an object*. Instead he says that the ideas which we have, and in particular those ideas or sensations produced by the movements of the eyes in the ways specified *suggest* further sensations of distance. Malebranche had also spoken of sensations in this context, but he had added that they were to be equated with a species of judgment. Berkeley shows no tendency to speak of judgment. He does not say that the sensations which we have enable us to judge the distance of objects from us; he thinks entirely in terms of one set of sensations suggesting others. The notion of 'suggestion' has much in common with the 'association' of ideas on which Hume relied so much. For Berkeley, perception is entirely passive, despite the occasional references to inference; and the connections between perceptions can only be of a more or less mechanical sort.

Whether or not it is right to say that the connection between the sensations derived from the movements of our eyes and that of distance is mechanical, it is certainly contingent. It is, that is to say, built up through experience. But how can this be, if we never immediately see distance itself? We immediately see only light and colours (*N.T.V.*, 130); these are the proper and primary objects of vision (cf. *N.T.V.*, 50). Distance, on the other hand, is immediately perceived by touch. It is by the habitual connection of the ideas of sight with those of touch that we come to think that we see things at a distance. Since this applies also to the size of things, Berkeley is quite definite (*N.T.V.*, 132 ff.) that Locke is right in his answer to Molyneux's question whether a man born blind could on receiving his sight distinguish by sight between a cube and a sphere. Berkeley agrees that the answer is 'No', because such a man could not have come by experience to connect the ideas of vision and touch. These ideas are, on Berkeley's view, quite distinct, and that they are in fact connected is merely a contingent fact.

Berkeley's explanation of the zenith-horizon illusion of the moon relies upon the analogous contingent connection which he takes to exist between the size and faintness of things. He maintains that when the moon is at the horizon its light has to pass through vapours arising from the earth. For this reason it appears fainter and in consequence larger; because, being fainter, it is taken to be farther away. This theory is, he thinks, confirmed by the apparent increase in the size of the moon in misty weather. He rejects the theory of a Dr. Wilks, a theory similar to that of Malebranche, that the phenomenon occurs because, when the moon is at the horizon we see things between us and it, and in consequence we see it as farther away. The illusion is not altered, he claims, when the moon is observed from behind a wall; and its size also appears different in different circumstances. But, throughout, Berkeley stresses that what is meant by the words 'appears of greater size at the horizon' is that the moon appears to have greater *tangible size* there. Its visible size is, he implies, the same in all circumstances.

A great deal of the *New Theory of Vision* is devoted to following out the consequence of his main view that the objects of the different senses are themselves different. He insists, for example, on what otherwise might seem a paradoxical notion, that the *minimum visibile* is the same for all creatures (*N.T.V.*, 80). That there is both a *minimum visibile* and *minimum tangibile* he takes as something that 'every one's experience will inform him' (*N.T.V.*, 54, and *Princ.*, 123 ff.), and he uses this view in order to criticize the ordinary interpretations of geometry. His reason for saying that the *minimum visibile* is the same for all creatures is that there is no other standard than that of vision itself by which to judge of the size of the *minimum visibile*. Hence the *minimum visibile* is that which is of the least size to vision itself. We think that different creatures can see things of different size because we think of the things of different *tactual* size which they can discriminate. But if we remove considerations of tactual size we have no other common standard by which to judge what creatures can discriminate; for it is only by touch that we, strictly speaking, perceive size. Hence *the* size of an object is its tactual size and there is only a contingent connection between this and visible size. Whereas we can say what is the smallest thing *tactually* that a creature can perceive, we can say nothing about the smallest thing *visually* that it can perceive, because the *minimum visibile* has no 'existence without the mind of him who sees it'.

Berkeley deals in a similar way with a fact that has seemed puzzling to some—the fact that we see things one way up while the retinal image is reversed. His recipe is in effect to deny that we see the retinal image and then correct it. But although he insists that the retinal images are not pictures of external objects (*N.T.V.*, 117), he dwells on this point less than on the point that it does not make sense to say of the retinal image that it is upside down in relation to what we see. To be able to say this we should have to relate what we see to the tangible earth, in relation to which in turn we decide which way up the retinal image is. But we cannot in fact bring the visible earth and the tangible earth into any relation. In other words being visibly head uppermost is connected only by experience with being tactually head uppermost. It is impossible to judge one by the other (*N.T.V.*, 115).

Berkeley takes to the extreme the view that each sense has its proper object and that they have nothing in common. He admits (*N.T.V.*, 142) that a 'visible square, is fitter than the visible circle, to represent the tangible square', but only because the former contains the necessary number of distinct parts, while the latter does not; and he denies that it follows that a visible square is *like* a tangible square. Nevertheless, in the *New Theory of Vision* he talks of the objects of touch as if these were in fact physical objects; touch, that is, informs us of the nature of physical things, while sight informs us only of light and colour. In the *Principles* he came to withdraw this suggestion (*Princ.*, 43 ff.), maintaining that the objects of touch were sensations equally with those of sight. This does not, however, alter his position in the *New Theory of Vision* that the objects of sight and touch have nothing in common; his later position is in general only the logical outcome of the earlier.

Berkeley's final view, as we have already seen, is that each sense is responsible for separate and distinct sensations, and these are connected only by experience. To perceive an object is merely to have a bundle of ideas or sensations. The only permanence given to that which we should ordinarily call an object is that God has the constituent ideas when we do not. Hume was to find this view unsatisfactory, especially when he tried to do without the notion of God. But provided that we understand by 'sensation' a kind of idea put into our minds by God, Berkeley's view provides an almost perfect example of an attempt to assimilate perception to sensation throughout. The notion of a sensation is such that it could rightly be said to be proper to a sense, and Berkeley relies on that fact. When the assimilation of perception to sensation is rejected, Berkeley's conclusions, including his somewhat paradoxical metaphysical views, no longer seem compelling.

(iv) HUME

There are differences of opinion concerning Hume's exact intentions in writing the first book of the *Treatise of Human Nature*, or rather concerning the nature of the philosophical theory that he was there trying to put forward. Some look at his conclusions as entirely sceptical, the result of a development to its extreme of British Empiricism. Others find something more positive there. N. Kemp Smith, for example, maintains that, influenced by Hutcheson, Hume wished to stress the part played by nature rather than reason in the formation of our beliefs about the world.[1] But whatever be Hume's actual intentions, the result in fact is that the principles of Empiricism, as founded by Locke and Berkeley, are pushed to their extreme, thus providing something of a *reductio ad absurdum* of those principles. Like most cases of a comparable *reductio ad absurdum*, however, Hume's theory contains suggestions for future development of a more positive nature.

Hume's theory of perception is one of the most sceptical parts of his work. He begins the chapter entitled 'Scepticism with Regard to the Senses' (*Treatise* I. iv. 2) by stressing how inevitable it is that we should believe in the existence of bodies independent of our minds. He says, 'We may well ask, *What causes induce us to believe in the existence of body?* but 'tis vain to ask, *Whether there be body or not?*' But he concludes the chapter by saying, with reference to scepticism concerning what our senses tell us about an independent world of objects, ''Tis impossible upon any system to defend either our understanding or senses', and he recommends carelessness and inattention with regard to them. He thinks nevertheless that some account of the matter is required and that

[1] N. Kemp Smith, *The Philosophy of David Hume*.

Berkeley's theory is insufficient. Berkeley's arguments, he thinks, are not really in accord with common-sense; they are in fact sceptical. 'They admit of no answer and produce no conviction' (*Enquiry Concerning the Human Understanding*, XII. pt. 1, Selby-Bigge, sect. 122, n. 1, p. 155).[1] What, then, did Hume put in their place?

Like many other philosophers of his time, Hume uses the term 'perception' for any content of the mind, and 'all the actions of seeing, hearing, judging, loving, hating, and thinking, fall under this denomination' (*Treatise* III. i. 1, p. 456). For this reason he thinks it axiomatic 'that nothing is ever present to the mind but its perceptions' (*Treatise*, ibid.). So far Hume uses the term as an equivalent of the 'ideas' of his Empiricist predecessors. An innovation on his part, which if largely terminological is nevertheless important, was to distinguish between two kinds of perceptions—namely, impressions and ideas—and he maintains that in making this distinction he is restoring 'the word, idea, to its original sense, from which Mr. *Locke* had perverted it, in making it stand for all our perceptions' (*Treatise* I. i. 1, p. 2, n. 1). Ideas, or at any rate the simple ones, are copies of impressions, and the latter may be distinguished from the former by their superior force and liveliness. Thus Hume seems to make the distinction between impressions and ideas both one of kind and one of degree. In some places (e.g. *Treatise* I. iii. 2, p. 73) he uses the term 'perception' instead of 'impression', speaking of it as passive in contrast with the active exercise of thought; and he occasionally uses the term 'sensation' as another equivalent of 'impression' (e.g. *Treatise* I. iv. 2, p. 189).

While Hume sometimes speaks of impressions as passive, and while the term itself suggests this, he does not initially make the distinction between impressions and ideas in terms of the passivity of the former. The explanation of this is that Hume in effect wishes to use impressions and ideas as building-blocks out of which knowledge of everything else is to be constructed. In *Treatise* I. iv. 5, p. 233, he admits that perceptions are equivalent to substances in his system, since they are the only distinct, separable and independent things. For the same reason he maintains

[1] References to the *Treatise* and the *Enquiry* are to the editions of L. A. Selby-Bigge (O.U.P.). The *Treatise* has page references only; the *Enquiry* has section-references as well.

that there is nothing impossible in the notion of an unperceived perception—a perception, that is, which is separable from the bundle of perceptions which in his view constitute the mind. Given this, it would be inconsistent for Hume to define an impression by its relation to a mind—in terms, for example, of its passivity—as Berkeley did in the case of the corresponding class of ideas. When Hume does speak in these terms he is being careless. When being precise he can look only to the qualities which impressions and ideas have as such, and he therefore finds the distinguishing marks of impressions and ideas only in the degree of force and liveliness that they possess. Despite this it must be admitted that Hume derives much from the suggestiveness of his terminology, i.e. the suggestions of passivity in the terms 'impression', 'sensation' and 'perception'.

The programme of distinguishing impressions from ideas of the imagination by reference to their relations to the mind demands, as Berkeley's theory does, an independent source of knowledge of an independently existing mind. Hume thought that there was no such knowledge to be obtained. He was similarly dissatisfied with the view that the permanence which, despite the fragmentary character of our ideas, we attribute to physical objects is due to a superior mind, namely God. Hume therefore tried to do without those features of Berkeley's philosophy which he must have thought of as something of a *deus ex machina* used to escape the otherwise sceptical conclusions of that philosophy. There is, nevertheless, something very unsatisfactory in Hume's own procedure. How is it possible to distinguish between an idea and an impression without reference to their owner? Ideas are always someone's ideas, and the same is true of sensations. Similarly, perceiving is always done by someone. Despite what Hume says, the notion of an unperceived perception, i.e. a perception which is unowned, not made by anyone, does appear to be an inconsistent one.

Hume is right in suggesting, however unwillingly, that his perceptions are the substances of the world in his theory. But what is wrong with ordinary substances? Hume objects to the notion that ordinary things can be regarded as substances, even in the minimal sense that he allows to that notion, i.e. as that of an independently existing thing. He does so because there seems to be no way of knowing them, once it is admitted that perceptions are the direct objects of the mind. Similar difficulties about knowledge of the mind itself leave only the perceptions themselves as that which is 'given'. Hume disagrees with Berkeley over the question whether we have knowledge of a mind independent of our perceptions, but he agrees with him in thinking that the only way to circumvent the difficulties of the representative theory of perception is to insist that we have knowledge of our perceptions only, i.e. we have no knowledge of independently existing objects. In this, Hume claims to agree with the 'vulgar' and to disagree with the 'philosophical system'. The 'vulgar' agree that perceptions are the only objects of which we are aware (*Treatise* I. iv. 2, p. 209; cf. p. 239), but they maintain that these have a continuous existence; the 'philosophical system' tries to distinguish between objects and perceptions, the former permanent, the latter not.

In agreeing with the 'vulgar' in this way, Hume may be accused of clinging to a prejudice. It will be remembered that Locke assimilated ideas of secondary qualities to feelings like pain, so making them subjective. In pointing out that there is nothing in respect of their variability to distinguish primary from secondary qualities Berkeley concluded that they were both subjective. Hume argues similarly. He maintains that there are 'three different kinds of impressions convey'd by the senses' (*Treatise* I. iv. 2, p. 192), i.e. those of primary qualities, those of secondary qualities, and pains and pleasures. The vulgar, Hume says, think that the first two have an independent existence, while the philosophers think that this can be said of the first only. But, he adds, ''Tis evident that, whatever may be our philosophical opinion, colours, sounds, heat and cold, as far as appears to the senses, exist after the same manner with motion and solidity'. Furthermore, ''Tis also evident, that colours, sounds, &c. are originally on the same footing with the pain which arises from steel, and pleasure that proceeds from a fire; and that the difference betwixt them is founded neither on perception nor reason, but on the imagination. For as they are confest to be, both of them, nothing but perceptions arising from the particular configurations and motions of the parts of body, wherein possibly can their difference consist?'[1]

Hume does not say who it is that confesses that secondary

[1] He has to admit later (*Treatise* I. iv. 5, p. 236) that whereas the perceptions of sight and feeling may be located at a place, those of the other senses cannot be. Hence they differ in that the latter exist and yet are not at a place.

qualities and pains are similar in this way, but he has clearly no right to assume that they are. Colours are not in fact *produced* in us in the way that pains are. But even if they were, Hume would have no right, on his principles, to claim knowledge to that effect; he ought to base his argument upon the intrinsic properties of the impressions alone, and not to behave as if he could, on his principles, know about the causes of these impressions. This is not to say that Hume could not give an account of the physiological causes of sensations in his own terms, invoking his own theory of causality. He might have done so, but he does not do so here. Hume accepts the bones of the representative theory of perception without the flesh. He accepts the apparatus of that theory—the impressions and the ideas—whilst explicitly denying, for the most part, that we can have any reason to believe that these are representative of anything.

Yet, as Hume admits, it is natural to believe in the evidence of our senses, and they seem to tell us that there is a world of independent objects. Since our belief in such a world cannot be a matter of perception, and since reason cannot justify it either, it must be due to the imagination (*Treatise* I. iv. 2, p. 193). Our impressions have a certain degree of coherence, and the imagination tends to act in such a way that it 'like a galley put in motion by the oars, carries on its course without any new impulse'. (*Treatise* I. iv. 2, p. 198.) The imagination thus tends to make us attribute greater regularity to the objects of perception than they really have. But this, Hume admits, is too weak a principle 'to support alone so vast an edifice, as is that of the continu'd existence of all external bodies'. Hence he adds, as a further factor on which the imagination relies, the constancy of our impressions—the fact that the same impressions tend to recur in the same order after intervals of one kind or another. Subjective impressions, like those of pleasure and pain, exhibit no such constancy. Reference to these factors is not meant to *justify* belief in an external world; it is meant only as a psychological explanation of such a belief. The conflict between what reason tells us about the interrupted existence of our perceptions and what imagination or our nature leads us to believe, we tend to reconcile by the philosophical belief in a distinction between continuously existing objects and a succession of perceptions (*Treatise* I. iv. 2, pp. 215–16). There nevertheless remains a 'direct and total opposition betwixt our reason and our senses' (*Treatise* I. iv. 4, p. 231). It is not reason or our senses which promote a belief in a world of independently existing objects, but nature by means of the imagination.

That which we should ordinarily call perception of an object is, for Hume, not just a matter of perception in his limited sense. It involves the imagination also, and this leads to belief in the existence of an independently existing object. Since Hume thinks that belief itself is constituted only by the force or liveliness of an impression or a connected idea, it might be suggested that the original distinction between impressions and ideas is founded upon the notion of belief. And so it has been argued by N. Kemp Smith.[1] This would amount to the view that the distinction between impressions and ideas is a distinction between perceptions which are inevitably combined with a tendency to believe in their objectivity and perceptions which are not so combined. Impressions would therefore involve belief. Yet if this is so, it is odd that Hume gives no clue to that effect. Moreover, the thesis runs counter to passages in which Hume's account of impressions can be interpreted only as an account of sensations such that there is no accompanying belief in their objectivity. It runs counter also to the fact that the impressions as originally defined include pain; and certainly no objectivity is claimed for that. The truth is that, given that the mind has to do with nothing except impressions and ideas, there is little but their relative liveliness which can serve to distinguish the one from the other.

Belief or judgment play a part in perception in other ways too, for example in the perception of the size and distance of things. In much of his account of this Hume follows Berkeley. He insists, for example, that the distance of things is not immediately perceived (*Treatise* I. ii. 5, p. 56; I. iv. 2, p. 191)—a thesis which he puts in a picturesque way by saying, 'All bodies, which discover themselves to the eye, appear as if painted on a plain surface'. The perception of distance must, therefore, be a product of reasoning and experience. By 'reasoning' Hume presumably means inference in accordance with knowledge of causes and effects; and this too is a product of experience. Hume initially explains our perception of the distance of things by reference to the visual angle which they subtend at the eye, but in the appendix to the *Treatise* (p. 636) he recants this view for Berkeleian reasons, and adopts

[1] N. Kemp Smith, op. cit., ch. 10.

Berkeley's view explicitly. Like Berkeley too he makes the perception of the size of things a product of experience; we infer their size from 'some peculiar qualities of the image', i.e. the impression (*Treatise* I. iii. 9, p. 112). In the appendix to the *Treatise* (p. 632) he puts the matter in an even more forceful way: 'The understanding corrects the appearances of the senses, and makes us imagine, that an object at twenty foot distance seems even to the eye as large as one of the same dimensions at ten.' In the earlier passage he says that in such cases people are liable to take the judgments which they make for sensations; in other words, they are not conscious of their judgments as such. It is an interesting corollary of this point of view that Hume has to say that we do not *actually see* a distant object as of the same size as one near to us; we only imagine that it seems so to the eye. This view is entailed by the initial position that we directly perceive only the impressions of our senses. If this initial position is given up there is nothing to prevent our saying that we do see things at a distance as of the same size as those which are near to us. To say this is not to commit oneself to how it comes about, although experience is the most likely explanation.

In general, therefore, Hume tends to take the implications of Berkeley's philosophy to their extreme. But in his urge to retain our natural beliefs about the world, while at the same time insisting that the only objects of perception are impressions, Hume contrives to sit on the fence. On occasion he talks of material objects, or what we should ordinarily call such, as mere bundles of impressions. For example, at *Treatise* I. iv. 5, p. 239, he says, 'That table, which just now appears to me, is only a perception, and all its qualities are qualities of a perception'; and at *Treatise* I. iv. 5, p. 241, he says, '. . . we may suppose, but never can conceive a specific difference betwixt an object and an impression'. But the general trend of *Treatise* I. iv. 2, seems to the contrary effect. Hume, in other words, holds to the view that reason can give no justification of our belief in material objects, but realizes also that it is both natural and meaningful to maintain that there are such material objects. If this is his real view it is both unsatisfactory and a prey to scepticism.

One further aspect of Hume's views must be mentioned—an aspect which is perhaps of less importance for itself than for its consequences. The distinction between simple and complex impressions and ideas, like the corresponding Lockean distinction from which it is derived, is a logical or epistemological distinction. If an impression of X is a simple impression there is no other impression which I can be said to have in having the impression of X. The information which I obtain in having a simple impression is basic in the sense that it is logically impossible to analyse it into constituent items of information. With a complex impression this is not so; if I have an impression of a tree I *eo ipso* have an impression of, for example, branches.[1] Now, any impression of something extended is, on Hume's view, complex, in that the extended object can be analysed into parts. Indeed, inasmuch as objects *are* impressions, an impression of something extended is itself extended (*Treatise* I. iv. 5, p. 240). It can therefore be analysed into simple impressions which are its constituents. Each simple impression will be of a part, and in having the complex impression of the whole extended object I *eo ipso* have impressions of the parts. Hume thinks that the analysis of a complex impression of extension into its constituent simple impressions must be of finite length (*Treatise* I. ii. 1). In this he follows Berkeley who had argued that there must be a *minimum visibile* and a *minimum tangibile*. Hume maintains (loc. cit., p. 27) that if an ink-spot on paper is removed to a distance 'the moment before it vanish'd the image or impression was perfectly indivisible'. Hence impressions are divisible to a *minimum* only.

In the succeeding sections (cf. *Enquiry*, sects. 124 ff.) Hume argues that since anything that has extension must have parts, the indivisible parts of extended objects cannot themselves be extended, though they must be coloured or tangible. Hence the impression of extension itself (and the same applies to the *idea* of extension) must be an impression of the *order or manner* in which the indivisible and hence non-extended parts are disposed. This implies firstly that it is possible to have an impression of something non-extended, and secondly that our impression of extension is something superimposed on the first-order impressions of non-extended points.[2] An impression of extension is, so to speak, an impression of the *relations* between non-extended points. While

[1] The fact that I can conceivably see something as a tree without seeing it as having branches shows the inadequacy of the impressions-terminology.

[2] In his discussion of size-perception Hume proceeds on the assumption that 'the eye at all times sees an equal number of physical points' (*Treatise*, I. iii. 9, p. 112), a view which is connected with the same general position.

Hume seems to allow impressions of relations in general, this particular impression the terms of which are perceptible but non-extended is very odd. Hume's position is indeed an extraordinary one, and he may have been influenced in it by Bayle's article on *Zeno* in his *Dictionary*; it has also affinities with Leibniz's views on space and time, for Leibniz too made these a matter of the relations between non-extended and non-temporal entities.

Hume's arguments for a *minimum visibile* are not so sophisticated as those of Berkeley, but like the latter they turn on the fact that no distinction is made between an impression and its object. If that distinction is made, it is possible to argue that the least perceptible area *is* divisible, at any rate in principle; if it is not made, it is indeed feasible to say that some impressions are not in fact analysable into constituents. It is, however, questionable whether Hume has any right to call these *impressions of points*, and whether he has the right to assume that everything that has extension has parts. Might it not be the case that some extended objects have no parts? If this cannot be so Hume has not explained why.

Nevertheless, Hume's conclusions are of importance historically, especially because they came to be treated as relevant to psychological doctrines about the nature of the visual field. Kant assumed that 'sensations' in themselves could give no knowledge of extension, and this was adopted as common doctrine by the Sensationalists of the 19th century.

(v) APPENDIX—REID

It is convenient to treat Reid as an Empiricist, although much of his writing is devoted to criticisms of the British Empiricists, especially Hume. Reid thought that the conclusions of Hume's *Treatise* were shattering but obviously false. As he could find nothing wrong with the arguments for those conclusions he decided that the trouble lay in the premises—in particular in the doctrine of ideas which had been inherited from Descartes and Locke. Hence a great part of his *Inquiry into the Human Mind on the Principles of Common Sense* is devoted to a criticism of that doctrine; and the same is true of his later *Essays on the Intellectual Powers of Man*.[1]

---

[1] There is a modern edition of Reid's *Essays* (ed. A. D. Woozley), but copies of the *Inquiry* are not always readily accessible. Hence, despite the fuller treatment in the *Inquiry*, most references are given to the *Essays*.

Reid thought that the secret lay in a strict distinction between sensation and perception. He was perhaps the first philosopher to insist upon this rigorously, and he was quite right in doing so, although he was not always clear about the consequences to be drawn. Sensation, he says (*Essays*, I. 1), 'is a name given by philosophers to an act of mind which may be distinguished from all others by this, that it hath no object distinct from the act itself'. And later (*Essays*, II. 16) he says, 'There is no difference between the sensation and the feeling of it.' A pain and the feeling of pain are one and the same thing. In this Reid seems to be right, or very largely so. Normally, we cannot be said to have a pain without our feeling it; although it does sometimes make sense to speak, for example, of our having had a pain in a tooth for some time, although we have felt it only on occasion. There are perhaps special reasons for such deviations from the norm in cases where the pain is long-lasting. Reid has a discussion of toothache at the beginning of *Essays*, II. 18, and he says there that there are two factors involved: (*a*) the feeling and (*b*) the belief that the disorder in the tooth is the cause of the feeling. It is the disorder which continues when the pain is intermittent. Reid also, however, stresses that attention is necessary to the experiencing of a sensation; that is to say that, despite what has been said so far, there *is* the possibility of having a sensation without our being aware of it, when we are not paying attention to it.

Reid takes pains and similar feelings, therefore, as the paradigm cases of sensations, and he shows some acuteness in his remarks about the status of these sensations. His view of sensations is in consequence very different from that of his immediate predecessors. But while pains are the paradigm cases of sensations, they are not the only examples. Reid thinks that we have sensations whenever we use any of our senses. Yet it is important not to confuse these sensations with perception, and equally important not to talk of sensations as we should talk of the objects of perception. To a very large extent Reid is careful in maintaining the distinction, although he does not fully appreciate what kind of distinction it is. Instead of saying that when we use our senses what happens may be viewed in two quite different ways, or subsumed under two different and perhaps exclusive concepts—those of sensation and perception—he says that two distinct processes occur simultaneously, one of which is the sensation and the other perception. The precise relationship between these two processes is in consequence an inevitable problem.

Reid says, 'Almost all our perceptions have corresponding sensations which constantly accompany them and, on that account, are very apt to be confounded with them' (*Essays*, II. 16). The qualification in the 'almost' is probably due to his belief that there are no sensations corresponding to perceived position or figure, or at any rate no sensation distinct from that corresponding to perceived colour. In this Reid is probably opposing Hume's view that the *minimum visibile* is, while coloured, not extended; he wishes to say, on the contrary, that everything which is coloured is also extended and that there is therefore no need for a separate sensation corresponding to extension. In all other respects there is a consistent correlation between perception and sensation. But, he adds, we ought not to expect that sensations and perceptions should be distinguished in ordinary life, because there is no need for them to be so distinguished (cf. *Inquiry*, vi. 20). If we fail to note sensations accompanying perceptions of colour, for example, this is due to inattention (*Essays*, II. 18). Without attention, he says, a sensation will pass through the mind instantaneously and unobserved.[1]

Despite the difference between sensation and perception, the words which we use of sensations and the corresponding perceived qualities are often the same. The word 'smell', for example, may be applied to the quality of a rose or, alternatively, to the sensation derived from this. 'All the names we have,' he says, 'for smells, tastes, sounds and for the various degrees of heat and cold, have a like ambiguity.' Yet the sensation is not at all like the perceived quality. 'Pressing my hand with force against the table, I feel pain, and I feel the table to be hard. The pain is a sensation of the mind, and there is nothing that resembles it in the table. The hardness is in the table, nor is there anything resembling it in the mind. Feeling is applied to both, but in a different sense; being a word common to the act of sensation, and to that of perceiving by the sense of touch.' (*Essays*, II. 16).

What then is perception? It is, Reid thinks, an act of mind which

[1] Sir William Hamilton was later to systematize this point under the heading of 'the inverse relation between Sensation and Perception', maintaining that the more intense the sensation the more indistinct the perception, and *vice versa*.

has three essential characteristics: (1) it involves a 'conception or notion of the object perceived', (2) it involves a 'strong and irresistible conviction and belief of its present existence', and (3) 'this conviction and belief are immediate, and not the effect of reasoning' (*Essays*, II. 5). An objection to this account is that while it may be necessary that such characteristics should obtain if there is to be perception, it is not clear that these characteristics provide a sufficient account of perception. Nevertheless they serve to distinguish perception clearly from sensation in a way in which the terminology of impressions and ideas cannot do so. If I am to perceive something, I must at least have some conception of that thing. And if it seems to me that I perceive it, I must have a disposition to believe in its existence, without this being a result of inference. Reid might have added, although he did not, that if I really do perceive it, that thing must actually exist.

At the same time more needs to be said in particular about the relationship between perception and sensation. In this respect Reid tends to fall short. He stresses the point that the objects of perception cannot be viewed as sensations, and also that there is no similarity between them. He insists that this is equally true of secondary qualities as of primary qualities (for he thinks that Locke was right to make the distinction, although he was wrong to make it in the way in which he did); in the case of secondary qualities, however, the accompanying sensations are more likely to become the objects of our attention. Such points, however, are negative. His positive view of the relation of perceived quality to sensation is in general that the former is the cause of the latter (*Inquiry*, v. 7 and *Essays*, II. 16). This view does not involve him in a causal theory of perception, since it is *sensations* which are caused, not *perceptions*. Sensations bear no resemblance to perceived qualities, and are quite distinct from perceptions.

For similar reasons, sensations can provide us with no basis for inference about the nature of perceived objects; they are epistemologically irrelevant. Sensations are of importance because they can be painful and pleasant; for this reason they can affect our interests and attention. Thus he says at the end of *Essays* II. 17, 'The external senses have a double province—to make us feel and to make us perceive. They furnish us with a variety of sensations, some pleasant, others painful, and others indifferent; at the same time, they give us a conception and an invincible belief of the existence of external objects.... The perception and its corresponding sensation are produced at the same time. In our experience we never find them disjoined. Hence we are led to consider them as one thing, to give them one name, and to confound their different attributes. It becomes very difficult to separate them in thought, to attend to each by itself, and to attribute nothing to it which belongs to the other.' Because sensations do not function as the basis for our perception of physical objects, they cannot be responsible for error. Perception alone, he says, can be fallacious (*Essays*, II. 18 and 22). 'If we will speak accurately, our sensations cannot be deceitful; they must be what we feel them to be, and can be nothing else.' Certainly they play no part in our mistakes about physical objects.

The account given by Reid so far would seem to imply that the relation between sensation and perception is purely coincidental; they just happen to occur together. But this is not Reid's real view of the situation, for he also speaks as if the relation between sensation and perception might after all be of an epistemological kind. He maintains that sensations are *natural signs* of perceptible qualities (*Inquiry*, v. 3; *Essays* VI. 5), not only the effects of those qualities. Something is a natural sign of another thing when the sign-significate relationship is a product not of habit or convention but of 'the original constitution of our minds'. Reid frequently says that perception and sensation are 'by our constitution united'. A sensation is said to be a natural sign of the perceived quality in the same way in which an expression on the face may be a natural sign of an emotion. Reid argues that in this latter case the connection between the sign and that which is signified cannot be something learned by experience, since the emotion is not itself perceptible to the person who sees its expression. The fact that the one is taken as a sign of the other must, therefore, be due to nature.

Because the sensation is a natural sign of the perceived quality, Reid says that it *suggests* the perception of that quality. He calls this 'natural suggestion' or 'judgment of nature'. His use of the notion of suggestion is almost entirely confined to the *Inquiry*, but it is not clearly explained there. Berkeley, it will be remembered, used the notion of suggestion in his treatment of our perception of things at a distance from us, saying that certain sensations suggest further sensations to us. The connection which Reid allows between a sensation and the perception of a quality cannot similarly be due to experience. His account implies that perception occurs because, *owing to nature*, we treat the sensation as a sign of a perceptible quality, although he explicitly denies that we make any inference from the one to the other. His incoherence here results from the fact that he supposes that sensations and perceptions are two simultaneously occuring processes which then have to be linked. The one experience, he thinks, must lead in some way to the other. Yet this cannot be a matter of inference because there is nothing in the sensation which in any way resembles the perceived quality. Reid's sensations are in no way like the sense-data referred to by modern philosophers.[1]

The fact that nature determines that when we have a sensation we also have a perception does not mean that experience plays no part in perception. Nature determines what Reid calls 'natural and original perceptions' (*Inquiry*, vi. 20; *Essays*, II. 21), e.g. our perception of a spherical figure as circular and two-dimensional, in accordance with Berkeleian theory. As a result of experience the natural and original perceptions come to suggest acquired perceptions, e.g. the perception of the sphere as spherical. It is as a consequence of having acquired perceptions that we come to be able to see things at a distance. Thus Reid adopts the Berkeleian theory of distance-perception, but interprets it not in terms of sensations but in terms of different kinds of perceptions. Reid tends to talk of the relationship between original and acquired perceptions in the same way as of that between sensations and original perceptions. He uses, for example, the terminology of suggestion and signs, and implies that original perceptions have no resemblance to those which are acquired[2] (although the sense in which these do not resemble each other cannot be anything like that in which sensations and original perceptions are dissimilar). Original perceptions are not, of course, natural signs of acquired perceptions, since the link is in this case due to experience; nor is the

---

[1] R. Chisholm, *Perceiving*, refers to Reid in several places, implying that Reid meant appearances by 'sensations'. This is not so. Reid does sometimes speak of appearances, e.g. *Inquiry*, vi. 2 and 3, but he there probably means what he elsewhere calls 'natural and original perceptions'. See the following paragraph and cf. P. G. Winch, 'The Notion of "Suggestion" in Thomas Reid's Theory of Perception', *Ph. Q.*, 1953, pp. 327–41. This article is invaluable for many points concerning Reid.

[2] See P. G. Winch, op. cit.

suggestion involved *natural* suggestion. But in treating them in this way at all Reid was undoing much of the good that his distinction between sensations and perceptions had served to produce. The concept of an original perception is in effect the same as the Berkeleian concept of immediate perception. Despite his criticisms of the British Empiricists, Reid was still very close to them in many respects.

Reid's distinction between sensation and perception is of the utmost importance, and Reid himself has been unduly neglected and misinterpreted. In making the distinction he did much to undermine the foundations of philosophical thought about perception in this time. His own view of perception is incomplete and in some parts incoherent. But the main difficulties in his view derive from the fact that he basically misunderstood the import of the distinction which he had drawn between sensation and perception. He understood it as a distinction between two kinds of process which, most often, take place simultaneously. He was therefore obliged to say something about the relations between these processes, with the consequence that his theory often seems far from the theory of common-sense which he claimed to be providing. But the distinction between sensation and perception is not one of this kind. While there may be certain occurrences or processes which are most appropriately subsumed under the concept of sensation rather than that of perception, or *vice versa*, it is a mistake to assume in consequence that the words 'sensation' and 'perception' are merely names for these processes, and that all that is required is that the processes should be distinguished. Fundamentally, Reid makes this mistake, taking 'sensation' to be the name of something like a pain, and 'perception' for the name of something different and more complicated. In truth, for an understanding of the distinction between sensation and perception, it is necessary to understand the differences between the *concepts* under which, for one reason or another, different processes (or perhaps even the same process considered from different points of view) may be subsumed. To understand a concept and to appreciate the reasons for subsuming something under it as an instance come to the same thing. In this sense Reid does not have a full understanding of his distinction.

7
KANT, HEGEL AND IDEALISM

(i) KANT

IT is well known that the effect which a reading of Hume had upon Kant was to awaken him from his 'dogmatic slumber'. As a result he set out to provide a 'critical philosophy' which would in effect constitute something of a reconciliation between Rationalism and Empiricism. In the field of sense-perception it might be expected that this reconciliation would take the form of an attempt to assess the relative parts played by passive sensation and active judgment or understanding; and so it turns out. The details of Kant's reconciliation between Rationalism and Empiricism are intricate, involved and obscure, and it would be impossible and unprofitable to follow through all the details here.[1] On the other hand, it is relatively easier to provide a general picture of Kant's programme,[2] which, as long as it remains in general terms, is extremely impressive. The detailed argument is not only tortuous but often inadequate for the ends to which it is directed. The following discussion of Kant's conception of sense-perception confines itself mainly to the general point of view.

Kant took over, lock, stock and barrel, the representative

[1] There are many commentaries on Kant's work available—notably H. J. Paton's *Kant's Metaphysic of Experience*—which attempt to provide such details.

[2] There is a well-known story about J. S. Mill's reaction to a quick reading of the *Critique of Pure Reason*—'I see well enough what poor Kant be about.'

theory of perception, and maintained that all knowledge is founded on subjective experiences produced by entities outside the mind. But, as against the Rationalist tradition, he maintained that, as a consequence, there could be no knowledge of those entities or 'things-in-themselves'. The mind is acquainted with phenomena or appearances only, and it can know nothing of Rationalist constructions such as the Leibnizian monads; nor, for that matter, can it know of Lockean substance. At the same time, Kant accepted the Lockean theory of knowledge, in particular its distinction between primary and secondary qualities, the latter being purely subjective (see, e.g., *Critique of Pure Reason*, A 28–30 = B 44–45). On Kant's view, however, secondary qualities are purely subjective in the sense that they are not even valid of phenomena, let alone of things-in-themselves. Kant signifies his agreement with Locke and his disagreement with Berkeley in this respect by allowing that primary qualities are 'empirically real'; that is to say that they may be validly attributed to phenomena. But he qualifies this by adding that they are 'transcendentally ideal'; that is to say that they are valid *only of phenomena* and not of things-in-themselves.

What then is the nature of the phenomena or appearances which are thus distinguished from things-in-themselves? That they cannot be characterized as purely subjective we have already seen. Kant begins the division of the *Critique of Pure Reason* known as the *Aesthetic* (the title is directly derived from the Greek *aesthesis*) by a series of definitions. Any presumed awareness of an object Kant calls intuition. That form of awareness which is an awareness of appearances is empirical intuition and arises as a result of sensibility. The last is the capacity of the mind for receiving impressions or sensations as the result of its being affected by an object. Kant is well aware that in vision, for example, light affects our senses, but this knowledge of the causes of our sensations is still confined to appearances or phenomena. Nevertheless, all our sensations are ultimately determined by things-in-themselves. Sensations are thus in all respects entirely passive, but through them we have the intuition of appearances. An intuition may be opposed to a concept, which is a product of thought, and it is an essential part of Kant's teaching that experience in the proper sense cannot arise without both intuitions and concepts. Hence his famous saying that 'thoughts without content (sc. intuition) are empty, intuitions without concepts are blind' (*C.P.R.*, A 51 = B 75).

We may have an empirical intuition of an object, therefore, because that object is *given* to us in sensation; but such objects are appearances only. The difference between the intuition and the sensation is constituted (1) by the fact that the intuition is the awareness of the object mediated by the sensation, and (2) by the connected point that the intuition itself may be analysed into matter and form, of which the sensation provides the matter. Roughly speaking, therefore, the appearance which Kant speaks of as the object of an intuition is the content of the sensation which constitutes the matter of the intuition. Thus the object of the intuition has no existence independently of the experience, although Kant often uses language which suggests that it has. While an appearance, as the content of a sensation, provides the matter of an intuition, the form of the latter is provided by the spatio-temporal relations between sensations. Kant is explicit that this form cannot be constituted by the sensations themselves.

It seems clear from this that on Kant's view sensations cannot themselves possess spatio-temporal properties, and it may be that Kant took over this view from Hume.[1] It was maintained by Hume that the impression of extension is an impression of the 'order or manner' in which coloured or tangible points are disposed. Whether or not he explicitly took over this notion, Kant certainly came to the conclusion that extension cannot be a property of sensations themselves. As he tries to show in the section of the *Critique* known as 'The Anticipations of Experience', sensations have intensive magnitude, but they apparently have no extensive magnitude. Kant seems never to have questioned this view.

The fact that Kant distinguishes between the matter and the form of an intuition does not mean that he supposes the form to be imposed upon sensations which have already been acquired. Kant says that the matter and the form may be distinguished in thought, but he does not say that they can be distinguished in fact. Indeed the import of his arguments is to the reverse effect: matter and form are always conjoined, and for this reason we view appearances as possessing spatial and temporal properties as well as properties of other kinds. Space and time are empirically

[1] Paton (op. cit., p. 138) denies, however, that this is so.

real. Spatio-temporal form is a form which appearances really have; it is not imposed upon them by the mind or imagination. But since that form is not given *in* sensation—it not being part of the content of our sensations—it cannot be *a posteriori*; that is to say that it is not a contingent matter of experience that appearances have a spatio-temporal form. Our intuition of the spatio-temporal form of appearances, and our 'pure intuition' of space and time in general, are *a priori*. Spatio-temporal relations constitute the order in which the mind cannot help having sensations, so that appearances necessarily have a spatio-temporal form. How the precise order which appearances have is determined, is not clear from this, since Kant's argument so far is designed to show only that appearances must have a spatio-temporal order of some kind. There are objections to the view that the precise order of appearances is determined by things-in-themselves and also to the view that it is determined by the mind.[1] It is not necessary to pursue these difficulties here, but they are an inevitable consequence of the position which Kant initially assumed in his premises.

It should be mentioned in passing that Kant maintains the existence of an inner sense as well as outer sense. We can become aware by the former only of our own states of mind; and these have only a temporal order. Hence their form is constituted by time, while the objects of outer sense are ordered by both spatial and temporal relations. Other philosophers, e.g. Locke (*Essay* II, 1, 2 ff.), had assumed the existence of such a sense. Undoubtedly we can become aware of our own states of mind if we attend to them, but to postulate an inner sense in this context adds nothing to our understanding of the phenomenon. Kant merely wishes to say that, as well as indulging in active self-consciousness, we can take up a passive attitude to our own states of mind. A consequence of this is that by 'inner sense' the mind knows only the appearances of itself; hence by it we can gain knowledge only of what Kant calls the 'empirical self', not the real or noumenal self.

To return to outer sense—we have been told so far that we can have intuitions of appearances by means of sensations and their order. Kant followed the prevalent tradition in using the notion of a sensation in such a way that sensations can be said to have an

[1] Cf. Paton (op. cit., pp. 139 ff.) and N. Kemp Smith (*Commentary to Kant's Critique of Pure Reason*, pp. 84 ff.).

object, even if that object is in fact merely the content of the sensation. Sensations can thus provide us with information about the world or about appearances. Unlike Reid, Kant is uncritical in following this tradition. But he realizes also that in order to perceive something—in order, that is, to become aware of phenomena in the proper sense, as opposed to the mere appearances which are the contents of our sensations—we need to do more than stand in a merely passive relationship to the world. Perception, that is to say, is not constituted solely by sensation or empirical intuition. In this respect, Kant is still following Hume, for whom perception of an objective world was not merely the having of impressions, but this *plus* the working of the imagination. To perceive a table we need more than a set of impressions, more than what Kant calls the manifold of appearances.

The additional factors which Kant believes to be involved are discussed in the section of the *Critique* known as the *Analytic*. The part of that section which is devoted to the Transcendental Deduction of the Categories is certainly one of the most complex and difficult in Kant's work; and the situation is not helped by the fact that Kant made changes in his exposition between the 1st and 2nd editions of the *Critique*. I shall make no attempt to expound the detailed arguments employed, but only to outline the conclusions.

Kant's general point is that the synthesis of the manifold of appearances, i.e. the joining together of the appearances to form a unity, cannot be a function of sense. It is ultimately a function of the understanding helped by the imagination. Hume had in effect made the synthesis of the manifold the work of the imagination. Kant divides the synthesis into three stages, the first of which he calls the 'synthesis of apprehension', and the second the 'synthesis of reproduction'. The imagination not only enables us to view the manifold *as* a manifold (or, in Hume's terminology, the bundle of impressions *as* a bundle), but also enables us at the same time to keep in mind previously given elements of the manifold. In his exposition Kant separates these two syntheses as if they were quite distinct, but what he appears to mean is that the synthesizing of a manifold entails the reproduction of elements already surveyed. If we were not able to keep in mind previously surveyed elements of a manifold, we should not be able to view the whole *as* a manifold.

The third stage of the 'threefold synthesis' is the synthesis of recognition. The manifold which has been unified in the imagination must be brought under a concept, under one *principle of unity*. We must not only be in a position to view all the appearances of a table together as one, we must also be in a position to view them as constituting a table. The bringing of the intuitions under a concept makes possible a unitary apprehension of what is experienced, and for this reason subsumption under a concept is a necessary ingredient in any sense-perception. As Reid saw, perception involves a conception of the object.

The processes so far described could be purely subjective, and their result could be a mere figment of the imagination, not an objective perception. In effect, Hume had been able to give an account of these processes alone, and had thus been able to give no justification of claims that what we experience is, in Kantian terms, objectively valid. That is to say that he had not been able to show that what we think to be judgments about the world *are* judgments about the world which are universally valid for all men, rather than the product of our imagination. In consequence he had contented himself with a psychological account of the origin of our beliefs that we are acquainted with an independently existing world. Kant wishes to specify what more is required if the gap in Hume's account is to be made good.

Firstly, all our experiences which purport to be experiences of an objective world must be such that they may be conceived of as united in an *object*. Only the understanding, Kant thinks, can make it possible that the manifold of appearances can be conceived of as attaining a unity in an object. Thus the provision of the conception of an object is the work of the understanding. Similarly, all our experiences or representations of sense must be such that they may be unified as part of one consciousness. The 'I think', Kant says, accompanies all my representations; they are all necessarily part of *my* consciousness. These two ways in which the manifold can be seen as a unity are the two features, the objective and the subjective, of the unity of apperception. Kant uses the term 'apperception' in Leibnizian fashion to stress self-consciousness. Apperception forms a unity in that it is always and necessarily capable of being conceived as belonging to someone and as having an object, although neither the owner nor the object of the experiences which constitute apperception can be discovered *in* those experiences. Hume had looked for impressions of the self and of physical objects among the impressions which he had, and had found none. To the extent that Kant maintains that neither the self nor the object of empirical knowledge can be detected by surveying appearances he agrees with Hume. But Hume had had to assert that our belief in the self and physical objects was due to the imagination only. It would thus seem to be only a contingent fact that impressions ever belong to a self and are ever organized in such a way as to make it possible to talk of physical objects. Kant does not claim that the understanding gives us knowledge of the self or physical objects, although pure reason may *claim* to provide such knowledge in the form of knowledge of the noumenal self and things-in-themselves. But the understanding does indicate that if the experiences which we have are to be considered as providing empirical knowledge they must be conceived as forming a unity in the two senses that they have an object and belong to a subject. As against Hume, Kant is undoubtedly right: impressions cannot be treated as independent entities with a substantial existence in their own right.

Secondly, in order that we may have objective empirical knowledge, the judgments which we make concerning our experiences must be made in terms of certain principles. We must, for example, so judge that what we judge to be the case is subsumable under the law of universal causality; the events concerning which we judge must, that is, have a cause. Just as the logical forms of judgment may be constructed out of their constituent ideas (for Kant, like Aristotle, thinks that a judgment consists in a combination of ideas or concepts), so there must be principles whereby different forms of objectively valid judgment may be constructed. That is to say that any judgment which purports to be a judgment about the world must be in accordance with one or other of the principles of the construction of an objectively valid judgment. The pure concepts under which the understanding views these principles Kant calls *categories*. Hence all objectively valid judgments presuppose the applicability of at least one of the categories. I omit here consideration of the schematism—the bridge which Kant thinks necessary between the purely formal categories and intuitions; but in general it can be said that on Kant's view the applicability of the categories is necessary if objective experience is to be possible. The categories and the principles which are derived from them are therefore necessary presuppositions of objective experience, and are in this sense *a priori*.

In his theory of knowledge Kant was not so much concerned to refute scepticism by showing that some truths can be known for certain, since they are necessary, as to show that our judgments about the world are not mere products of the imagination. His aim was to show that there are objectively valid judgments—that is to say, judgments that are capable of being universally accepted as true of the world. This world, it is true, is still the world of appearances only, not that of things-in-themselves; but to call the former a world of appearances is not in itself to imply that it is illusory or delusive. Objectively valid judgments are necessarily valid for all and opposed to judgments which are subjectively valid only—judgments which are the product of the imagination alone and which are true, if at all, only for oneself. In Kant's view, Hume had denied the possibility of objectively valid judgments, since he had attributed our beliefs about the world to the imagination alone. Kant himself wished to distinguish clearly between those judgments which are due to the imagination alone and those which also involve the understanding. This could be done only by showing that objectively valid judgments *necessarily* conform to certain principles of the understanding (not merely that in our experience they do so as a matter of fact).

The task of showing that the existence of categories must be assumed Kant calls a *deduction* of the categories. The point of the so-called 'Transcendental Deduction' is to show that categories in general are necessarily presupposed in the making of any objectively valid judgment about the world. The precise categories which are so presupposed can be discovered only by the 'Metaphysical Deduction'—an analysis of the different forms of the understanding—and Kant thinks that the clue to this is provided by the traditional classification of the logical forms of judgment. This part of Kant's argument—the Metaphysical Deduction—is now almost universally rejected, but this does not mean that there is nothing to be said for the Transcendental Deduction. It has been shown by P. F. Strawson that the way in which it is natural to look at the world presupposes a set of basic concepts or categories, and it is at least arguable that any way of looking at the world necessarily presupposes certain categories, such as that of a thing.[1] But to pursue this idea here would take us too far from our main purpose.

In sum, Kant does not view perception as either the passive reception of sensations of the activity of judgment by itself. Perception is the result of the working of sensation, imagination and understanding together. It consists firstly in the having of empirical intuitions, which themselves consist of sensations which give us an awareness of the content of experience. But the form of experience is given by the relations between sensations, not by the sensations themselves, and since it is not a contingent fact that sensations are related spatio-temporally, the form of experience is *a priori*. Kant's treatment here is vitiated by his acceptance of the view that in having sensations in an entirely passive way we have experiences which may be said to have an object; it is vitiated also by his acceptance of the derivative point that the object of such a sensation cannot possess spatio-temporal characteristics.

Perception consists secondly in the fact that the imagination tends to unify the manifold of appearances which intuition provides. In Humean language, we tend, because of the imagination, to treat the bundles of impressions *as bundles* and not as separate impressions. So far, Kant's account could be translated into Humean terms without much in the way of modification. But perception consists, thirdly, in the fact that the understanding subsumes the manifold under a concept, in such a way that the experiences constituted by any given manifold are always experiences of a unitary object and belong to a single unitary consciousness. It is the understanding which turns the mere awareness of a bundle of impressions into a judgment by a subject about an object. Finally, such judgments necessarily conform to certain principles and necessarily presuppose the applicability of certain categories.

The whole of this account is applicable to appearances only. Behind appearances stand things-in-themselves of which the understanding can know nothing; and the claims which people make to knowledge of things-in-themselves by means of pure reason turn out, Kant thinks, to be unavailing and contradictory. Much of this programme is carried out within terms of reference which are more or less those laid down by Hume. Kant's arguments concerning the unity of apperception, for example, appear

[1] See P. F. Strawson, *Individuals* and my 'Formal Concepts, Categories and Metaphysics', *Philosophy*, 1959.

impressive and valid as against Hume, but outside this context they have a certain awkwardness and obscurity. They are, that is to say, of great value from a 'critical' point of view, but if we adopt another frame of reference and start from the concept of a person perceiving the world, rather than from the notion of appearances or experiences which then have to be attributed to a subject, the situation looks rather different.[1] Nevertheless, Kant's emphasis on the part which concepts play in perception is of the utmost importance, and his views on the role of categories are at the least arguable and probably more than this.

Kant provides one account of how passive sensation and active judgment are to be brought together in perception, and he deserves due credit for the attempt. Yet his account cannot be considered the final answer. The fact that he works within certain terms of reference is not a point of merely incidental interest. One point of vital importance remains. In Kant's theory sensations are like perceptions to the extent that they have an object and thus have an epistemological function. It is because of this feature that it is possible to suggest that the understanding subsumes their contents under concepts. We can subsume something under a concept only when in some sense we have knowledge of that thing. To perceive something as ϕ does indeed seem to involve subsuming it under a concept, and in consequence Kant's emphasis on this element seems justified. But if it is supposed that all perception involves the subsumption of something under a concept, it follows that it is necessary to have knowledge of that something in other ways than by perception. It is because of this that Kant treats sensations in the way in which he does; something has to be given in sensation if his theory is to work. Once this notion that something is given in sensation is repudiated the theory loses its foundations and the relationship between sensation and perception becomes obscure. The Idealist reaction to Kant was in this direction.

(ii) HEGEL AND IDEALISM

The idealist movement in philosophy, which became such a force in the 19th century, began in effect when Fichte rejected the Kantian things-in-themselves. As long as belief in things-in-

---
[1] See P. F. Strawson's discussion of persons in *Individuals*, ch. 3.

themselves was retained, the idea that it was possible to distinguish among the contents of the mind between those which are due to the mind itself and those which are due to things outside it received at least a persuasive support. The rejection of things-in-themselves resulted inevitably in a form of subjective idealism in which phenomena and the experiencing subject were only two sides of the same coin. In such circumstances the problem of perception becomes the problem whether it is possible at all to distinguish between perception and other forms of mental activity. Common sense seems to tell us that when we perceive something we are confronted with an object. But what is it about the nature of experience itself which indicates this?

The basic form of experience is, in Hegelian terms, an apprehension of the immediate (*Phenomenology*, ch. 1). This form of experience seems to present us with that which *is*, independently of its subsumption under concepts. It seems as if two individuals, one the Ego, the other the object, confront each other. But, Hegel asks, is this the truth? In dealing with this question he follows a procedure which is typical of Idealism—that of pointing out that all the knowledge which we can have of anything is a knowledge of universals, of the properties which that thing possesses. Thus, if we are to have knowledge, that which *is* must be subsumed under concepts. How, then, can we grasp the particular which we assume, in perception, is confronting us? All thoughts and words which we can use, it is maintained, are general, not particular: even our use of such words as 'this', 'here' and 'now', let alone our use of proper-names, fails to guarantee particularity. Hegel[1] points out that at different times and places many things can be spoken of as this, here or now. Hence he concludes that these words—words which were later to be thought of by Logical Atomists such a Russell as the paradigm cases of expressions used to refer to particulars—are just as general as words like 'red'.

From this it is argued that if there are no words by means of which we can think of anything which is particular there can be no knowledge of anything particular as such. In sense-knowledge we appear to have an immediate knowledge of the existence of a particular; but, for the reasons given, Hegel takes this to be impossible. It is the universal, not the particular, of which we have

[1] Cf. F. H. Bradley, *Principles of Logic*, ch. 2, sects. 21-7.

immediate knowledge. Sense-knowledge is after all a mediated knowledge; our apparent awareness of a particular is mediated through the knowledge of the universals or concepts under which it can be subsumed. It is only experience as a whole of whose existence we can be certain through sense-experience; we have no right to claim certainty about any of the specific contents of experience. Hence it is that F. H. Bradley insists that the subject of all judgments, even those ostensibly about perceived objects, is in fact Reality as a whole; for in his view Reality and experience are identical.

The precedents for the Hegelian doctrine that there can be no immediate knowledge of particulars is the Aristotelian view that knowledge is of the universal and the Kantian view that knowledge is ultimately a question of fitting something under a concept in judgment. The Idealists objected to Kant that he had no right to claim knowledge of the existence of things-in-themselves. But, if these were rejected, how could one know about that which is given in sensation. If knowledge presupposes subsumption under concepts it is impossible to know about the 'given' apart from concepts. In other words, by giving sensations an epistemological status Kant belied his main theory.

On the other hand, the Hegelian argument concerning expressions such as 'this' is clearly unsatisfactory. From the fact that we use the word 'this' of many things it does not immediately follow that it is a general word. Granted that general words *are* used of many things, and that this is the main reason why they are general, it is important also to notice the *way* in which they are applied to many things. Words like 'red' are normally applied to many things predicatively; we use such words to characterize things. We do not normally use 'this' in that way, but in order to refer to things. The fact that we use the word 'this' to refer to a number of different things on different occasions does not show that it is like 'red' in its use. Words like 'this' were fastened on by Hegelians for the same reason as they were fastened on by their later opponents—e.g. Russell—because they were supposed to be the last ditch in a defence of knowledge of particulars. If these words did not guarantee particularity, what would? But the considerations which make it implausible to treat these words as general words of the same kind as 'red' apply equally to all those words which we use to refer to particular things, e.g. proper-names. If we have, therefore, the means of referring to particulars, there seems no remaining objection to the view that we may have knowledge of particulars also.

Hegel's conclusions follow, therefore, only if it be granted that all knowledge is knowledge of universals. In sense-experience, he thinks, it is universals of sense which provide the materials of knowledge. But this is not the end of the matter. In perception, common-sense takes it that we are concerned with things. How are the universals out of which perceptual knowledge is created related to those things? We think of an object of perception as a unity, and yet the properties which we attribute to it are in themselves quite unconnected. In a lump of sugar, the sweetness and the whiteness are quite distinct (*Phenomenology*, ch. 2; cf. F. H. Bradley, *Appearance and Reality*, ch. 2). For this reason, it is argued, if we consider the thing by itself, sense-perception can be seen to involve a contradiction—the contradiction between the unity of the thing and the plurality of its properties, and again between the unity of each property and the plurality of the constituents of the thing which exemplify it.

Bradley argues to some length (*Principles of Logic*, ch. 2, sects. 58 ff.) that even judgments which purport to involve an analysis of immediate experience, e.g. 'This is a bird', are, if true, only conditionally true. As Hegel puts it, there is in perception only a conditional universality, and this must rest upon a higher unconditional universality. The universals which we apply to experience in perceptual judgments are conditional upon the fact that other universals are also applicable. Thus Bradley's argument amounts to the thesis that I can say 'This is a bird' only because of a knowledge of connections between the elements of experience. That is to say that while there is no intrinsic connection between the properties possessed by a lump of sugar, my knowledge about the lump of sugar rests upon knowledge of the connections between the universals 'sugar', 'sweetness', 'whiteness', etc. Singular judgments of sense are in effect disguised hypothetical judgments; they are judgments stating that if some universal is present, then there are also other universals present. But because the connection which is stated to hold between the universals is applied to some selection of reality or experience only, judgments of sense are not pure hypothetical judgments.

Hegel argues that since sense-universals are conditional universals, i.e. universals which apply to experience only on the condition that other universals do so, there must be an unconditional universal which is the object of the understanding. This is something which perception alone cannot grasp: perception is irrevocably committed to the so-called contradictions already noted, e.g. that between the unity of the object and the plurality of its properties. Perception is inevitably faced with the problem of the one and the many. The understanding can surmount this problem by reference to the unconditional universal. Hegel calls this unconditional universal 'Force'; it is in fact the idea of lawlikeness. The law-like connections between the properties of a thing determine its unity. The same point is brought out by Bradley's argument that singular judgments of sense are really hypothetical in form. Hypothetical judgments state law-like connections—if p, then q. Any judgment about an object of perception, therefore, implicitly states and also presupposes law-like connections between attributes. To see this is a function of the understanding: perception alone cannot grasp it, and hence the world of perception is appearance only.

In a sense, much of the foregoing is implicit in Kant. On his view also it is only because of the fact that the understanding plays a part in determining empirical knowledge that such empirical knowledge is possible at all. It is the understanding which attaches the notion of law-likeness to phenomena. Kant and Hegel differ in that the former, by stressing the existence of sensible intuition, maintains that there is something which, if not knowledge in the full sense, is at any rate very like knowledge, although non-conceptual. A certain backing to this view is provided by the belief in the existence of things-in-themselves, since they might be assumed to be the causes of the sensations which provide sensible intuitions.[1] By rejecting things-in-themselves and at the same time taking to its extreme the view that all knowledge is knowledge of the universal, Idealism makes it difficult for itself to justify the claim that anything independent of ourselves exists. Even the assertion of the existence of something could, in its terms, be put down as purely conceptual, in that existence also is a concept. If this is so, how can the world of perception be distinguished from a

[1] Even on Kant's view it is impossible to have knowledge to this effect.

world which is purely a creation of the mind?[1] The remedy is not to restore things-in-themselves, but to abandon the whole conceptual framework from which both Kantianism and Hegelianism are derived. It is a presupposition of that conceptual framework that something is 'given' in experience, and that subsequent modifications are due to judgment.

In Hegelianism the only thing which is 'given' is experience as a whole; and specification of this is due to the mind. But it is questionable whether it makes sense to speak of experience as a whole being the only thing that is 'given'. For what may this be opposed to? If we are to approach the matter from the inside of experience, so to speak, without any assumptions about an independent world such as things-in-themselves, perception can be distinguished from other forms of experience only by the supposed contradictoriness of its findings. These 'contradictions' rest upon an inability from this point of view to explain how the set of properties which we attach to a thing, the concepts under which we subsume it, can add up to the unitary thing of which we are supposed to have knowledge. The problems here are at least as old as Plato;[2] they arise also for the more recent phenomenalists who have wished to regard things as logical constructions out of a plurality of sense-data. For Idealists the problem is increased by the fact that, if objects are to be constructed at all, that out of which they must be constructed is mind-dependent.

In giving the minimum of attention to the role of sensation in perception and the maximum of attention to the role of judgment, Idealism presents something of a *reductio ad absurdum* of the view that in perceiving something I am making a judgment. To put the matter in the most direct way—if, in perceiving, I am making a judgment, what is it that I am making the judgment about and how do I know of this? The Idealist emphasis upon concepts or ideas resulted in the position that the only thing which could act as the subject of our judgments must be experience as a whole. While Idealists themselves show no sign of considering this view

---

[1] The inability to cope with knowledge of existences in any full sense is the burden of criticisms levelled against Hegel by Existentialists. There is no room in Hegel's theory for any belief in the contingency of things.

[2] Plato is mainly interested in the question of how one thing can be many rather than how the many can add up to the one. But the latter problem also appears in his writings, e.g. *Theaetetus* 204 ff.

paradoxical, it is considered so by others, and it is an indication that for a satisfactory account of perception we must, while taking account of judgment, look elsewhere also. The philosophers who must be considered next went to the other extreme, paying every attention to sensation and the minimum to judgment. This view produced paradoxes of its own in turn, and the Idealists were among the first to point this out.

8

NINETEENTH-CENTURY SENSATIONALISM

THE Sensationalism (with its accompanying Associationism) which became the most prevalent philosophical and psychological view in this country during the first half of the 19th century owed its origins to the much earlier Hartley, who wrote his *Observations on Man* in 1749. Hartley was a doctor, perhaps a significant fact; he claimed that his theory was suggested to him by a certain 'Rev. Mr. Gay', who is otherwise unknown.

Hartley's theory was in effect physiological in character. He postulated vibrations which were set up in the nerves by stimulation of the sense-organs. Where one vibration was followed by another, the occurrence of the first vibration on another occasion was supposed to have a tendency to set up the second vibration in the brain, without further stimulation of the sense-organ. According to Hartley, each nerve vibrates in a characteristic way, and it is noteworthy that although this was pure speculation on Hartley's part, a similar theory was put forward in the 1830s by the physiologist J. Müller, under the title of 'specific nervous energies'. Each nerve, it was claimed, has its own specific function and cannot take over that of another.

One consequence of this theory was the following: It could be inferred from the theory of specific nervous energies that each nerve is responsible for a single experience or sensation. Since our sense-organs are served by a plurality of nerve-endings, it could also be inferred that any experience derived from the stimulation of a sense-organ must consist of a plurality of distinct sensations. This view could be, and indeed was, taken as confirmatory of the epistemological or psychological atomism which Hume put forward—the view that each impression is distinct and separable and that the impression of extension is dependent upon a number of distinct, atomic impressions of coloured or tangible points. For this reason, the Sensationalists took the physiological theory to be confirmatory of what they already expected on philosophical grounds. The use of words like 'mosaic' in order to describe sensory experience became common.[1] Not everyone, however, found Hartley's own physiological speculation acceptable, and Priestley produced an expurgated text of Hartley's work, with the references to vibrations deleted.

Hartley defined sensations as (*Observations on Man*, Introduction) 'those internal feelings of the mind which arise from the impressions made by external objects upon the several parts of our bodies'. He thus equated sensations with feelings, a move which was typical of the Sensationalists, although Bain was later to have scruples. 'All our other internal feelings may be called ideas,' Hartley goes on, and he makes it clear that sensations may be distinguished from ideas only by their intensity—so agreeing with Hume. He adds, 'It will appear in the course of these observations, that the ideas of sensation are the elements of which all the rest are compounded. Hence ideas of sensation may be termed simple, intellectual ones complex.' The complex ideas are built up out of simple ones by the mechanical processes of association. Hartley was a mechanist in the extreme; he reduced even association by similarity, which, generally speaking, might be looked upon as an exception to the otherwise purely mechanical processes of association, to association by contiguity. The latter could be treated mechanically.

Associationism, as put forward by Hume and Hartley, was taken over in a modified form by the Scottish school of philosophers who succeeded Reid. The general tendency of the school was to explain associationism in terms of principles inherited from Reid. Thomas Brown, for example, used the notion of 'suggestion' in place of association, and introduced 'relative suggestion' in order to account for our recognition of relations. When it is main-

---

[1] The inadequacy of the analogy between a field of sensations and a mosaic becomes obvious when it is considered that a mosaic must have a background. What is the background against which the sensations are set?

tained that our experience of things can be broken down into atomic perceptions, it becomes a problem how we become aware of the relations between perceptions. It was a problem for most of the Sensationalists, and Brown's notion of relative suggestion was meant to deal with it. Still later, Sir William Hamilton combined this tradition with the Kantian one, maintaining that our perception of spatial and temporal relations is as direct as our perception of colour.[1]

The most clear-cut and direct exposition of Sensationalism and Associationism is to be found in *The Analysis of the Phenomena of the Human Mind* by James Mill, the father of John Stuart Mill. Later, J. S. Mill himself and Alexander Bain introduced refinements upon James Mill's theory, and like most attempts to add sophistication the result showed a partial awareness of the theory's general inadequacy. Like Hartley, James Mill used the notion of a feeling as the basic notion of his system. He says (op. cit., I. p. 52),[2] 'We have two classes of feelings; one, that which exists when the object of sense is present; another, that which exists after the object of sense has ceased to be present. The one class of feelings I call "sensations"; the other class of feelings I call "ideas".' This is very much in the tradition of Hartley. Later Mill adds (op. cit., I. p. 116), 'The proper attribute of a sensation or an idea, considered as an *intellectual* element, is greater or less distinctness. . . . A feeling is more or less strong or intense.' So it is that once having adopted the position that the contents of the mind consist only of feelings, Mill is forced to distinguish between those contents by reference only to those characteristics which can belong to feelings.

Mill is very forthright in this respect. Some quotations will reveal the spirit with which he tackles his problem:

'Having a *sensation*, and having a feeling, are not two things.' (I. p. 224.)

'To have an idea, and the feeling of that idea, are not two things; they are one and the same thing.' (I. p. 225.)

[1] Though not directly connected with the Sensationalist school, Ernst Mach, the philosopher of science, followed very much the same tradition. In his work, *The Analysis of Sensations*, he suggested that there are sensations of relations. Cf. William James' 'feelings of relations'.

[2] References to James Mill's work are to the 1869 edition edited by J. S. Mill.

'To have a sensation, and to believe that we have it, are not distinguishable things.' (I. p. 342.)

'Having *two* sensations, therefore, is not only having sensation, but the only thing which can, in strictness, be called having sensation ... The having a new sensation, and knowing that it is new, are not two things, but one and the same thing.' (II. p. 11.)

'Having a change of sensation, and knowing I have it are not two things but one and the same thing.' (II. p. 14.)

Much of this is little more than a development of Hume or Hartley, but the insistence with which Mill reduces everything mental to feelings is notable.

Since he has made perception a matter of feeling, Mill is faced with the problem how it comes about that we think that we have knowledge of material objects. He does not tackle this problem directly, however; he contents himself with the view that when, as it seems to us, we refer to material objects, we are in fact referring to sensations. In other words, he adopts Berkeley's point of view in a rather crude way. Thus he says (op. cit., I. p. 93), 'In using the names, tree, man, the names of what I call objects, I am referring, and can be referring, only to my own sensations.' J. S. Mill, with more sophistication, was to show more concern for the problem of our knowledge of material objects, but starting from the same premises, he could give only a psychological explanation of our belief that we have such knowledge.

Mill follows and even develops Berkeley's views in another respect also. Berkeley's *New Theory of Vision* was designed to explain our visual perception of the distance of things, by saying that visual sensations suggest or become associated with ideas derived from touch. Mill and all the other Sensationalists accepted this view, although it was not without its critics in the 19th century, e.g. T. K. Abbott and S. Bailey. But following the influence of Hume's view that simple impressions are atomic and hence that the perception of extension is a perception of the order of impressions, the Sensationalists extended Berkeley's view to the perception of spatial extension also. Mill admits that the eye may give rise to a number of sensations at once—synchronous sensations as he calls them—but this was more than Bain wished to admit. In commenting upon this view in J. S. Mill's edition of his father's work, Bain tries to play down the notion of synchronous sensations in favour of temporal sequences of sensations due to changes in muscular activity. Nevertheless, while James Mill himself admits that there may be synchronous sensations, he does not think that this is enough to produce perception of spatial extension. The mind, that is, cannot immediately perceive the order of those sensations. Thus he says (op. cit., I. p. 95), 'Yet, philosophy has ascertained that we derive nothing from the eye whatever, but sensations of colour; that the idea of extension, in which size, and form, and distance are included, is derived from sensations, not in the eye, but in the muscular part of our frame.' We learn to perceive the extension of bodies only by association of sensations of colour with sensations from muscular activity, e.g. from movements in the eyes.

It is Bain who is most explicit in this view. Bain was perhaps the first psychologist in whose writings a physiological approach was united with an approach to the subject derived from philosophy or philosophical psychology. He begins his work *The Senses and the Intellect* with a consideration of the physiology of the nervous system, and his approach to this is admirable. He has much of sense, for example, to say about the *function* of the eye. But when he turns to the experiences which are derived from the eye's functioning he is chained to the Sensationalist tradition, according to which sensations and the perceptible qualities of objects are to be identified.

Like James Mill, Bain starts from sensations, which he defines as 'mental impressions, feelings, or states of consciousness, resulting from the action of external things on some part of the body' (*Senses and the Intellect*, 3rd ed., p. 101). But in commenting on James Mill's use of the term 'feeling' in J. S. Mill's edition of his father's work (I. pp. 65 ff.), he makes careful distinctions between different things to which the term 'sensation' has been or might be applied. In particular, he distinguishes between sensations of the objective consciousness and those of the subjective consciousness. To the former he allocates the perceived qualities of things, and to the latter feelings of pleasure and pain; and he adds, 'Now the word "Sensation" covers both, though to object consciousness, "Perception" is more strictly applicable.' But he draws no conclusion from this terminological point, except in so far as he tends to distinguish systematically between 'sensations of organic life, taste and smell' and 'sensations of the intellectual senses'. For he treats such matters as the perception of colour, distance and material objects in general under the heading of the 'Intellect'.

The sensations of sight, he thinks, are partly due to the effect of light on the retina of the eye, and partly due to the movements of the muscles of the eye. Apart from its muscular activity the functioning of the eye results in sensations of light and colour alone. Hence apart from the muscular activity there could be no perception of the extension of objects. But the movements of the muscles of the eye are, while necessary, not sufficient to produce perception of spatial extension. They only make possible the production of a series of varying sensations of colour. The sensations which we have of the muscular movements in the eye themselves produce a perception of the sweep of the eye, but the exact nature and degree of that sweep can be learned only from the association of those sensations with the ideas of the movement of our body. The eye alone cannot give us an impression of extension, let alone of distance. Our perception of extension and distance is a complicated matter of sensations plus associated ideas. There is no immediate visual perception of extension; we perceive extension indirectly *via* a series of sensations of movement in the eye which are associated with ideas of the movement of our body.

Bain sums this up epigrammatically in his more popular *Mental Science* (p. 49), 'Time or succession is the simpler fact; co-existence or extension in space is a complex fact; and the serial fixedness of sensation is one element of the complication.' In effect, Bain wishes to analyse space or our awareness of it into awareness of temporal change. Although he is not quite definite on the matter, his tendency is to say that there is no direct perception of spatial extension. The problem immediately arises how in that case it comes about that we have any idea of extension at all. Bain gives no explanation how, as a result of having a series of sensations, we come to associate them with ideas of extension. For this association to be possible, it would be necessary to have an *independent* knowledge of extension, and this Bain all but denies. It is impossible to explain our perception of the spatial properties of things merely by reference to a temporal series of experiences. Spatiality, as Kant saw, is a necessary feature of the objects of experience.

A reluctant admission of this fact is to be found in J. S. Mill's discussion of a similar point in his *Examination of Sir William Hamilton's Philosophy*. Hamilton had maintained in Kantian fashion that we have a direct perception of spatial extension, and J. S. Mill wished to dispute this. He asserts that if it is asked how one obtains a perception of spatial extension *via* a series of sensations of muscular movements, the answer might be provided by reference to a person born blind who happens to be a metaphysician! This, J. S. Mill thinks, would at least show that the Sensationalist theory concerning our perception of spatial extension is a possible theory. For this reason he attempts to describe how a blind man finds out about the spatial extension possessed by objects, e.g. by passing his hand along those objects, or by walking over them if they are large. But he adds in a characteristically honest way (op. cit., 6th ed., p. 283), 'The parts of extension which it is possible for him to perceive simultaneously, are only very small parts, almost the minima of extension.' Thus he does not deny that the parts of an object which such a man could see simultaneously are extended, even if they are very small. Later (op. cit., p. 293) he asserts that if it were not for the movement of the eye, 'the impression we should have of a boundary between two colours would be so vague and indistinct as to be merely rudimentary'. But he goes on to say, 'A rudimentary conception must be allowed, for it is evident that even without moving the eye we are capable of having two sensations of colour at once.' Yet he refuses to allow that the 'discriminative impressions' derived from the boundary between two colours are enough to give us an impression of extension. 'To confer on these discriminative impressions', he says, 'the name which denotes our matured and perfected cognition of Extension, or even to assume that they have anything in common with it, seems to be going beyond the evidence.'

J. S. Mill is here in an ambivalent position and he is honest enough to admit the difficulties. These difficulties are made worse by the failure to distinguish quite different questions: (*a*) How do we come to see things as extended at all? (*b*) How do we come to see that things have the size or shape that they do have? (*c*) How do we come to have the idea or concept of extension or spatiality? In the quotation from J. S. Mill given above there is an evident confusion between questions (*a*) and (*c*), for Mill speaks of a 'perfected cognition of Extension' when he is really concerned with how we come to see things as extended. Moreover, the answer 'By learning' is quite appropriate to question (*b*), but is utterly inappropriate to question (*a*). That is to say that it does not make sense to say that we come by learning to see things as extended, unless this means only that it is by learning that we come to apply the *expression* 'extended' to them. On the other hand it makes very good sense to suggest that we learn to see that things have whatever size or shape that they do have. How else could we come to do this?

The failure to distinguish these questions not only made the Sensationalist thesis confused; it also caused confusion in some of the reactions to that thesis. The dispute between Nativism and Empiricism concerning space-perception, which arose during the latter half of the 19th century, turned largely on this point. Nativists tended to follow Kant in asserting that extension was an essential characteristic of the objects of perception, and that knowledge of it was therefore not acquired by learning. Their opponents took the opposite point of view. The issue emerges most clearly over the localization of sensations. The question how sensations are localized arises most obviously in connection with bodily sensations, but because of the 19th-century tendency to treat the perception of objects as a matter of having sensations, the question how we localize objects was also treated as a matter of how we localize sensations. Hence the problem was raised in a quite general form.

Bain's treatment of this matter is most obscure (*Senses and the Intellect*, 3rd ed., pp. 396 ff.). He suggests that there may be certain sensations which are 'in themselves, or as originally felt' identical, but which become distinguished as a result of their associations. A touch on the left and right hands, for example, may give rise to qualitatively identical feelings; but these feelings are associated with quite different ideas and sensations, so that we distinguish them, the one as being derived from the left hand, the other as derived from the right. How this could be a matter of association, when the original sensations are indistinguishable, Bain does not explain. But he adds, 'This possibility of suspending associations proves that there is a real difference in the sensations, that they are not confounded in the brain, though we may not trace this difference in the immediate consciousness. Association alone brings it out.' Hence it appears that on his view qualitatively indistinguishable sensations may nevertheless really be different, and this difference is 'taken account of' in the brain.

Bain's view is far from clear, but he opposes it to another view which was more current in the 19th century—the local-sign theory, associated chiefly with the name of Lotze. Herbart had already maintained that spatially different sensations are also qualitatively different, and that our localization of a sensation, and indeed of our impressions of external objects in general, is due to these qualitative differences. The local-sign theory is somewhat more complex. On this theory every sensation provides a sign of its locality as well as possessing a specific qualitative character. Lotze maintained that in the case of the eye, a sensation derived from a particular part of the retina produces a reaction in the shape of a tendency to turn the head in that direction. As a result every sensation comes by reason of its local-sign to be associated with certain movements; and in this way it becomes localized. Similar considerations apply to bodily sensations.[1]

This view was adopted by most 19th-century psychologists, especially Wundt and Helmholtz. Wundt pointed out in addition that sensations derived from the eye vary qualitatively according to the part of the retina stimulated. But the theory was not unopposed, and Hering in particular maintained that we directly perceive the locality of a sensation without having to learn of it through its connection with movements. Behind the dispute, however, can be detected the same confusion as that involved in the Sensationalist theory of our perception of spatial extension. If sensations differ qualitatively only, no amount of association can provide a knowledge of either the extension or the localization of the objects which produce them. This result might be achieved if the sensations of the associated movements themselves provided the knowledge; but if these sensations in turn constitute merely a series of sensations in time, there is no hope. We may not know exactly in which tooth we have toothache, and we may be able to find this out only by prodding our teeth and so learning by experience. But a necessary condition of our being able to discover that a pain is in one tooth rather than another is that there should

[1] Something very like the local-sign theory can be found in Gilbert Ryle's *Concept of Mind*, p. 105. I owe this observation to an unpublished paper by Mr. G. N. A. Vesey.

be a general way of distinguishing the places of origin of our feelings. That is to say that in order that we may be able to localize feelings exactly, their places of origin must themselves be capable of being distinguished spatially. This is not something that could be learned from other kinds of data. But if all perception is a matter of having sensations only, and if sensations differ in quality but not intrinsically in locality, the places of origin of sensations must be learned from other data, if at all.

There is a sense in which if we feel a pain to be in a tooth, it is in that tooth even if tests, e.g. by prodding, suggest that its *cause* lies in another tooth. While we could not feel the pain as in a certain tooth unless we already knew what it was like to discover by tests where its origin really was (unless, that is, there were some way in which we might have acquired the general concept of 'being in a tooth'), it makes no sense to suggest that we might come by further tests to discover where we *feel* the pain to be. For in the latter case there are no criteria of being right or wrong, and hence no criteria of whether it is in place to talk of a discovery.[1] The local-sign theory suggests that sensations are in some way inspected and that the result of the inspection will tell us where they are to be located. But finding out that a pain is due to something in a specific tooth is a matter of objective tests, not inspection of the pain; while feeling it to be in that tooth is not a matter of having the pain, inspecting it and then concluding that it is in that tooth. It is purely and simply feeling it to be in that tooth. In this last case the question 'How do we come to do this?' makes no sense, unless it means only 'What has to be the case for me to feel a pain to be in a tooth?' And to this one answer is 'I must have acquired already the concept of being in a tooth'.[2]

This is far from the references to learning and association to be found in 19th-century discussions of the local-sign theory. As already indicated, those discussions are made worse by the fact that the objects which we perceive and localize were treated as sensations on the same level as pains. Indeed, it is possible to argue that the notion of localization as applied to sensations is a notion which is transferred from the context in which we talk of localizing or locating objects of perception. Sensations, that is,

---

[1] Cf. L. Wittgenstein, *Philosophical Investigations*, I. 258 ff.

[2] I owe much here to discussion with Mr. A. P. Griffiths and to the paper by Mr. G. N. A. Vesey previously referred to.

are treated as objects of perception, when we talk of their localization in the literal sense.

One more feature of the Sensationalist point of view merits discussion—namely, their views concerning our perception of the material world. As might be expected, they were less interested in the epistemological problems involved than in psychology. Bain contents himself with the assertion that belief in the externality of the causes of our sensations arises from the fact that our own actions modify our sensations, or bring them into play or cause them to cease. While it is true and important that our actions do have these effects, reference to them provides no justification for our belief in an external world. It gives one explanation only of how we could come to believe in the existence of things causing our sensations, if it were the case that we were acquainted with nothing but sensations. But for a thorough-going Sensationalist it is not a satisfactory explanation either, unless it is possible to give some independent sense to the notion of 'things causing our sensations'. In other words, Sensationalism leaves the matter just where Hume left it, and Bain's discussion is in fact rather cruder than Hume's.

The same may be said of J. S. Mill's account of the matter, although here there is greater sophistication. The chapter in the *Examination of Sir William Hamilton's Philosophy* which deals with these matters is entitled 'The Psychological Theory of the Belief in an External World', and this title sums up the chapter admirably. It is notorious that Mill holds that all that is contained in our idea of material objects is the idea of permanent possibilities of sensation. Hence he attempts to explain, by reference to the principles of Associationism, why it is that we come to believe in such possibilities—why, that is, we come to have expectations which take us beyond the immediate sensation. To this extent his view is like that of Hume. But he also tends to say that a permanent possibility of sensation is what we *mean* by matter, a view which Hume held more equivocally. Mill is, philosophically, a proponent of phenomenalism—the view that what we mean by material objects is to be analysed purely in terms of sensation or sense-data. In this respect also Mill begins to go beyond the straightforward Sensationalist position.

9
THE REACTION

WHEN a reaction against the Sensationalist view began it had many sources. In consequence the philosophers and psychologists who will be considered in this chapter are rather a mixed bag. They are united only in their opposition to the main features of Sensationalism. These features are particularly (1) the view that all mental contents can be reduced to sensations, and (2) the view that these sensations are atomic and point-like. J. S. Mill had already sensed some of the difficulties involved in each of these views. He had realized that not all mental functions can be regarded as the result of a simple compounding of different sensations, and he had used the notions of 'mental chemistry' in an attempt to deal with the matter. Just as quite new compounds can be formed out of chemical elements, so, he supposed, new mental contents could be formed out of sensations. His hesitations over the second view have been noted in the previous chapter. But there remained the problem how it is that, if I am confronted with a series of distinct, point-like sensations, I come to see continuous objects. Earlier in the 19th century Herbart had used the Leibnizian notion of apperception to explain how experience as a whole could be constituted out of individual 'presentations'. According to Herbart, apperception provides a mental frame of reference into which presentations can be fitted. Wundt used the same notion in perhaps a cruder way, with the result that apperception became a conscious process which functioned as a sort of glue by which sensations could be united.[1] The problem was clearly pressing.

[1] That is to say that the sense-field may consist of sensations of which we know nothing in detail. By means of apperception we come to be clearly

THE REACTION

The main reaction against Sensationalism began round about 1890, but there was a straw in the wind earlier in Brentano's *Psychology from an Empiricist Standpoint* (1874). In the main, Brentano was reacting against the German romantic tradition, but his views had influence upon philosophers of a different persuasion. Brentano maintained that the knowledge which introspection brings is a knowledge of mental acts, and for this reason psychology should consist in the study of such acts. This view constituted a quite different approach to the mind from that of the Sensationalists. Brentano held that every mental act is related to an immanent object, and in order to characterize this he revived the scholastic terminology of 'intentional objects'—an intentional object being a sort of cognate or internal accusative to the act, e.g. the judgment to the act of judgment. He thought that three main classes of mental act could be distinguished: presentation, judgment and interest. The first is that act by which the mind has awareness of an object, and although he maintained that no sensation is independent of judgment, he thought that it was *in principle* possible to distinguish presentation from judgment. The importance of this view lies not only in the fact that he gave a new orientation to psychology, but also in the fact that he revived the view that sensation is not *actually* separable from judgment. This in turn led to a general acceptance of the view that pure sensations are a fiction.

Conscious opposition to Sensationalism as such began a little later. F. H. Bradley wrote his *Principles of Logic* in 1883, and he thereafter wrote many articles on matters related to philosophical psychology. William James wrote his *Principles of Psychology* in 1890, H. Bergson his *Les données immédiates de la conscience* in 1889 and G. F. Stout his *Analytic Psychology* in 1896. But the first publication which constituted a direct reaction to Sensationalism was James Ward's *Encyclopaedia Britannica* article on 'Psychology', which he wrote in 1885. This article was sufficient to exact

---

aware of whole objects, i.e. by it sensations are synthesized in clear consciousness. The Wundtian approach was taken further by E. B. Titchener, who substituted 'attention' for 'apperception'. Titchenerian 'structuralism' consisted of attempts to analyse all mental contents into sensations, images and feelings with varying degrees of clarity. Attention is merely the process whereby sensations or images attain such clarity. There is little which is active about it.

a number of concessions from Bain. Ward's views were incorporated much later in the more accessible *Psychological Principles*.

Ward uses the term 'sensation' in roughly the same way in which the Sensationalists had used it, although he often substitutes for it the term 'presentation' (from the German *vorstellung*). He distinguishes between sensation and perception (*Psych. Princ.*, p. 142) by saying that perception involves the *recognition* of a sensation, its location and its reference to a thing. To perceive something is thus not merely to have a sensation. Sensations are, to use a term which Stout was to use and which Ward later adopted, *anoetic* (op. cit., p. 317)—a sensation 'brings along with it' nothing but itself. But Ward stresses also that pure sensations are really a product of analysis only: that is to say that we do not in our experience find sensations which are then combined and connected to form higher types of consciousness. 'The pure sensation', Ward says, 'we may regard as a psychological myth' (op. cit., p. 143). This view was to provide the keynote of much of the succeeding discussion of Sensationalist principles; it did indeed reverse the whole tendency of those principles. Ward was strongly opposed to the view which he called 'Presentationism'—the view that in discussing mental phenomena it is possible to leave out of consideration altogether the part played by the 'active subject'. The Sensationalists had done exactly this. Ward sought to restore a Kantian emphasis upon the understanding. To this end he lays emphasis upon the notion of 'attention', stressing the point that the mind must *attend* to presentations as well as receive them. Some part of any account of psychological functions must therefore be concerned with the results of such attention.

The second point which Ward stresses is that it is impossible to conceive of sensations or presentations as point-like or atomic. He insists that sensations must be thought to have not only intensive qualities but also what he called 'extensity'. This extensity must be distinguished from extension; for sensations are not literally extended. Unless sensations had extensity, Ward thinks, spatial perception would be impossible. Thus he says (op. cit., p. 145), 'The first condition of spatial experience seems to lie in what has been noted above as the extensity of sensation. This much we may allow is original; for the longer we reflect the more clearly we see that no combination or association of sensations varying only in intensity and quality, not even if motor presentations were among them, will account for this element in our spatial perception.' Later (op. cit., p. 149) he expresses surprise that this has not been noticed before. Ward is here still operating within the terms of reference provided by the view that he is disputing. He accepts the view that perception consists, at any rate in part, of sensations which can properly be said to refer to something; he wishes only to argue about the character of those sensations. Nevertheless his general point remains—that unless we had some way of perceiving in general that things are extended, we could not perceive where they are or of what size they are. And this is enough to upset the foundations on which Sensationalism was built.

On Ward's view, consciousness consists not of a series of discrete sensations but primarily of what he calls the 'presentational continuum'. Experience presents a continuum both in spatial extensity and in time. Individual presentations are differentiated out of this continuum. It is for this reason, among others, that the pure sensation is a psychological myth; it is at the most an artificial product of analysis. This notion of the continuity of consciousness came to play a large part in the writings of the period.

In several articles written in succeeding years Bradley points to the same moral. In the paper on 'Association and Thought' (*Collected Essays*, I. p. 209), he says, 'We must get rid of the idea that our mind is a train of perishing existences, that so long as they exist have separate being and, so to speak, are coupled up by another sort of thing which we call relations. If we turn to what is given this is not what we find, but rather a continuous mass of presentation in which the separation of a single element from all context is never observed, and where, if I may use the expression, no one ever saw a carriage, and still less a coupling, divided from its train. . . . Hence the Atomism must go wholly, and the associative links must be connexions of content, not conjunctions of existences; in other words, Association marries only universals.'[1] And he goes on later to say (p. 212), 'Every mental

[1] Cf. F. H. Bradley, *Collected Essays*, II. p. 376, 'What is immediately experienced is not a collection of pellets or a "cluster", as it used to be called, of things like grapes, together with other things called relations that serve as

element (to use a metaphor) strives to make itself a whole or to lose itself in one, and it will not have its company assigned to it by mere conjunction in presentation. . . . To speak more strictly, each element tends (that is, moves unless prevented) by means of fusion and redintegration to give itself a context through identity of content, and in the result which is so made the element may not survive in a distinguishable form.' This second passage indicates that while insisting on the continuity of consciousness Bradley still feels compelled to talk of elements. But he also distinguishes between the elements of consciousness and the thought which is expressed through them. Thought is concerned only with universals, and it is that which is universal which provides the connection between the parts of consciousness.

The effect of Bradley's view is to distinguish (as the Sensationalists would not) between thought and mere presentation; it is also to stress again that pure presentation is an artificial abstraction. Hence when Bradley comes to discuss space-perception (in the paper entitled 'In What Sense are Psychical States Extended?' —*Collected Papers*, II. pp. 349 ff.), he hesitates to follow Ward in attributing extensity to sensations. While he agrees that 'the perceived spatial world' cannot arise from 'what is quite non-spatial', he hesitates about the notion of extensity. He does so because he thinks that (1) when we observe something, either we seem to become acquainted with something which implies space outright or we are confronted with mere volume, and (2) volume is not identical with space. In other words, the qualities which sensations may possess include something which may be called 'volume', but this is not in itself sufficient to give an idea of extension. Perceiving things as extended is different from merely having sensations which possess volume, and if we do perceive things as extended we must already have the concept of space.

Similar tendencies can be seen in Stout's writings, although here perhaps the influence of Brentano shows itself to a greater extent. Stout distinguishes explicitly between sentience and thought as quite distinct mental functions. 'Presentation considered as having an existence relatively independent of thought,' he says (*Analytic Psychology*, I. p. 50), 'may be called Sentience, or

---

a kind of stalk to the cluster. On the contrary, what at any time is experienced is a whole with certain aspects which can be distinguished but, as so distinguished, are abstractions'.

anoetic consciousness. Thought and sentience are fundamentally different functions.' But he does not think that a purely anoetic consciousness can in fact be detected. 'We have no sufficient warrant for asserting that any experience of a normal human being is so completely anoetic that it has no objective reference whatever' (op. cit., p. 180). Hence in giving an analysis of the phenomena of the mind it is necessary to start first with forms of apprehension; and the apprehension of a whole need not entail apprehension of its details. We can have an implicit apprehension of an object without apprehending its parts. Since the Sensationalists had held that any apprehension of a whole must be built up out of individual sensations, Stout's view amounts once again to an explicit rejection of Sensationalism.

Stout classifies perception as a form of apprehension, and he insists that, like other forms of cognition, it always involves a reference to something other than the modification of subjective consciousness.[1] 'By simple perception', he says (op. cit., II. p. 4), 'is meant the immediate identification and distinction of an object presented to the senses.' Because perception involves the recognition of an object and the discrimination of it from other objects, it involves what Stout calls 'noetic synthesis'. This, he maintains, differs fundamentally from mere association. Recognition, for example, is not merely the having of an idea which happens to have been triggered off by association with whatever is presented to the senses; it involves the bringing of what is presented to the senses under an ordered system of ideas. Stout stresses the mechanical nature of association and the consequent applicability of the notion only to the more mechanical forms of thought. At the same time he stresses that thought proper, which is to be brought under the general heading of 'apperception', is not mechanical in this way. He does not deny that association may play a part in the perception of objects, but he insists that there must also be 'apprehension of the whole which determines the order and connection of the apprehensions of the parts' (op. cit., II. p. 41). In other words, recognition of an object involves the

[1] Stout sometimes says that the experience itself is apprehended as part of something other than itself. Cf. *Manual of Psychology* 5th ed., p. 676—'The sensible appearance is itself an actual sensation. But it is also an appearance of something other than itself. It is an appearance of what seems to the percipient to be a physical object.'

bringing to bear upon it of a system of concepts which determines how we see the parts of the object also.

Stout's discussion is not always very clear, although his later *Manual of Psychology* is much clearer. But the general trend of his argument is to reverse the tendencies of Sensationalism in a direction which is more like that taken by Kant and the Idealists. Atomism is rejected and emphasis is laid upon the part played in perception by understanding and thought. With this goes the view that sensations as such are, if anything, a product of analysis. In contradistinction to Sensationalism, it is Stout's view that we may have an implicit awareness of a whole before explicit awareness of the parts. This view has been taken as an anticipation of Gestalt Psychology, but, while it is so, it should be noted that Bradley and many others at this time made similar anticipations. Indeed, Gestalt Theory is, *via* Husserl, part of the same reaction to Sensationalism.

It is perhaps in William James and in Bergson that the issues emerge most clearly. Both of these philosophers wished to take a biological and functional view of the mind. That is to say that they wished in the main to treat man and his psychological function from a biological point of view, stressing what we *do* in thinking, perceiving, etc., rather than what passes through our minds. But their tendencies in this direction are within the context of the older tradition. Because philosophers of this tradition, like the Sensationalists, tried to deal with all mental phenomena by discussing the structure of the contents of the mind—how they are built up from initial sensations—they may be called by contrast 'structuralists'. Ward still shows evidence of structuralism in his view of presentations, despite his emphasis on activity. Bradley and Stout perhaps show less evidence of it, the former because of his emphasis on thought and understanding, the latter because of the influence of Brentano's act-psychology. Both James and Bergson, on the other hand, give the appearance of wishing to discuss psychological functions *via* a discussion of the contents of the mind. This produces interesting though confused doctrines.

The central notion with which James operates is that of a feeling or state of consciousness. In using the term 'feeling' he shows what he has inherited from the Sensationalists, and he is very much opposed to the notion of 'a permanently existing "idea" or *Vorstellung* which makes its appearance before the footlights of consciousness at periodical intervals' (*Principles of Psychology*, I. p. 236). Indeed, anything savouring of Idealism was to James a *bête-noire*. He is, on the other hand, equally opposed to what he calls the 'mind-stuff theory', with its assumption of a kind of mind-dust. This latter theory is in effect Sensationalism given an epiphenomenalist twist (e.g. by Herbert Spencer); according to it sensations may be viewed as mental particles which can be loose or detached from the mind. James rejects the theory on two main grounds. Firstly, sensations do not combine in an arithmetical way (cf. J. S. Mill on 'mental chemistry'). One state of consciousness is, he says, a single thing, and the taste of lemonade is not the taste of lemon plus the taste of sugar, nor is a 'feeling of yellowness' the 'feeling of redness' plus the 'feeling of greenness', even though when red and green light fall together on the same retina we see yellow (op. cit., I. pp. 157–8—the awkwardness of his use of the word 'feeling' is here obvious). Secondly, as he says in his chapter on 'The Stream of Thought', all states of consciousness are one's own—although he fears that the facts of dissociation of personality may require a gesture towards the mind-stuff theory. After his earlier discussion of that theory (op. cit., I. p. 180), he said, 'Many readers have certainly been saying to themselves for the last few pages: "Why on earth doesn't the poor man say *the Soul* and have done with it?"' James has no wish to say that, but he is continually in the position where he feels that he may have to do so.

James feels that too great a stress on the fact that states of consciousness are the property of a person may lead him to espouse the notion of a soul. It is partly because of this that, despite his general functionalist leanings, he tries in effect to construct mental activities out of mental contents. That is to say that he tends to start from the contents of the mind, the states of consciousness, and only then goes on to ask how the activities of the mind manifest themselves in these. This sometimes leads to paradoxical results. Like Hume, for example, James thinks that by mere inspection of states of consciousness it is impossible to discover one which corresponds to the self purely and simply; although he also thinks that it is certain feelings of motions in the head and throat that make us suppose that we have a self. What then is the self? James believes that it must be constituted by each passing thought. We are, as it were, a series of selves, not just one.

James is forced into this position only because, like Hume, he starts from states of consciousness, or impressions and ideas, rather than from the fact that we think, perceive, etc.

The ambiguity of his position is nowhere more clear than in his famous chapter on 'The Stream of Thought'. He begins the chapter by stating five propositions which he proposes to discuss: '(1) Every thought tends to be part of a personal consciousness; (2) Within each personal consciousness thought is always changing; (3) Within each personal consciousness thought is sensibly continuous; (4) It always appears to deal with objects independent of itself; (5) It is interested in some parts of these objects to the exclusion of others, and welcomes or rejects—*chooses* from among them, in a word—all the while.' James spends relatively the biggest amount of time in discussing propositions 2 and 3. He says very little *à propos* of proposition 1, and, as we have already seen, he gets into further difficulties on this issue in the next chapter, on 'The Consciousness of Self'. His main interest in discussing propositions 4 and 5 is to attack his *bête-noire*, Idealism. Hence most of his positive views are to be found in the discussion of propositions 2 and 3. The outcome of this discussion is the doctrine of the stream of thought.

James maintains that no state of consciousness 'once gone can recur and be identical with what it was before' (op. cit., I. p. 230). The contents of the mind, that is, are always changing. Hume had thought that this entailed that the mind is like a theatre in which separate and distinct scenes are staged. James does not accept this conclusion, for he says (op. cit., I. p. 239), 'Consciousness, then, does not appear to itself chopped up in bits. Such words as "chain" or "train" do not describe it fitly as it presents itself in the first instance. It is nothing jointed; it flows. A "river" or a "stream" are the metaphors by which it is most naturally described. *In talking of it hereafter, let us call it the stream of thought, of consciousness, or of subjective life.*' In some respects James presents his view as if it were meant merely to be a description of our thought, but it is really more than this.[1] The fact that he applies his view to 'subjective life' in general shows that it is meant to provide a new account of the mind which will be an antithesis to Sensationalism. James is thus in company with Bradley, Ward and Stout.

While James represents thought as a stream, he realizes also

---
[1] Cf. my 'The Stream of Thought', *Proc. Arist. Soc.*, 1955–56.

that we suppose ourselves to have distinct thoughts. For this reason he describes the stream as having variations in its rate of flow. Altering his simile, he says that thought is 'like a bird's life: it seems to be made of an alternation of flights and perches'. And combining the two similes, he calls the 'resting-places' the 'substantive parts', and the places of flight the 'transitive parts' of 'the stream of thought'. But how can a continuous stream be made up of parts some of which are substantive? James' solution is to argue, as against the Sensationalists, that there must be, firstly, feelings of relations, and secondly, feelings of tendency. The feelings of relations link the substantive parts of the stream, and the feelings of tendency guarantee that when we begin a train of thought we know how to go on and know roughly where the train of thought is going to take us. But these additional feelings add only to the variety of the feelings in the stream of consciousness; they do not make that stream literally continuous. To achieve this result James supposes that each thought or state of consciousness has a 'psychic-fringe' (due to faint brain-processes). The fringes of succcessive thoughts overlap, so providing a kind of continuity. Each thought is like a saddle-back in the specious present, and each thought overlaps other saddle-backs in the past and future.

In a footnote (op. cit., I. p. 258) James tries to meet a criticism to the effect that his psychic fringe acts as a kind of glue with which sensations are stuck together (Wundt's *apperception* had had something of this role). He replies that the fringe is in fact 'part of the *object cognized*,—substantive *qualities* and *things* appearing to the mind in a *fringe of* relations'. And he denies that there are any discrete sensations in the stream.[1] Here James appears to be on the threshold of distinguishing between thinking and that of which we think, and the consistent retention of that distinction would do much to resolve his problem. That problem arises from the fact that while consciousness appears continuous we have individual thoughts and experiences. But the continuity results from the fact that thoughts are always *someone's* thoughts; they are not loose. The discreteness, on the other hand, results from the fact that there are distinguishable items which we have thoughts *of.*

[1] In James' view all relations are external, not internal to their terms as the Idealists supposed. There could, therefore, be no solution of his problem by appeal to Idealist principles.

Accounts of what is going on in my mind and accounts of what I am thinking *of* may be accounts of thinking at different levels and from different points of view.[1] One needs, indeed, to distinguish between the thinking, the words, images or ideas which may be the vehicles of thought, and the objects of thought. James makes no such distinctions, at any rate consistently. Feelings of relations, for example, are meant to provide both an awareness of the relations between the objects of thought and a link between the images, sensations or other vehicles of thought which constitute the substantive parts of the stream of consciousness. In sum, instead of seeing that the continuity of thought or consciousness is provided by the fact that it is we who think and that all our thoughts are *our* thoughts—instead, that is, of stressing the active part which we play in thinking—James tries to build up a continuum out of elements of which consciousness is supposed to consist. The Sensationalist tradition dies hard.

James' treatment of sensation and perception rests in part upon proposition 5 of the chapter on 'The Stream of Thought'—the proposition which asserts that thought selects from its objects. It rests also upon the distinction which he makes between 'knowledge by acquaintance' and 'knowledge about'. Sensation differs from perception firstly in the simplicity of its contents (although James emphasizes that in ordinary usage the words 'sensation' and 'perception' are not definitely distinguished), and secondly in that the function of sensations is to provide acquaintance with a fact, while that of perception is to provide knowledge about a fact. But James stresses also the point that the pure sensation is an abstraction, or rather that such sensations 'can only be realized in the earliest days of life' (op. cit., II. p. 7). The mind of a baby, James says, may be a 'blooming, buzzing confusion'. By his first sensation the baby is acquainted with the Universe, but he *perceives* nothing, because perception involves selection from this mass of sensations. Perception of objects, being a knowledge about objects, involves learning—'every perception is an acquired perception'.

While perception involves selection from sensations, it is not in itself a mere complex of sensations. It is, James says, 'one state of mind or nothing' (op. cit., II. p. 80). It cannot be a mere complex of sensations, because it is a knowledge about, not a mere

[1] See again my 'The Stream of Thought', *Proc. Arist. Soc.*, 1955-56.

acquaintance with, objects. Hence it is that perception involves selection from the stream of consciousness plus the processes of association and reproduction. In discussing space-perception, James insists in a similar way that whereas sensations themselves have the original property of 'voluminousness' (cf. Bradley's 'volume' and Ward's 'extensity'), the actual perception of the details of the spatial properties of things can come only through learning. But he adds that it would be wrong to think that perception involves inference, whether conscious or unconscious. Helmholtz had used the notion of unconscious inferences in cases where what is seen is perceived differently from what would be expected on the assumption that the way in which one sees a thing is determined by sensations alone. That is to say that he used the notion when perception does not correspond exactly to the details of the 'retinal image', as it should do according to what the Gestalt Psychologists called the 'constancy hypothesis'. On that hypothesis the pattern of stimulation on the retina of the eye should result in sensations exactly corresponding to it. We nevertheless sometimes perceive things differently from what would be expected on that assumption; in these cases Helmholtz suggested that the deviation from expectation is due to inferences which we make. But since we are not generally aware of making such inferences they were supposed to be unconscious. James is opposed to this view and to any suggestion that perception involves judgment. On this view, the 'knowledge about' which comprises perception is a result of the formation of habits due to physiological activity. James' views on space-perception and our perception of objects are developed in this spirit.

Bergson's point of view is remarkably similar to that of James, and although their views were evolved independently of each other, James welcomed Bergson's conclusions, especially in formulating the theory which he called 'Radical Empiricism'.[1] Like James, Bergson takes a biological view of our perception of objects. What we distinguish in the world around us is, he thinks, a function of the needs of our organism (*Matière et Mémoire*, 2nd ed., p. 258). The space and time of which we are conscious are both continuous. For that reason the movements which we make are also continuous, since they involve both space and time. Because space and time are continuous it is impossible to build up

[1] See W. James, *Essays in Radical Empiricism*.

our perception of them from unextended sensations, as the Sensationalists supposed. Such sensations, which Bergson calls *perceptions pures*, are a product of analysis only. More than this—Bergson thinks it important to draw a general distinction between sensations or affections and perceptions. An affection is something which may be experienced in our body, but we perceive things outside us; and, as already indicated, these things are distinguished, according to the needs of the organism, out of the continuity which is space and time.

According to Bergson, the body possesses automatic tendencies to respond to a stimulus. Affections correspond to such simple movements of the body in response to a stimulus; but a perception is not composed of affections of this kind, for it is *inversely proportional* to the tendency to automatic response to a stimulus. For this reason, perception and sensation themselves are in a sense inversely proportional. Perception corresponds not to an actual movement in response to a stimulus but to a possible one (op. cit., p. 50). But that perception has its rationale in the tendency of the body to movement is central to the theory and gives it its biological flavour. It is only through such movements that we gain a consciousness of an extended world. Our ideas of movement are indivisible and constitute the stuff of consciousness (op. cit., pp. 207, 258). Perception of an object is founded upon an awareness of the movements of our body which are possible in relation to it. In so far as an object stimulates our body in such a way as to call out an automatic movement, we may have a sensation, but no perception. For the latter to occur, there must be no automatic response, but an awareness of what responses might have been made. In this way Bergson distinguishes sensation from perception and at the same time founds both upon the biological functioning of the body. Perception involves the active projection on to an object of an image similar to it—an image which is a function of the possible movements of our body in relation to that object.

Like James, Bergson stresses the continuity of consciousness in time as well as the continuity of space of which we are conscious. The discrimination of things out of space and the separation of elements out of the stream of consciousness are both a product of our biological needs. In *Matière et Mémoire* Bergson concentrates on the former point, but in the earlier *Les Données Immédiates de la*

Conscience he faces the same problem as that which James faced in his chapter on 'The Stream of Thought'—i.e. how the continuity of consciousness in time can be formed out of the ideas of which we are aware. There Bergson is concerned to distinguish between the time with which physics deals by spatializing it and the time of which we are conscious, the time which we live through. This latter time Bergson calls *durée*, and since the series of events which constitute consciousness forms a developing series, Bergson holds that there are in consciousness no repeatable events, any more than there are such in the history of the *whole* universe.[1] For where every event is a development of what has gone before, each event is unique by definition. But how can we reconcile the fact that we live through a continuous consciousness with the fact that we find ourselves having distinct ideas and perceptions? This is the same problem as that of James, and Bergson deals with it in a similar way. Instead of saying that each idea has a fringe which overlaps that of other ideas, he says that the ideas themselves interpenetrate (a *pénétration mutuelle*). And the development which is constituted by the interpenetrating ideas which we have is determined by a vital impulse (the *élan vital*).

This last motion signalizes Bergson's tendency (and the same tendency is there in a lesser form in James) to depreciate 'intellectualism' in favour of 'life'. His reaction against the more mechanical aspects of Sensationalism was in part a reaction in accordance with that tendency—a rather mystical reaction. But this does not mean that the reaction was not in any way justified. James and Bergson, indeed, form a reaction against Sensationalism which is determined by biological considerations. But in distinguishing as they do between sensation and perception, bringing perception into relation with the workings of the organism, they make an important contribution to the philosophy of mind. In other respects they are at one with the other philosophers discussed in this section, in stressing the continuity of consciousness.

[1] Cf. Bergson's *Creative Evolution*, ch. 1.

10
THE 20th CENTURY—
SENSE DATA
AND PHENOMENOLOGY

(i) INTRODUCTION

THE reaction discussed in the last chapter was primarily a reaction against a certain philosophy of mind, and it came from philosophers of quite different schools. The prime reaction in philosophy at the beginning of this century, however, was one of a metaphysical sort—a reaction against Idealism. As such it was not in the main concerned with the philosophy of mind for its own sake. The move towards Realism which took place in Great Britain and America, and to some extent on the continent of Europe, in the early years of this century resulted from a preoccupation with the problem of the nature of reality. For this reason, most discussions of perception carried on during this period and since have been discussions within a certain metaphysical and epistemological context. Less interest has been shown in the nature of perception for its own sake. The main philosophical trend has been to assume that in perception we are directly aware of something 'given', something which is independent of our judgments. There have been occasional disputes concerning the exact nature of the 'given', but philosophers have more often devoted themselves to the problem of the relation between that which is given and our perception of the everyday world around us. They have not questioned the statement that *something* is 'given'.

20TH CENTURY—SENSE-DATA AND PHENOMENOLOGY

Phenomenology, which is perhaps the dominant philosophical theory in this field on the continent of Europe, had a somewhat similar realist ancestry. Brentano's emphasis on the objects of mental acts led to an attempt on the part of Meinong to assess the constitution of the world in terms of such objects. Since these objects can be opposed to the mental acts which we perform with regard to them, Meinong's view may be classified as a form of Realism. It has seemed an extreme view to many, and Russell has called it a 'Meinongian jungle' because of the numerous kinds of entity with which Meinong supposed the world to be populated.[1] Husserl, the founder of phenomenology, started from somewhat the same point of view, although his Realism was to become one which, because of its emphasis on essences, may be characterized as 'Platonic'. Husserl also came to stress the point that philosophical inquiry necessitates the 'bracketing-off' of all presuppositions. The consequent search for the pure experience, free from all presuppositions, has had, therefore, something in common with the search for sense-data, or immediate objects of perception, in 20th-century Empiricism. Nevertheless the findings which have been claimed to result from the 'bracketing-off' technique have had little in common with the sensations of Sensationalism, and Phenomenology might therefore be included among the reactions to that theory. The same may be said of Gestalt Theory in psychology; fo that theory stems from Phenomenology. Husserl's epistemology is more in the Cartesian tradition than in that of British Empiricism (as is manifest from his *Méditations Cartésiennes*). In consequence he finds that ultimately the only 'given', the only absolute, is consciousness itself. In this respect, his views have points in common with Hegel and German Idealism.[2]

A phenomenological account of the world of perception, being an account of how the world directly appears to us, may have bearings upon certain views of sense-data. Any attempt to give an exact account of what is 'given' in perception may be described as 'phenomenological'. Some of H. H. Price's views on perception (in his book *Perception*) are phenomenological in this sense—especially his claim that sense-data must be considered to have

[1] It is only fair to point out that the extent of Meinong's jungle has often been exaggerated.
[2] That a realist ancestry should thus lead back to idealism is a curious fact noted by J. A. Passmore, *A Hundred Years of Philosophy*, p. 197.

depth or voluminousness. Other British philosophers, however, have shown little interest in such matters, since they have been concerned only with the *logical* requirements of the notion of a 'given'. Indeed, A. J. Ayer (*Foundations of Empirical Knowledge*, p. 116) explicitly denies any concern with empirical facts about the 'given'. More interest has been shown in the relation of what is 'given' to what is not, and attacks on 'sense-datum philosophy' have largely been directed at the accounts of this relation. But any theory concerned with the relation between sense-data and so-called material objects which neglects to demonstrate the existence of sense-data and explain their nature is, to say the least of it, rather unreal.

The truth of the matter is that the notion of a sense-datum was introduced in the first place to fulfil certain logical or epistemological requirements, and these requirements have always seemed more fundamental to sense-datum theorists than the requirement that the notion should be given content by reference to the facts of experience. To phenomenologists, on the other hand, the nature of experience has been the main thing, although here again the belief has been expressed that some experience may be discovered which is pure in the sense that it is free from judgments or inferences on our part.

(ii) SENSE-DATA

The term 'sense-datum' was probably first introduced into philosophy by G. E. Moore in lectures given in 1910–11 but published only in 1953 under the title *Some Main Problems of Philosophy*. Bertrand Russell read these lectures and used the term in his own *Problems of Philosophy* (1913). Even before this, Moore had, in his famous paper *The Refutation of Idealism*, sought to make a distinction between yellow and a sensation of yellow, with the aim of making a general distinction between objects and our experience of them. In this way, he thought, it could be shown that it is not true that 'to be is to be perceived'. And in his paper *The Nature and Reality of Objects of Perception* (1905)[1] he distinguished between physical objects and what we 'actually see', e.g. a coloured patch. In *Some Main Problems of Philosophy* he called that which we actually

[1] Both this paper and that previously mentioned are to be found in his *Philosophical Studies*.

see or 'directly apprehend' a sense-datum, and identified sense-data with entities such as coloured patches. Russell used the notion in a similar way, although he applied it, not to the coloured patch, but to its colour, shape or size (as Moore also did on occasion). Moreover, in *Problems of Philosophy*, ch. 5, Russell listed sense-data as one of the kinds of thing of which we have knowledge by acquaintance, as opposed to knowledge by description.

The connection of the notion of a sense-datum with the notions of direct apprehension or knowledge by acquaintance is important. For, however sense-data are to be identified (and, as we have already seen, they were not identified unequivocally even by Moore), it is as objects of direct apprehension that they are to be defined. It is to apply to such an object that the notion was first introduced. A sense-datum is supposed to be the one firm thing in what we take ourselves to perceive; it is literally a *datum*. Moore always found great difficulty in deciding how sense-data are to be identified. He was never sure whether they are to be considered as parts of the surfaces of physical objects. If they are, what of illusions and hallucinations? For in these cases we are still having experiences which are perceptual, and they are thus to be interpreted in terms of the apprehension of sense-data. If, on the other hand, sense-data are not parts of the surfaces of physical objects, what is the relation between them and physical objects?

It is tempting to say that in illusions and hallucinations we must be seeing *something*. Since the experience is perceptual, what we see must be something common to veridical perceptions, illusions and hallucinations. It cannot be a physical object, since in an hallucination there is no such object there, and in an illusion the object is either not there or is not seen as it actually is. What we see, it may be said, is always a sense-datum. But this argument is highly questionable. While in these cases we are certainly having experiences of a certain kind—we are, perhaps, having analogous sensations—we are certainly not *seeing* something in every case. In an hallucination we are *ex hypothesi* seeing nothing, since there is nothing there to see; in an illusion we may be seeing something, namely an object, but we are not seeing it *as* it is. It may be granted that ordinary language permits us to speak of people seeing a mirage and perhaps of people seeing ghosts; but the conventions for the use of these expressions are well understood, and they certainly provide no warrant for invoking the notion of a sense-datum.[1]

Illusions and hallucinations do, however, provide the most persuasive reasons for invoking sense-data, since in these cases we are not seeing what is actually there. We are seeing an 'appearance', it is sometimes said—either the appearance of what is actually there or an appearance in the sense of what appears to us to be there. But even if this move be admitted (as it should *not*, since, as already indicated, there is no general warrant for saying that we see anything in these cases), not *any* way in which things appear to us could provide the justification for saying that we are then confronted with a sense-datum. Sense-data are that which we directly apprehend; or, in other words, something about which it is logically impossible to be mistaken. As Russell puts it, a sense-datum must be the object of knowledge by acquaintance, not merely of knowledge by description. Being the one firm thing in what we see, the sense-datum must be such as to provide the basis for our judgments about that which is not 'given'.[2]

The question that next arises is whether the descriptions 'appearance' and 'object of direct apprehension' which are applied to sense-data are mutually compatible. As already indicated, the primary notion here is that of direct apprehension, a notion which brings with it that of incorrigibility or indubitability. Whatever else sense-data are, it should be impossible to be mistaken about them. The reasons for saying that we do not directly perceive physical objects are that we are sometimes mistaken in our identification or description of them and it is always logically possible that we should be so. It is supposed that if this is so there must be *something* which we directly perceive and about which we cannot be mistaken. This is the so-called 'argument from illusion'. The use of the expression 'directly' here is not the ordinary one; we are not said to perceive physical objects indirectly in the same sense as that in which we might be said to perceive something indirectly

---

[1] Such usages, however, should prevent too cavalier an assertion that we speak only of seeing what is actually there. In ordinary language, we may be said to see whatever it is *contextually correct* to say that we see.

[2] Cf. H. H. Price, *Perception*, ch. 1, for the view that something 'given' is required to be the object of thought. It must be admitted that H. A. Prichard denied that sense-data were objects of knowledge at all, but the subsequent account given by him of the relation between our sensing of sense-data and our perception of material objects is exceedingly obscure.

in a mirror. We would not, in the use in question, be said to perceive something directly (and the same considerations apply to the use of the word 'actually') unless there were no room for doubt about that something. As it is always logically, if not practically, possible to raise doubts about what we suppose ourselves to see, we may in the search for the sense-datum find ourselves progressively reducing our claims to what we directly perceive. But the distinction between logical and practical possibility is here important. There comes a stage when it is in practice impossible to have doubts concerning what one is seeing; but this is no guarantee that one has reached the stage at which one can be said to perceive the thing in question directly (in the meaning of that word which is here in question). In other words, the question what we directly perceive is a metaphysical question, not a practical one. And it may well be asked what it has to do with perception in the ordinary sense.

The notion of a sense-datum can be given a formal definition in terms of the impossibility of error, and we have then an adequately defined metaphysical notion (a notion, incidentally, which makes it possible also to define that of a 'material object', since in discussions about perception the motion of a material object is generally opposed to that of a sense-datum and is given a sense only thereby). But metaphysical notions are of little use unless they can be given an application. How then is one to identify a sense-datum? It has been seen that Moore tended to identify sense-data with coloured patches; but it does not, on the face of it, seem that coloured patches are such that we cannot make mistakes about them. Indeed Moore often expressed doubt, despite protests to the contrary by, for example, Ayer,[1] whether a sense-datum could not be other than it appears to be. Such doubts seem possible about coloured patches but not about sense-data if defined in the way already outlined. What then is to count as a sense-datum? Not sensations, clearly, for, as Moore pointed out, a sense-datum is the object of an experience, while a sensation is an experience itself. But what else can it be?

Some sense-datum philosophers have tended to proceed as if the notion of a sense-datum has been given an application, and have gone on to ask what theory about the perception of material objects is made plausible thereby. Are material objects to be

[1] See his 'The Terminology of Sense-data' in *Philosophical Essays*, ch. 4.

considered as objects whose existence is inferred from that of sense-data (according to the causal or representative theory of perception)? But if that is so, what is the basis of the inference? Or is one version or another of phenomenalism to be adopted, i.e. the view that material objects can be reduced to sense-data, either because they are mere bundles of sense-data or because they are logical constructions out of sense-data (i.e. because any statement about a material object is translatable into a series of statements about sense-data)? But no finite number of sense-datum statements can ever be equivalent to a material object statement, since the number of possible appearances which an object may manifest are unlimited in number. Hence it seems that the translation cannot be carried out, and material objects cannot be reduced to sense-data. In sum, neither the representative theory nor phenomenalism is a satisfactory theory of perception.[1] But the whole discussion is unreal if no application is first given to the notion of a sense-datum. The phenomenalist theories which Berkeley and Mill put forward (if they can be called phenomenalist) at least identified the direct objects of perception with sensations.

It is at this point that it is tempting to have recourse to phenomenology, to approach the matter from the opposite direction, so to speak. Might it not be better to study how things appear to us and then ask whether any of these appearances can be characterized as basic? It has already been noted that Price's account of sense-data is in part phenomenological in this sense. He sets out to describe how things appear to us in the most basic sense, and he concludes, for example, that sense-data must at least have the property of depth, and not be mere patches. But how can any such account of sense-data provide a *logical* guarantee of freedom from error? What is perhaps a final attempt to deal with the matter along these lines has been made by Ayer in his *Problem of Knowledge* (ch. 3, esp. section iii).

Ayer attempts to introduce sense-data by considering the progressive reductions which we should make in our claims concerning what we see, if we were to consider the possibilities of error. If I take myself to see a cigarette-case on the table, the errors which are at any rate logically possible owing to illusion and hallucination prevent there being a guarantee that I really do see a

[1] See A. J. Ayer, *The Problem of Knowledge*, ch. 3, sects. 5, 6, for further reasons for this conclusion.

cigarette-case. If I am persuaded by this point I may instead say that there appears or seems to be a cigarette-case there. Further, I may pass from this again to saying that there is an appearance of a cigarette-case or a seeming cigarette-case there, and this may be called a sense-datum. In this way sense-data are introduced *via* the notion of an appearance.

Various steps of this argument may be questioned. It is possible, for example, to dispute the move from saying that there appears to be an X to saying that there is an appearance of an X. Again, it might be pointed out that the ordinary use of 'appears' is to suggest that the object in question is other than it seems, so that doubt is conveyed by that use rather than certainty; but sense-data are thought to be, in some sense, epistemologically basic. It is this last notion, however, which provides the most pertinent objection. Sense-data must be basic in that, if a justification of our claims to perceive physical objects is to be provided by reference to them, an application must be given to the notion of a sense-datum which is independent of our knowledge of physical objects. Ayer has not done this; for he started from the notion of physical objects in considering the reduction of perceptual claims. Later in the chapter he maintains that it is only a contingent, psychological impossibility that we should not be able to fill out the notion of a sense-datum without reference to physical objects; it is not, he maintains, a logical impossibility. But on his account of the matter it *is* a logical impossibility. For, not only has he given no independent application to the notion of a sense-datum, but he has also given it no independent *sense*. That is to say that, on the account given in the *Problem of Knowledge*, sense-data are defined in terms of the appearances of physical objects. The only account given is phenomenological, so that to make reference to sense-data is to say how things appear to us. It is *not* claimed that sense-data are objects of direct perception, and thus incapable of giving rise to error.

This is the crux. It is possible to define a sense-datum by reference to direct apprehension, but one is then confronted with the problem of giving the notion so defined an application. What sort of thing is it of which we have a direct apprehension? But whether or not the notion can be given an application, it has been defined and given a sense by this procedure, and it has been established thereby as something basic. Alternatively, it is possible to give the notion a phenomenological application, i.e. an application in terms of appearances. In that case, however, it will not be epistemologically basic in the sense that our perception of physical objects can be explained and justified by reference to sense-data. For that to be possible it is necessary to give the notion of a sense-datum a sense which is independent of that of a physical object. The only possible way out seems to be to maintain that there are certain experiences which are epistemologically basic and which nevertheless have a phenomenological content, i.e. they must provide information about the world or its appearances. They must provide us with a direct acquaintance with something which is independent of ourselves.

Gilbert Ryle has objected to such an experience (*Concept of Mind*, ch. 7, esp. sections 3 and 4) on the grounds that it would be one drawn from two quite different categories: those of sensing and observing. A sense-datum is supposed to be the object which one senses, and yet the information which it provides can only be the result of observation. For this reason he argues that any attempt to justify what one observes in the world around us in terms of sense-data will generate an infinite regress; for the information given in the sense-datum—what one observes in sensing it—will itself require justification. Any resort to further sense-data can only have the same result, and so on *ad infinitum*. In other words, the information provided by any experience can always logically be called in question, while the bare experience itself can provide no backing for any information about the world. It would never be possible to make inferences from our sensations to the nature of the so-called external world if we had no prior knowledge of that world.

Wittgenstein, on the other hand, has made what is perhaps a more fundamental objection (*Philosophical Investigations*, I. 242–316)—that the whole notion of a language used of experiences prior to actual perception of objects is senseless. The usual way in which we speak of our experiences is derived from the ways in which we speak of things around us. The words which we use of our sensations, words like 'burning' and 'shooting' as used of pains, depend on analogies with physical processes. Could there be a language which we might use of our experiences which is independent of such analogies? Could there, in other words, be an intrinsically private language? Wittgenstein answers 'No', on the grounds that in such a context the essential conditions of a language are lacking. There could be no rules for the application of expressions, since there could be no criteria for the correct or incorrect application of these rules themselves. In using an expression of one experience when one had already used it of another, it would be impossible to say whether one was making a new decision to use that expression or whether one was acting in accordance with precedent. When a connection is made with a language used of a common world so that the application of rules of usage is publicly checkable, the use of language with regard to experiences is possible—but not otherwise.[1]

These arguments are, in my opinion, well taken. A pre-perceptual language is impossible. The notion of an experience which can provide us with information about the things around us (information which is thus in principle statable in language) is secondary to the notion of such things. Phenomenology is logically dependent upon our knowledge of a world independent of ourselves, and while the phenomenology of our experiences may be extremely rich and varied, it can never constitute a datum upon which our perception of the world may depend.

(iii) PHENOMENOLOGY

Since the issues have already been presented, it is possible to deal with phenomenology itself in a relatively brief way. It has already been pointed out that phenomenology is an attempt to give an account of the ways in which different things appear to consciousness. Included among those things will of course be the phenomena of perception. In consequence, Husserl initially defined phenomenology as a form of descriptive psychology. This account of the matter is in part true. Phenomenologists have provided interesting accounts of how things appear to us—the role which our body plays in how we see things, and so on. The phenomenological method has had some results within empirical psychology in so far as its aim is to provide an adequate and unprejudiced account of the phenomena to be dealt with. A by-product of this may well be the rejection of accounts of those phenomena

[1] Later at *Philosophical Investigations*, II. xi, Wittgenstein reinforces these conclusions by a discussion of seeing and 'seeing-as'.

arrived at, as a result of certain theories, in a relatively *a priori* way.

One of the results of Phenomenology was thus a further rejection of Sensationalism. Husserl noted this explicitly. In his *Méditations Cartésiennes* (p. 33) he says that in an analysis of perception it seems natural to start from sensations as 'given' and to suppose that we impose upon them a form (a *gestaltqualität*, as Von Ehrenfels called it). 'It may be added, however, as a refutation of "atomism" that the form (*gestalt*) is necessarily implied in the given, such that the whole is in itself prior to the parts.' It is just this notion which had been seized upon by the Gestalt Psychologists. Gestalt Theory stands upon the notion that we are 'given' wholes which are more than the sum of the parts.[1] It thus accepts the previous tradition in which Sensationalism stood, but rejects its detailed findings. According to Gestalt Theory the most important aspect of what we see and how we see it is the form or structure of the object, the perception of which, it is claimed, does not require learning because it is innately determined. Gestalt Psychology is essentially the application of this idea to different psychological problems.[2]

Similar refutations of 'sensory atomism' have been noted by other phenomenologists, e.g. by M. Merleau-Ponty, in his *La Phénoménologie de la Perception*. But Husserl is not prepared to leave the matter there. It is not in his view sufficient to say that in perception we are 'given' wholes rather than discrete sensations, as the Gestaltists insisted. And despite the fact that the Gestaltists have claimed that the perception of wholes is innately determined because such wholes are the object of a pure experience, Husserl has denied that pure experience is of this kind. Indeed, he has sometimes maintained that phenomenological reduction cannot be complete. In other words, what Husserl thinks of as a stage in phenomenological reduction—in the bracketing-off of all the presuppositions which experience involves—the Gestaltists have thought of as the end.

At other times Phenomenologists have behaved as if the pure experience can be isolated, although it is not what the Sensa-

---

[1] See Gestaltist writings *passim*, but especially M. Wertheimer, 'The General Theoretical Situation' in W. D. Ellis *A Source Book of Gestalt Psychology*, ch. 2.
[2] For further details see my *The Psychology of Perception*, ch. 4.

tionalists or the Gestaltists supposed it to be. In the passage mentioned above Husserl goes on to say, 'But the descriptive theory of consciousness, if it proceeds with an absolute radicalism, knows nothing of the given and wholes of that kind, except as preconceived notions. The starting-point is the pure, and for that matter inchoate, experience, which has to be brought to the pure expression of its own sense.' Merleau-Ponty argues similarly that it is necessary to isolate the phenomenal field, the pre-objective world, and discover its properties. The pre-objective world is that which is the object of perceptual consciousness when all ideas concerning the objective world around us have been 'bracketed-off'. In this it is important to avoid what Merleau-Ponty calls *le préjugé du monde*; that is to say that it is important to avoid attributing to experience properties which we already know to belong to the world which experience has discovered. It is this mistake (a mistake akin to that which William James called the 'stimulus error') which, in Merleau-Ponty's view, was committed by the Sensationalists.

An investigation of this pre-objective world would be an investigation of the categories applicable to perceptual consciousness prior (logically and perhaps temporally prior) to the construction of an objective world. Merleau-Ponty has much of interest to say about this. But the question may still be asked whether he has any right to assume that the necessary 'bracketing-off' has been complete.[1] May his account not be after all another account of how things appear to us under very special conditions?[2] As befits a 'descriptive psychology', phenomenology may largely be looked upon as an attempt to describe how things appear under different conditions. But once it is assumed that a pure experience can be discovered, the use of words like 'appears' becomes inappropriate. In saying that we are studying how things appear to us, we presuppose the notion of things and how they really are (for we use the word 'appears' very largely to make a contrast with how things really are). It is difficult in consequence to see how a description of appearances can be a description of pure experience.

[1] Cf. M. Kullman and C. Taylor, 'The Pre-objective World', *Rev. Metaphysics*, 1958.
[2] Cf. J. J. Gibson's account of the visual field in his *Perception of the Visual World* and my criticism that his visual field is merely the world as it appears to us under certain special conditions in 'The Visual Field and Perception', *Proc. Arist. Soc.*, Supp. Vol., 1957.

In this respect Phenomenology finds itself in the same dilemma as Ayer. Either we can look on the experience as basic or we can define it in terms of appearances, *but not both*. In so far as Phenomenology deserts descriptive psychology and enters epistemology it is confronted with this dilemma. The same may be said of Gestalt Theory. Its description of how things appear to us, i.e. as wholes and not as mere aggregates of parts, may be perfectly fair description, but the claim that such experiences are basic is as much an epistomological claim as the contrary theory of the Sensationalists. It is in consequence open to many of the same objections.

One final point is that, despite the richness of Phenomenologist descriptions of appearances, the concept of consciousness upon which so much weight is laid is a concept of a very general sort. I have throughout my discussion used terms like 'perceptual consciousness', but such terms give rise to as many questions as they answer. Husserl claimed that the final result of the bracketing-off process—that which cannot be bracketed off—is pure consciousness, and he has been followed in this by others, e.g. Merleau-Ponty and J. P. Sartre. But the notion of consciousness in general is as crude and indeterminate as the Cartesian *cogitatio* or *perception*. As such it may cover a multitude of sins. While it may be important to distinguish what may be said about forms of consciousness in general (the *pour soi*) from what may be said about physical things (the *en soi*), the details of forms of consciousness can scarcely be distinguished by relying on so general a concept. Sense-datum philosophers have shown little interest in the question of the nature of perception, except by assuming that something is 'given' in experience and that the rest is a matter of inference or construction. But the Phenomenologist concept of consciousness does little more of itself. Both the terms 'experience' and 'consciousness' are umbrella-words, and it is important to distinguish the different things that they may cover.

(iv) APPENDIX—20TH-CENTURY NEUROLOGY

The notion of sense-data has also seemed attractive to some 20th-century neurologists, e.g. Sir Russell Brain and J. R. Smythies.[1] It has seemed attractive because it has been taken as

[1] See Sir Russell Brain *Mind Perception and Science* and J. R. Smythies *Analysis of Perception*.

more or less axiomatic that perception is an experience which comes at the end of a number of physical and neurological processes. It is by dwelling on this that the representative theory of perception becomes apparently compelling. For it seems that the experience can be connected only indirectly with its cause. If perception is the having of an experience, it would seem that we cannot be directly aware of objects around us.

This conclusion, however, does not follow, since the whole question is whether perceiving is merely the having of an experience, whether, that is, it is constituted by the having of sensations or their equivalent. Sense-data have seemed attractive because they are a cross between sensations and objects of perception. In so far as they are like sensations they can be postulated as the end-term in a process of stimulation; in so far as they are objects of perception they can be thought of as more than bare experiences, something that we can be *aware of*. But it should be noted that *sensations* played a somewhat similar role in the 17th century, and this gives rise to a crucial point. It has sometimes been thought that the developments in modern knowledge about the processes underlying perception *must* shed light on the nature of perception itself, and that in consequence philosophers should pay a great deal of attention to physiological findings.[1] But while these findings are real enough they are essentially *of the same kind* as those of the 17th century, or indeed of the Presocratics. All the issues were available for consideration in those earlier periods of thought, and the central problem is that of the relevance of the processes underlying perception to the nature of perception itself. Because the problem is general, i.e. conceptual, no greater resort to details of factual knowledge will provide fresh insight.

[1] For a recent suggestion in this direction see R. J. Hirst *The Problems of Perception*.

11
CONCLUSION—
SENSATION AND
PERCEPTION

A HISTORY of a particular branch of philosophy would be of little *philosophical* value did it not lead, in one way or another, to further insights into the nature of the problems involved, and perhaps, to their solution. What then are sensation and perception?

The discussions in the previous chapters have at least revealed the following points. Firstly, an explicit distinction between sensation and perception has only rarely been made. It was made by Reid and Bergson, for example, but by few others. One reason for the failure to make this distinction may be that in many languages words connected with sensation and words connected with perception are interchangeable. Thus the Greek 'αἰσθάνεσθαι' (*aisthanesthai*), the Latin *sentire* and the French *sentir*, to take only some examples, can be translated equally 'to sense', 'to feel' or 'to perceive'. It would, however, be unwise to build any theory on this fact, since, as I pointed out at the beginning of this work, the fact that a linguistic distinction is not made does not automatically show that there is no conceptual distinction to be made.

Secondly, there have been two main tendencies in giving an account of perception. The first is to assimilate perception to something passive, as sensations might be supposed to be. The second is to assimilate it to judgment.[1] The difficulties involved in following the first tendency have been amply pointed out by

[1] Cf. M. Merleau-Ponty, *La Phénoménologie de la Perception*, Introd.

CONCLUSION—SENSATION AND PERCEPTION

those following the second. Perception does not seem to be an entirely passive matter and sensations do not in themselves provide us with the information about things around us that we believe perception does provide. The difficulties involved in following the second tendency seems to centre round the problem how, if perception is a matter of judgment, we know that which we judge about. Unless there is some other way of coming to know the object of perceptual judgment we would seem, like Kant, to be put in the position of being confronted with an unknowable 'thing-in-itself'. Perhaps for this very reason, most philosophers have attempted a compromise view—suggesting that we are given some information about the world in sensation and that we then elaborate this in judgment. The difficulties, however, remain that (a) in the ordinary sense of 'sensation' to have a sensation is not in itself to become aware of anything outside us, and (b) when perceiving we are not generally aware of making judgments in any explicit form.

In the face of these difficulties, it is tempting to say that, because perception is in some respects passive (i.e. in so far as it is dependent upon things affecting our senses) and in other respects active (i.e. in so far as it involves interpretation, classification and the like), but is neither entirely, it is really like nothing else. There is, in fact, nothing so like perception as perception. To adopt this view would not only be a counsel of despair, it would also be a mistake. In the first place it implies that nothing can be done by way of answering the question 'What is perception?', and in the second place it presupposes that the question demands a single answer—that there is, in other words, one thing, an activity, process or experience, which is named 'perception'. These two mistakes are of course connected, since the view that the question demands an answer of this sort and the view that it is impossible to specify or categorize what perception is together entail that no answer can be given to the question at all.

At the beginning of section xi of part 2 of his *Philosophical Investigations* Wittgenstein says, 'Two uses of the word "see". The one: "What do you see there?"—"I see *this*" (and then a description, a drawing, a copy). The other: "I see a likeness between these two faces"—let the man I tell this to be seeing the faces as clearly as I do myself. The importance of this is the categorial difference between the two "objects" of sight.' He goes on to provide an

CONCLUSION—SENSATION AND PERCEPTION

extensive discussion of this difference, the aim of which, I believe, is to make criticisms of the notion of 'sense-data' as objects of sight in the second sense which he specifies. The target of his attack is the notion that when we see something *in a certain way* or see it *as* something this is to be explained by saying that what we see, the aspect or appearance of the object in question, is itself an object. Hence, later in his discussion (p. 197e) he says, ' "Seeing as . . ." is not part of perception. And for that reason it is like seeing and and again not like.' This remark is of great importance. It cuts across the presumption that the word 'perception' is the name of a single kind of experience—a presumption which has caused great difficulties both for philosophers and for psychologists in their more theoretical moments.

It may seem obvious that by 'sensation' is meant any experience which we have when our senses are stimulated. In the *Concept of Mind*[1] (pp. 240 ff.), however, Ryle has criticized the notion of sensations as applied to senses like that of sight. He maintains that there are two ordinary senses of the word 'sensation'—one applicable to feelings such as pains and feelings of discomfort, the other applicable to the way in which we find out about things by means of touch. It is by sensation, he says, that we find out that things are sticky or rough. Hence, he goes on to maintain, the idea that we have sensations when we see is a 'para-mechanical' theory, in which sensations are the ghostly impressions set up by para-mechanical causes. The existence of sensations in this context is a myth, smuggled in from the fact that we can call the way in which we perceive things by touch 'sensation'.

Of these two senses of 'sensation' the first may seem perspicuous. In his discussion of the second Ryle appears to be talking about the *faculty* of sensation. He is pointing out that one *species* of perception may be called 'sensation'. It is doubtful, however, whether this is more than a linguistic point, like the linguistic point that in French it is possible to call perception *le sentir*. (That it is a linguistic point only does not, of course, mean that it has not been misleading.) There can be no objection to calling touch 'sensation', or indeed to calling other senses the same,[2]

---

[1] See also his article on 'Sensations' in *Contemporary British Philosophy*, 3rd Series, ed. H. D. Lewis.

[2] Cf. P. Geach, *Mental Acts*, p. 122, n. 1.

CONCLUSION—SENSATION AND PERCEPTION

as long as one is not misled by so doing. And Ryle may well be right in saying that some philosophers have been misled. But the mere fact that we may use the expression 'sensation' in this way has no *conceptual* significance. This faculty of sensation is, on Ryle's own showing, a species of perception and may be treated accordingly.

Of the other use of 'sensation' there is, despite its apparent perspicuity, more to be said. It is clear that we do sometimes use 'sensation' as a synonym for 'feeling'. Thus itches, pains and titillations are bodily sensations. To have a sensation in this sense is to have an experience which is more or less passive; that is to say that it is something which is caused by stimuli affecting our body. That the sensation must have or attract our attention is no objection to the general principle. But while sensations may be caused by stimuli affecting our body, to have a sensation is not necessarily, or even generally, to know anything about its cause. In certain cases we may be able to make inferences about the causes of our sensations from the character of those sensations themselves; but we can do this only if we have an independent means of coming to know about that which acts as the cause. Nothing in the sensation itself, *apart from other knowledge*, can tell us anything about its cause. In order to make an inference from a sensation to its cause we need to know the connection which in general holds between sensations of this kind and certain stimuli. The same considerations apply to our knowledge of the location of our sensations. The location of the physical cause of a sensation is something which can be learned only through experience, even if we cannot be said to learn where we *feel* the sensation to be.[1]

This raises a further point. Not only does knowledge of the actual causes of our sensations presuppose knowledge of more than those sensations themselves, but our ability to talk of sensations presupposes that we already have the *concept* of something independent of our sensations. This point arose in the earlier discussion about the localization of our sensations, in that in order to be able to express where we *feel* our sensations to be we must already have the concept of a physical locality—and this is something independent of our sensations. But the point has a general application. We describe our sensations by means of words which suggest analogies with physical processes; e.g. we may describe

[1] See the previous discussion on pp. 155–6.

CONCLUSION—SENSATION AND PERCEPTION

pains as shooting or searing. This fact is no coincidence. For the reasons given by Wittgenstein and discussed in the previous chapter, an intrinsically private language, designed to deal with sensations alone, is impossible. There is no neat sensation-language, to use Ryle's terms. Descriptions of sensations which did not depend upon analogies with physical processes or other public phenomena, if *per impossibile* they could be called descriptions, would convey nothing. We sometimes depend upon our sensations in order to make inferences about their causes, as we have already seen. This may be so whether the causes are something in the world around us or something in our own bodies. But we need the *concept* of something independent of our sensations even to characterize those sensations, let alone to specify the information which they may provide by way of inference. For this reason it is useless to consider sensations as a 'given' from which all else is to be constructed.

In the light of these considerations we can now ask again whether it is correct to say that we have sensations when we see. In a sense it would be foolish to deny this; yet in another sense it is possible to see why scruples may be raised. Why should we deny that, if we have experiences of a certain kind when some of our sense-organs are stimulated, we have them too when the retinae of our eyes are stimulated? Yet normally we should describe the experiences which we have from the use of our eyes by saying that we see light of a certain colour, for example; and this description of our experience is unlike that which we give when we say that we feel a shooting pain. It is unlike it if only because while the latter description depends upon *analogies* with an objective phenomenon, i.e. shooting, the former description is a description of our *perception of* an objective phenomenon, i.e. colour. The term 'experience' can be used of our feelings and sensations, and also of what we find out by perception. If we are to say that we have sensations when our eyes are stimulated, and if they are sensations akin to those received from the other senses, they must not be described in terms which liken them to objects of perception. Normally the descriptions which we give of our visual experiences are descriptions of what we see and how we see it. We seldom, if ever, have recourse to descriptions of experiences which might be called 'visual sensations'. In the case of the bodily senses we need on occasion to describe our bodily sensations as an aid in the

CONCLUSION—SENSATION AND PERCEPTION

diagnosis of bodily ills. In the same way it might be necessary to describe the pains or feelings of discomfort in our eyes. But there is no parallel situation which makes it necessary to refer to sensations of a different sort which may be said to be peculiar to vision. Yet if we did need to describe the sensations derived from the stimulation of our eyes, the descriptions would have to be essentially of the same logical type as those of bodily sensations.

There is indeed an oddity about the phrase 'visual sensation'. But the oddity arises from the fact that vision is a form of perception; hence to speak of visual *sensations* is to combine two quite different concepts. Nevertheless, the fact that there are difficulties about the *concept* of a visual sensation provides no reason for doubting that our eyes furnish experiences which could be called sensations. Those experiences can be subsumed under the concept of sensation, although, owing to lack of interest in them and of vocabulary for them, we should have great difficulty in saying anything more about them from that point of view. But they can also be subsumed under the concept of perception, and that the more easily since when we describe our visual experiences we normally describe what we see or take ourselves to see.

The point which I have just made I made also in relation to Reid. It will be remembered that Reid distinguished clearly between the concepts of sensation and perception, saying that the former is constituted by the fact that there is 'no object distinct from the act itself', while perception is a more complicated matter involving a conception of the object and a belief in its existence. But having clearly distinguished the concepts in this way, he went on to talk as if there were also two quite different processes or experiences involved. When we perceive something not only the process or experience of perception occurs, but also at the same time a different process or experience called 'sensation'. It is, however, evident that in some cases of perception it is extremely difficult and indeed impossible to distinguish a separate experience or process which is the sensation; on the other hand, in having some sensations we seem *ipso facto* to perceive something, e.g. when we feel a pain in a foot we seem *ipso facto* to perceive where it is. Such facts presented Reid with a problem. But there is no need for the problem if it is realized that the conceptual distinction of itself is both sufficient and appropriate. We may be likely to call an experience a sensation in so far as it is relatively passive and forced

CONCLUSION—SENSATION AND PERCEPTION

upon us; but it is noteworthy that we may sometimes be forced to *perceive* something in a certain way—the *perception* may be relatively passive also. The distinction between sensation and perception cannot indeed be made in terms of the character of the experiences which we have, even if perhaps the paradigm cases of the application of the concept of a sensation are experiences which are passive.

If we ask whether in perceiving we are having sensations or making judgments we ask the wrong question. We ask for an analysis of an experience or process, as if it were obvious that the word 'perception' is the name of such an experience or process. But this is the very point at issue. An understanding of what perception is cannot be arrived at *via* the presupposition that it is the kind of thing which admits of the analyses in question. It is characteristic of some philosophical concepts—perception is one, belief is another—that we may not only fail to understand them in detail but also be unable to say even under which *category* they are to be subsumed. Our list of categories is likely to be determined by the more obvious features of the world which we detect in our thought about it. Aristotle's attempts to subsume perception under the categories of passivity and activity were dictated by the analogies which he saw between perception and sensation on the one hand and between perception and judgment on the other. His whole programme, however, presupposes that perception is a process, though whether active or passive is not clear.

What a man does and what happens to him are the most obvious things about him from the point of view of an outsider. They thus provide the biological and psychological starting-point for an inquiry into his faculties. Because perception is not obviously something that just happens to a man or that he just does, it may seem feasible to introduce the notion of a disposition. Bergson, it will be remembered, described perception as related to possible action—what one is disposed to do. Yet while our *evidence* concerning what a man perceives and how he perceives it may be derived from what he is disposed to do, it scarcely seems right to say that by perception is *meant* a form of disposition to action. The necessity of recognizing further categories seems forced upon us.

Terms like 'perception' belong to a family of terms which may be described as epistemological—they centre round the concept

CONCLUSION—SENSATION AND PERCEPTION

of knowledge. The most important features of this last concept are that we should not allow that a man knows some truth unless what he claims to know is in fact true and unless he has good reason for asserting it as true. In saying that he knows p, we not only register his belief, his state of mind; we also register the fact that his belief is both true and well-founded. It comes up to a standard in these respects. Perception is analogous in that we should not allow that someone could have seen something unless that something was in some sense there, or unless it was, given certain presuppositions, appropriate or correct to assume this. (The latter qualification is necessary, since *in certain contexts* it might be quite legitimate to speak of seeing ghosts, for example, even if we believed that there are no such things as ghosts. It all depends upon what is, in the context, taken for granted.) Moreover, we should not allow that he could have seen it unless he had the proper grounds for claiming to know that it was there, i.e. unless he had used his eyes and was in the position to observe it.

If a man sincerely claims to know something but is not in the position to know it, either because what he claims to know is not true or because he claims to know it on insufficient grounds, we normally say that he does not know it although he may think that he does. Likewise, when a man sincerely claims to see something but is not in the position to do so, either because that something is not there or because he has not sufficient warrant for claiming to see it, we normally say that he does not see it although he may think that he does. When a man is mistaken in what he claims to know, we may say that he only supposes it to be so; when a man is mistaken in what he claims to see, we may say that he only sees it *as* such and such or that it appears to him to be such and such. In saying this we imply a contrast with genuine knowledge and genuine perception; and the application of these latter concepts implies or presupposes the notion of a standard, as already noted. The family of concepts to which similar considerations apply is fairly extensive; it includes, for example, insight, awareness and recognition. Any account of perception which is to be at all adequate must proceed by way of the invocation of concepts which belong to this same family. Locke was thus right in maintaining, implicitly at any rate, the connection of perception with awareness. And it is because of such connections that by analogy

CONCLUSION—SENSATION AND PERCEPTION

with the more straightforward cases of perception we speak of seeing the answer to a problem, of perceiving the truth, and so on.

Even in the more straightforward cases of perception, we speak not only of perceiving an object, or of perceiving that object as such and such; we speak also of perceiving that something is the case. Perception, one might say, may take as its object not only physical things and their properties, but also facts. There is no difficulty about this, since, in the primary sense, 'perception' can signify any means whereby we come to recognize, identify or characterize something by means of the senses. It is possible both to recognize an object and to recognize that the facts are what they are. It may of course be the case that an object cannot be recognized or identified without its first being characterized in a certain way; but whether this is so is not a problem which is peculiar to the philosophy of perception. It is a general problem concerning the presuppositions involved in the identification of things, however that identification is carried out.[1]

The experiences which a man has enable him to identify or characterize physical objects or facts about them. By this I do not mean that he somehow surveys his experiences and uses them in order to carry out the subsequent processes of identification or characterization. This is the mistake made by those who think of sensations as providing a 'given' which furnishes a basis for future judgment about objects. Sense-experiences are necessary but not sufficient for the identification or characterization of physical objects; and they are necessary just because those physical objects are empirical objects. There is no way other than by sense-perception by which they could be identified or characterized.

It is possible to imagine a race of beings who had no experiences, but who were capable of coming to behave towards things as we now do. This might be because, as in our case, they had sense-organs in a physiological sense, which were stimulated by external stimuli, and a nervous system in many ways like ours; but they were unlike us in that the stimulation of their 'sense-organs' resulted in no experiences. It is by no means impossible to conceive of such beings, because it is clear that, in principle at any rate, a

[1] See P. F. Strawson, *Individuals*. The same considerations apply to the traditional problem of knowledge with its attempt to answer scepticism. This also is not a problem peculiar to the philosophy of perception.

CONCLUSION—SENSATION AND PERCEPTION

machine might be built just like this. Should we describe such a being or such a machine as able to perceive things? With the lack of experiences thus made explicit and with our present concept of perception, we should, I think, be reluctant to do so. Yet it would seem that the absence of those experiences which are so necessary to the application of the concept of perception need not detract from the ability of those beings to behave in some sense like us. (It may be, however, that in the absence of those experiences we should not have the right to apply concepts like that of learning to such beings. In that case, we might be hesitant to apply that of behaviour also. Yet the connection between sense-experience and behaviour is sufficiently indirect to make it *prima facie* plausible to talk of behaviour in the absence of experiences.)

In other words, an essential condition of our application of the concept of perception to a being of any kind is that such a being should have sense-experiences or sensations. Yet those sensations need play no part in the mechanism which makes it possible to behave in ways which, but for the absence of experiences, we should describe as behaviour in the light of perception. Our nervous system is of itself capable of responding differentially towards things, and of coming in time to acquire further differential responses as a result of certain patterns of stimulus and response. The description of these responses as behaviour brings with it the application of a whole scheme of concepts like those of intention and knowledge; and we should not apply the concept of behaviour except where the application of the others is possible. The description of the situation in perceptual terms brings with it not only the application of scheme of concepts but also as a presupposition that of the concept of sense-experience (although, as already noted, it may be that this concept is really already presupposed by the application of the scheme applicable to behaviour). The fact that the concept of perception presupposes these other concepts implies that it cannot be elucidated without reference to them. It is for this reason that I can say that if I now see this page in front of me as a page with writing on it I must have so identified it. There is of course derivatively a sense in which I could be said to see the page without my having identified anything—in that I am in the position so to identify it, although I do not actually do so. Thus someone may say, 'You *must* have seen it.' But this use of 'see' is derivative from the primary one, and in

CONCLUSION—SENSATION AND PERCEPTION

that primary use perception and identification must go hand in hand.

The relation of sensation to perception is that the first is a necessary condition of the second (and conversely, of course, that the second is a sufficient condition of the first). This is so only because there is a *conceptual* link between the two concepts. Not only would we not have the concept of perception if we did not have that of sensation, but in order to apply the concept of perception to anything, it must be possible to apply to it that of sensation. There is, however, no other link. In particular, the having of a sensation is not a *part* of perceiving, in the sense that perceiving is a process the mechanics of which include sensations. Indeed, it shows a misunderstanding of the problem if one is tempted to ask what experiences, processes or activities constitute perception. But this is just the question which has so often been asked in the history of philosophy and psychology. It has been asked, for example, whether in perceiving something one is having sensations, making judgments or having a belief about the object.

While the having of sensations is, in the sense specified, necessary to perceiving, it is not sufficient. And the same applies to judgment and belief. We sometimes make judgments concerning what we see; we sometimes believe in what our senses 'tell' us. But not always. Even the distinction between veridical and illusory perception is not a straight-forward distinction between being right and being wrong about what we perceive; for it is possible to 'perceive an illusion' without believing or judging that things are as they appear to be. If a stick in water looks bent we do not have to believe or even judge that it is so. The application of the concept of an illusion in general presupposes the concept of being wrong in the sense that were we never wrong in what we perceive, were we never to make a false judgment about what we perceive, we should not have the concept of an illusion. But it certainly is not true that whenever we 'perceive an illusion' we have an erroneous belief or judgment. The same considerations apply to hallucinations, except that here the error, if it exists, is concerned primarily with the existence of an object rather than its nature. Thus while we can speak of perceiving something rightly or wrongly, this is not sufficient to warrant identification of perception with belief or judgment. Indeed to suppose that it might be so identified is to misinterpret the problem. Reid's 'conception

CONCLUSION—SENSATION AND PERCEPTION

or notion of the object perceived' and 'strong and irresistible conviction and belief of its present existence' may be features necessary to the application of the concept of perception; they do not themselves constitute the nature of perception.

An understanding of the concepts of sensation and perception comes, therefore, not by asking what experiences, processes or activities these terms stand for. It can come only as the result of an inquiry into the concepts which form the schemes to which these particular concepts belong, together with the conditions for the application of those schemes. In indicating the connection between perception, identification, characterization, recognition, awareness and the like, I have sought to reveal the skeleton of that conceptual scheme. Its application presupposes that there are standards with reference to which it may be asserted that someone has perceived, identified, etc., a given object. Hence the concepts of this class could have evolved only in a situation where the notion of a standard could evolve. Such a notion could not itself have arisen except within a *society* in which one man can assess another's judgments. The notion of a standard is thus essentially a social concept.[1] That which distinguishes the concept of perception from other concepts in the scheme is that *its* application also presupposes the applicability of that of a sensation or sense-experience.

Since the elucidation of the concept of perception involves reference to many other concepts which belong to the same conceptual scheme, and can proceed only thereby, there can be no short cut for anyone who genuinely fails to understand the concept. The fatal mistake is again to seek to study the concepts of sensation and perception by way of an investigation of one's own experiences. As Wittgenstein says in an extremely important remark (*Philosophical Investigations*, I. 314), 'It shows a fundamental misunderstanding if I am inclined to study the headache I have now in order to get clear about the philosophical problem of sensation.'

[1] See my *The Psychology of Perception*, pp. 17, 24.

BIBLIOGRAPHY

(*a*) = Sources.   (*b*) = Works of reference.

GENERAL WORKS

F. C. Coplestone: *History of Philosophy* (Burns, Oates and Washbourne, 1950–).
J. A. Passmore: *A Hundred Years of Philosophy* (Duckworth, 1957).
G. S. Brett: *History of Psychology* (Allen and Unwin, 1912–21: one-volume edition, ed. R. S. Peters, 1953).
G. Murphy: *An Historical Introduction to Modern Psychology* (Routledge and Kegan Paul, 1928).
E. G. Boring: *Sensation and Perception in the History of Experimental Psychology* (New York; Appleton-Century-Crofts, 1942).

CHAPTER 1

(*a*)

H. Diels (ed. W. Kranz): *Die Fragmente der Vorsokratiker* (Berlin: Weidman, 1954).
G. S. Kirk and J. Raven: *The Presocratic Philosophers* (C.U.P., 1957). (These two works contain relevant passages from Theophrastus *De Sensu*.)
Plato: *Republic*, esp. Bks. 5–7; *Timaeus*; *Theaetetus*.
Aristotle: *De Anima*; *De Sensu*; *Metaphysics* Γ. 5; *Post. An.*, II. 19.

(*b*)

J. I. Beare: *Greek Theories of Elementary Cognition* (O.U.P., 1906).
B. Snell: *The Discovery of the Mind* (Blackwell, 1953).
G. S. Kirk and J. Raven: *The Presocratic Philosophers* (C.U.P., 1957).

BIBLIOGRAPHY

J. Burnet: *Early Greek Philosophy* (Black, 4th ed., 1930).
F. M. Cornford: *Plato's Theory of Knowledge* (Routledge and Kegan Paul, 1935).
W. F. R. Hardie: *A Study in Plato*, esp. chs. 3, 4 (O.U.P., 1936).
D. W. Hamlyn: 'Eikasia in Plato's Republic,' *Philosophical Quarterly*, Vol. 8, No. 30, 1958.
G. E. L. Owen: 'A Proof in the Peri Ideon,' *Journal of Hellenic Studies*, Vol. 77, 1957.
W. D. Ross: *Aristotle* (Methuen, 4th ed., 1944).
R. D. Hicks: *De Anima*, Introduction, Text and Commentary (C.U.P., 1907).
D. W. Hamlyn: 'Aristotle's Account of Aesthesis in the De Anima,' *Classical Quarterly*, N.S., Vol. 9, 1959.

CHAPTER 2

(*a*)

H. Usener: *Epicurea* (Teubner, 1887).
Diogenes Laertius: *Lives of Eminent Philosophers*, 7 and 10 (Loeb).
Lucretius: *De Rerum Natura*.
H. Von Arnim: *Stoicorum Veterum Fragmenta* (Teubner, 1903–5).
Sextus Empiricus: *Adversus Mathematicos*, 7 and 8 (Loeb, Vol. 2).
Plotinus: *Enneads* (esp. iv. 6 and ii. 8).
C. J. de Vogel: *Greek Philosophy*, Vol. III (Leiden: Brill).

(*b*)

A. Zeller: *Stoics, Epicureans and Sceptics* (Longmans Green, 1892).
R. D. Hicks: *Stoic and Epicurean* (London, 1910).
C. Bailey: *Epicurus and the Greek Atomists* (O.U.P., 1926).
M. Pohlenz: *Die Stoa* (Gottingen: Vandenhoeck und Ruprecht, 1948).
S. Sambursky: *The Physics of the Stoics* (Routledge and Kegan Paul, 1959).
T. Whittaker: *The Neo-Platonists* (C.U.P., 1928).
E. Brehier: *Plotin* (Paris: Boivin, 1928).

CHAPTER 3

St. Augustine: *De Musica*, esp. vi. v. 9–10; *De Libero Arbitrio*, esp. ii, 7–8; *De Quantitate Animae*, 23 ff.

BIBLIOGRAPHY

St. Thomas Aquinas: *Summa Theologica*, 1a, 78 ff.; *Commentary on the De Anima*.
William of Ockham: *Sententiae*, Prol.; *Quodlibeta*, i and vi. (For extracts see P. Boehner: *Ockham, Philosophical Writings* (Nelson).)
Ed. R. McKeon: *Mediaeval Philosophers* (Scribner).

(*b*)

E. Gilson: *Christian Philosophy in the Middle Ages* (Sheed and Ward, 1953).
Idem: *Introduction à l'étude de St. Augustine* (Paris: Vrin, 1943).
Idem: *The Christian Philosophy of St. Thomas Aquinas* (New York Random House, 1956).
Idem: *The Philosophy of St. Bonaventure* (Sheed and Ward, 1940).
C. R. S. Harris: *Duns Scotus* (O.U.P., 1927).
M. H. Carré: *Realists and Nominalists* (O.U.P., 1946).

CHAPTERS 4 AND 5
(*a*)

F. Bacon: *Novum Organon*.
T. Hobbes: *Leviathan*, Pt. I.
R. Descartes: *Regulae*; *Discourse on Method*; *Meditations*; *Principles of Philosophy*; *Dioptric*.
(For selections see N. Kemp Smith: *Descartes, Philosophical Writings* (Macmillan, 1952).)
N. Malebranche: *Recherche de la Vérité*. I: *Dialogues on Metaphysics*, 12.
B. de Spinoza: *Ethics*, esp. Bk. II.
G. Leibniz: *Nouveaux Essais*; *Correspondence with Clarke*; *Monadology*; *Reflections on Knowledge, Truth and Ideas*; *What is an Idea?*; *Discourse on Metaphysics*.
(For selections, see P. Wiener: *Leibniz* (Scribner).)

(*b*)

R. S. Peters: *Hobbes* (Penguin, 1956).
F. Brandt: *Hobbes' Mechanical Conception of Nature* (Copenhagen: Levin & Munksgaard, 1928).
N. Kemp Smith: *New Studies in the Philosophy of Descartes* (Macmillan, 1952).

BIBLIOGRAPHY

A. Boyce Gibson: *The Philosophy of Descartes* (Methuen, 1932).
A. H. Joachim: *A Study in Spinoza's Ethics* (O.U.P., 1901).
S. Hampshire: *Spinoza* (Penguin, 1951).
B. Russell: *The Philosophy of Leibniz* (Allen and Unwin, 1900).
R. L. Saw: *Leibniz* (Penguin, 1954).

CHAPTER 6

(a)

J. Locke: *Essay Concerning Human Understanding*.
G. Berkeley: *New Theory of Vision; Principles of Human Knowledge; Three Dialogues of Hylas and Philonous*.
D. Hume: *Treatise of Human Nature; Enquiry Concerning the Human Understanding*.
T. Reid: *Inquiry into the Human Mind on the Principles of Common Sense; Essays on the Intellectual Powers of Man* (ed. A. D. Woozley: Macmillan, 1941).

(b)

R. I. Aaron: *John Locke* (O.U.P., 1937).
D. J. O'Connor: *John Locke* (Penguin, 1952).
G. J. Warnock: *Berkeley* (Penguin, 1953).
G. N. A. Vesey: 'Berkeley and Sensations of Heat'; *Philosophical Review*, Vol. LXIX, 1960.
N. Kemp Smith: *The Philosophy of David Hume* (Macmillan, 1949).
D. G. C. MacNabb: *David Hume, His Theory of Knowledge and Morality* (Hutchinson, 1951).
A. H. Basson: *David Hume* (Penguin, 1958).
H. H. Price: *Hume's Theory of the External World* (O.U.P., 1940).
P. G. Winch: 'The Notion of "Suggestion" in Thomas Reid's Theory of Perception,' *Philosophical Quarterly*, Vol. 3, 1953.
T. J. Duggan: 'Thomas Reid's Theory of Sensation', *Philosophical Review*, Vol. LXIX, 1960.

CHAPTER 7

(a)

I. Kant: *Critique of Pure Reason; Prolegomena to Every Future Metaphysics; Anthropologie*, Bk. I.
G. W. F. Hegel: *Phenomenology of Mind* (ed. J. B. Bailey: Allen and Unwin, 1910).

BIBLIOGRAPHY

F. H. Bradley: *Appearance and Reality* (Sonnenschein, 1893); *Principles of Logic* (O.U.P., 1883).

(b)

H. J. Paton: *Kant's Metaphysic of Experience* (Allen and Unwin, 1936).
N. Kemp Smith: *Commentary to Kant's Critique of Pure Reason* (Macmillan, 1918).
S. Korner: *Kant* (Penguin, 1955).
W. T. Stace: *The Philosophy of Hegel* (Dover, 1955).
J. N. Findlay: *Hegel: A Re-Examination* (Macmillan, 1958).
R. Wollheim: *F. H. Bradley* (Penguin, 1959).

CHAPTER 8

(a)

D. Hartley: *Observations on Man*.
J. Mill: *Analysis of the Phenomena of the Human Mind* (ed. J. S. Mill, 1869).
A. Bain: *The Senses and the Intellect*; *Mental Science*.
J. S. Mill: *An Examination of Sir William Hamilton's Philosophy*.
H. Lotze: *Metaphysic*, III, ch. 4.

(b)

H. C. Warren: *A History of the Association Psychology* (New York, 1921).
K. Britton: *John Stuart Mill* (Penguin, 1953).
J. A. Passmore: *A Hundred Years of Philosophy*, ch. 1 (Duckworth, 1957).
G. S. Brett: *History of Psychology*, Vol. 3 (Allen and Unwin, 1921).
G. Bergmann: 'The Problem of Relations in Classical Psychology,' *Philosophical Quarterly*, Vol. 2, 1952.

CHAPTER 9

(a)

F. C. Brentano: *Psychologie vom empirischen Standpunkte* (1874).
F. H. Bradley: *Collected Essays* (O.U.P., 1935).
W. James: *Principles of Psychology*, esp. chs. 9 and 17–21 (Macmillan, 1890); *Essays in Radical Empiricism* (1912).
H. Bergson: *Les données immédiates de la conscience* (Paris: Alcan, 1889; trans. into English 1910); *Matière et Mémoire* (Paris: Alcan, 1896; trans., 1911).

BIBLIOGRAPHY

J. Ward: *Psychological Principles* (C.U.P., 1920).
G. F. Stout: *Analytic Psychology* (Sonnenschein, 1890); *Manual of Psychology* (University Tutorial Press, 5th ed., 1938).

(b)

J. A. Passmore: *A Hundred Years of Philosophy*, chs. 3-5, 7, 8 (Duckworth, 1957).
R. Wollheim: *F. H. Bradley* (Penguin, 1959).
A. D. Lindsay: *The Philosophy of Bergson* (Dent, 1911).
J. N. Findlay: *Meinong's Theory of Objects*, ch. 1 (O.U.P., 1933).
D. W. Hamlyn: 'The Stream of Thought,' *Proc. Arist. Soc.*, 1955-56.

(Passmore's book provides a multitude of further references.)

CHAPTERS 10 AND 11

G. E. Moore: *Philosophical Studies* (Routledge and Kegan Paul, 1922); *Some Main Problems of Philosophy* (Allen and Unwin, 1953).
B. Russell: *Problems of Philosophy* (O.U.P., 1912); *Our Knowledge of the External World* (Allen and Unwin, 1914); *Analysis of Mind* (Allen and Unwin, 1921).
A. J. Ayer: *Language, Truth and Logic* (Gollancz, 1936); *Foundations of Empirical Knowledge* (Macmillan, 1941); *Philosophical Essays* (Macmillan, 1954); *The Problem of Knowledge* (Macmillan and Penguin, 1956).
H. H. Price: *Perception* (Methuen, 1932).
G. Ryle: *The Concept of Mind* (Hutchinson, 1949); *Dilemmas*, ch. 7 (C.U.P., 1954); *Sensation* in *Contemporary British Philosophy*, III (Allen and Unwin, 1956).
L. Wittgenstein: *Philosophical Investigations*, esp. I. 242-316 and II. xi (Blackwell, 1953).
R. Chisholm: *Perceiving* (Cornell U.P., 1957).
C. F. Strawson: *Individuals* (Methuen, 1959).
R. J. Hirst: *The Problems of Perception* (Allen and Unwin, 1959).
G. Paul: 'Is there a Problem about Sense-data?' *Proc. Arist. Soc.*, Supp., Vol. 15, 1936.
A. M. Quinton and K. Britton: 'Seeming,' *Proc. Arist. Soc.*, *Supp*. Vol. 26, 1952.
A. M. Quinton: 'The Problem of Perception,' *Mind*, N.S., Vol. LXIV., 1955.

BIBLIOGRAPHY

G. N. A. Vesey: 'Seeing and Seeing-as,' *Proc. Arist. Soc.*, 1955–56.

D. W. Hamlyn: 'The Visual Field and Perception,' *Proc. Arist. Soc.*, Supp., Vol. 31, 1957.

P. T. Geach: *Mental Acts*, Sects. 25 ff. (Routledge and Kegan Paul, 1957).

E. Husserl: *Logische Untersuchungen* (1900–1); *Ideas* (Allen and Unwin, 1931); *Méditations Cartésiennes* (Paris: Colin, 1931).

M. Merleau-Ponty: *La Phénoménologie de la Perception* (Paris: Gallimard, 1945).

J. P. Sartre: *L'Etre et le Néant* (Paris: Gallimard, 1943; English translation, Methuen, 1957).

M. Kullman and C. Taylor: 'The Preobjective World,' *Review of Metaphysics*, Vol. 12, 1958.

C. Taylor and A. J. Ayer: 'Phenomenology and Linguistic Analysis,' *Proc. Arist. Soc.*, Supp. Vol. 33, 1959.

G. Ryle: 'Phenomenology,' *Proc. Arist. Soc.*, Supp. Vol. 11, 1932.

K. Koffka: *Principles of Gestalt Psychology* (Routledge and Kegan Paul, 1935).

W. D. Ellis: *A Source Book of Gestalt Psychology* (Routlege and Kegan Paul, 1938).

J. J. Gibson: *The Perception of the Visual World* (Houghton Mifflin, 1950).

D. W. Hamlyn: *The Psychology of Perception* (Routledge and Kegan Paul, 1957).

Sir Russell Brain: *Mind, Perception and Science* (Oxford, 1951).

J. R. Smythies: *Analysis of Perception* (Routledge and Kegan Paul, 1956).

(The above bibliography is by no means comprehensive and further references may be found in many of the books mentioned, especially, for recent work, in Passmore's *A Hundred Years of Philosophy*.)

INDEX

Aaron, R. I., 101 n.
Abbott, T. K., 150
Academy, of Plato, 12, 31, 39
Ackrill, J., 14 n.
acquaintance, 10, 14, 53-4, 168, 175, 176
activity (*v.* passivity), 19 ff., 26-7, 40, 44, 52, 75, 84, 87 ff., 91, 92, 96 ff., 105, 111, 164—5, 192
actuality, *v.* potentiality
aesthesis, 1, 3, 9, 13 ff., 17 ff., 37
Aëtius, 32
Alcmaeon, 5
Anaxagoras, 7, 9
animal spirits, 57, 70, 96
appearances, 27, 31, 107, 129 n., 132 ff., 176, 179, 183-4, 193
apperception, 88 ff., 136, 158, 163, 167
apprehension, 38, 46, 141, 163, 175, 179
Aquinas, St. T., 17-18, 42, 43, 45, 46-51, 52, 58, 67, 94 n.
Arcesilaus, 31, 39
Aristotelianism, 42, 43, 46, 47, 56
Aristotle, x, 2, 3, 5 n., 10, 11 n., 17-30, 34, 35, 38, 39, 41, 44, 45, 46-51, 60, 64, 110-11, 137, 142, 192
Arnauld, A., 87

assent, 37-8
association of ideas, 113, 147-8, 161
Associationism, 147 ff.
Atomism, 7-8, 32-5, 47, 51, 56-7
attention, 7, 44, 98-9, 125-6, 159 n., 160
Augustine, St., 41, 43-6, 48, 51, 52, 54, 70, 75
Avicenna, 47
awareness, 97, 132, 193
Ayer, A. J., 62 n., 174, 177, 178-80, 184

Bacon, F., 56
Bailey, S., 150
Bain, A., 148, 149, 150-2, 154-5, 157, 160
Bayle, P., 124
belief, 121, 127, 192, 193, 196-7
Bergson, H., 159, 164, 169-71, 186, 192
Berkeley, G., 41, 49, 55, 93, 94, 101, 103, 104-16, 118, 119, 121-2, 124, 129, 130, 132, 150, 178
Bluck, R. S., 14 n.
Bonaventure, St., 43, 51-2
Bradley, F. H., 141 n., 142-4, 159, 161-2, 164, 166, 169
Brain, Sir R., 184-5
Brandt, F., 57 n.

INDEX

Brentano, F. C., 159, 162, 164, 173
Brown, T., 148

Carneades, 31, 39
categories, 3, 4, 19, 135, 137-40, 192
Chrysippus, 36, 37
Chisholm, R., 129 n.
Cicero, 38, 43
Clarke, S., 87
cogito, 62-4
colour, perception of, 23, 26, 41, 110
concepts, 16, 45, 48, 132, 140, 142, 144
and words, 2 ff.
conceptual schemes, 192 ff., 195 ff., 197
consciousness, 181 ff., 184
continuity of, 161-2, 166 ff., 170-1
constancy hypothesis, 80, 169
Cratylus, 12, 13

delusions, 13, 27, 31, 102, 103
Democritus, 7-8, 32, 35, 47, 56
Descartes, R., 31, 38, 44, 54, 55 ff., 62-75, 76, 79, 82, 85, 95, 97, 101, 102, 124, 173, 184
Diogenes Laertius, 33, 34, 35 n., 36, 37 n.
Duns Scotus, 52

effluences, 6-7, 8
Ehrenfels, C. Von, 182
Elizabeth, Princess, 69
Empedocles, 6, 8, 13, 20, 40
Empiricism, 50, 51, 59-60, 93 ff., 110, 116, 131, 154, 173
Epicurus, 31, 32-5, 36, 37, 38, 45, 50, 56-7, 101
epistemology, x, 9, 17-19, 32, 33, 51, 58 ff., 110, 127, 140, 172, 184
error, 11, 15, 26-7, 34, 38, 66, 76 ff., 90, 102 ff., 110 ff., 178
Existentialism, 145 n.
extensity, 160, 162, 169

faculty of sense-perception, 21 ff., 51
Fichte, J. G., 140
Forms, Platonic theory of, 2, 10 ff., 16, 40

Galileo, 55
Gassendi, P., 56, 101 n.
Geach, P., 48 n., 62 n., 188 n.
Gestalt Psychology, 80, 164, 169, 173, 182
Geulincx, A., 69, 75
Gibson, J. J., 112 n., 183 n.
God, 43-4, 64 ff., 72 ff., 75, 82, 86, 90, 102, 104, 110, 115
Gorgias, 9
Griffiths, A. P., 64 n., 156 n.

hallucinations, 175-6, 178, 196
Hamilton, Sir W., 126 n., 149
Hamlyn, D. W., 13 n., 14 n., 139 n., 166 n., 168 n., 182 n., 183 n.
Hartley, D., 147 ff.
Harvey, W., 57
hearing, 7, 8, 22, 37
Hegel, G. W. F., x, 140 ff., 173
Helmholtz, H. Von, 155, 169
Heraclitus, 5, 12, 13
Herbart, J. F., 158
Hering, E., 155
Herodotus, 2
Hippocratic medical school, 6
Hirst, R. J., 185 n.
Hobbes, T., 56-7
Homer, 1

INDEX

Hume, D., 49, 55, 59, 93, 94, 113, 116–24, 126, 133, 135 ff., 148, 150, 157, 165
Husserl, E., 164, 173, 181 ff.

Idealism, 140 ff., 164, 166, 167 n., 172, 173
ideas, 62 ff., 66, 68, 70 ff., 82 ff., 94 ff., 105 ff., 117
  clear and distinct, 62, 66, 68, 69, 73, 75, 88
  simple and complex, 95, 102, 123
identification, 25, 194, 197
illusion, 13, 27, 34, 53, 102, 103, 175–6, 178, 196
  argument from, 32, 176
  zenith-horizon, 68, 81, 114
images, 17, 18, 44, 47, 85
  after-images, 54
  retinal images, 8, 79, 115
  sensory images, 47, 49
imagination, 27, 84, 102, 105, 110, 135 ff.
impressions, 14 ff., 18 n., 36 ff., 44 ff., 93, 96, 99, 117 ff., 132, 135, 137
  and ideas, 117, 121
  simple and complex, 123
incorrigibility, indubitability, infallibility, 13, 17, 25 ff., 33, 58 ff., 176 ff.
inference, 109 ff., 169, 178
  unconscious, 169
inner sense, 134
intellect, 26, 39–40, 48, 53, 84, 152
  active and passive, 18, 48, 50, 51
intentional objects, 159
intuition, 38, 52 ff., 64, 84, 95, 132 ff., 144

James, W., 149 n., 159, 164–9, 170, 171, 183

judgment, 12, 14 ff., 19, 20, 30, 38, 44 ff., 53–4, 77, 84, 97–8, 113, 121, 139, 145, 159, 169, 196
  natural judgments (or judgments of sense), 79 ff.
  perception assimilated to judgment, x, 26, 82, 140 ff., 186, 196

Kant, I., 29, 131–40, 142, 144, 149, 160, 164, 187
Kemp Smith, N., 58 n., 65 n., 116, 121, 134 n.
knowledge, 13 ff., 38, 58 ff., 75, 84, 93–5, 102, 110, 137–8, 141–2, 144, 175, 193
Kullman, M., 183 n.

Leibniz, G., 55, 64, 85–92, 103–4, 132, 136, 158
Leucippus, 7
Locke, J., 45, 49, 55, 59, 88–9, 93–104, 105, 106 ff., 116, 124, 127, 132, 134, 193
Logical Atomism, 141–2
Lotze, H., 155
Lucretius, 34, 35

Mach, E., 149 n.
Malebranche, N., 64, 69, 75–82, 103 n., 108 n., 113, 114
mathematics, 74, 76
Meinong, A., 173
memory, 15, 40, 44, 105, 135
mental chemistry, 158, 165
Merleau-Ponty, M., 182 ff.
metaphysics, 5, 33, 44, 90, 94, 105, 177
Mill, James, 149 ff.
Mill, J. S., 131 n., 149, 150, 151, 152–4, 157, 158, 165, 178

INDEX

mind (*v.* soul), 14–15, 44, 46, 51, 64 ff., 83, 118
minimum visibile, tangibile, 114–15, 123–4, 126
Molyneux, W., 103
monads, 85 ff.
Moore, G. E., 174 ff.
Müller, J., 147

Nativism, 154
Neo-Platonism, 39 ff., 43–6, 64
Newton, Sir I., 55

Occasionalism, 69, 75, 77, 86
Ockham, William of, 43, 52–4
opinion, 34, 38, 84
optics, 68, 103, 112
Owen, G. E. L., 12 n.

pain, 7, 99–100, 107–8, 120, 125, 156, 190
Parmenides, 5, 6, 9
particulars, knowledge of, 21, 141 ff.
passivity (*v.* activity), 18 ff., 28, 34, 75, 84, 87 ff., 91, 96 ff., 105, 111, 117–18, 191–2
Passmore, J. A., 173 n.
Paton, H. J., 131 n., 133 n., 134 n.
perception (*v.* sensation, judgment)
    causal theory of perception, 13, 15, 33, 46, 49, 82, 98, 101, 104
    immediate perception, 109 ff., 130
    natural and original perception, 129–30
    nature of perception, 130, 187, 192 ff.
    perception of distance, 35, 41, 44, 68, 79, 112–14, 121–2, 129, 150

perception (*contd.*)
    perception of extension, 123–4, 133–4, 150 ff., 160–1
    perception of shape, 79–80
    perception of size, 68, 78 ff., 114, 121, 153
    representative theory of perception, 46, 53, 73, 78, 95 ff., 102, 120, 131–2
    unperceived perception, 118
    unconscious perception, 89 ff.
    use of term 'perception' by 17th-century philosophers, 66, 83, 96, 117
Peters, R. S., 56 n.
phantasiae, 27, 31 ff., 36 ff.
phantasmata, 31 ff., 36, 47 ff., 67
phenomenalism, 107, 145, 157, 178
phenomenology, 173–4, 181–4
physics, 55 ff., 67–8, 101
physiology, 4, 5, 6, 20, 28, 68, 70, 147, 151, 184–5
Plato, 2, 3, 7, 10–16, 17, 18 n., 19, 27, 34, 35, 38, 40, 45, 58, 60, 64, 145
Platonism, 39, 43, 45, 70, 74, 173
Plotinus, 39–42, 43, 44
pneuma, 36, 37, 58
potentiality and actuality, 17–18, 21, 39, 46
Porphyry, 41
presentations, 158, 160 ff.
Presocratics, 4, 5–10, 20, 185
Price, H. H., 173, 176 n.
Prichard, H. A., 176 n.
Priestley, J., 148
private languages, 180–1
Protagoras, 8, 9, 13–14, 18–19, 25, 29
psychology, 7, 28, 50–1, 91, 94, 124, 157, 159, 164, 181–2

208

qualities, 2–3, 21, 109
  primary and secondary, 8, 35, 56, 67, 73–4, 99 ff., 107–8, 111, 119, 127

Rationalism, 55, 59–60, 62 ff., 65, 75, 83, 84, 85, 91, 92, 131
Realism, 172 ff.
reason (*v.* intellect), 121
recognition, 136, 160, 163, 194
Régis, P. S. (Regius), 69, 81
Reid, T., 124–30, 135, 136, 148, 186, 191, 196
Russell, B., 86, 87, 141, 142, 173, 174 ff.
Ryle, G., 50, 155 n., 180, 188 ff.

Sambursky, S., 37 n.
Sartre, J. P., 184
scepticism, x, 9, 35, 44 ff., 60, 110, 116, 122
Sceptics, 31–2, 39
Scholasticism, 49, 51, 55
seeing-as, 29, 181 n., 193
self, knowledge of, 54, 134, 137, 165
sensations, 23, 33, 44, 47, 53, 67, 78, 80, 96, 108, 125 ff., 133, 134–5, 148 ff., 151, 168, 174, 177, 180, 185, 188 ff., 195 ff.
  complex sensations, 80 ff.
  distinction between sensation and perception, 9, 28, 125 ff., 130, 160, 168, 170, 186, 191, 196 ff.
  localization of sensations, 154 ff.
  perception assimilated to sensation, ix, 66, 101, 116, 147 ff., 186
  synchronous sensations, 150–1
  visual sensations, 188 ff.

Sensationalism, 147 ff., 159, 160, 163, 164, 166, 173, 182, 184
sense-data, 14, 34, 129, 145, 173, 174–81, 184–5
sense-objects,
  common, 24, 27
  incidental, 25, 27, 29
  proper, 103, 110, 111 ff., 115
  special, 23, 24 ff., 110
sense-organs, physiology of, 6 ff., 20, 22, 32, 37, 56, 67–8, 96, 147, 152
sensus communis, 24–5, 44, 47, 70
Sextus Empiricus, 32, 36, 37–8
sight, *v.* vision
signs,
  natural, 128 ff.
  local, 155 ff.
simulacra, 32, 34–5
Snell, B., 1
Socrates, 2, 7, 10
Sophists, 9
soul (*v.* mind), 12, 27–8, 32, 36, 40, 44, 46, 51, 69 ff., 76, 165
species, 48, 49, 53, 57, 67, 87
Spencer, H., 165
Spinoza, B. de, 55, 59, 82–5, 86, 87, 91
spirit, 46, 106, 110–11
standards, 11–13, 19, 29, 193, 197
Stoics, 31, 35–9, 52, 53, 58, 101
Stout, G. F., 159, 160, 162–4, 166
Strawson, P. F., 138, 139 n., 194 n.
suggestion, 113, 128 ff., 148

Taylor, C., 183 n.
Theophrastus, 5, 6, 7, 8
things-in-themselves, 29, 132, 134, 140–1, 144–5, 187
Thomism, 46, 47, 49
Titchener, E. B., 159 n.
touch, 23, 113, 115

INDEX

understanding, 135 ff., 144
universals, 21, 141 ff., 162

Vesey, G. N. A., 100 n., 155 n., 156 n.
Victorinus, Marius, 43
vision, 8, 32, 37, 67, 103, 110 ff., 150 ff., 188 ff.

Ward, J., 159–61, 166, 169
Warnock, G. J., 23 n., 109 n.

Wertheimer, M., 182 n.
will, 38, 44, 52, 66, 84, 91, 105, 110–11
Winch, P. G., 129 n.
Wittgenstein, L., 156 n., 180–1, 187–8, 197
Wolff, C., 91–2
Wundt, W. M., 155, 159 n., 167

Zeno, of Citium, 36, 38

For Product Safety Concerns and Information please contact our EU representative GPSR@taylorandfrancis.com
Taylor & Francis Verlag GmbH, Kaufingerstraße 24, 80331 München, Germany

www.ingramcontent.com/pod-product-compliance
Lightning Source LLC
Chambersburg PA
CBHW062224300426

44115CB00012BA/2204